TO THE RESCUE!

True Stories of Tragedy and Survival

Carolyn Matthews

Copy-Editor: Lloyd Davis
Design: Andrew Roberts
Printer: Webcom

Library and Archives Canada Cataloguing in Publication

Matthews, Carolyn
     To the rescue! : true stories of tragedy and survival / Carolyn Matthews.

ISBN-10: 1-55002-561-9
ISBN-13: 978-1-55002-561-3

     1. Rescues--Canada. 2. Rescues--United States. I. Title.

G525.M374 2005   363.34'81'0971
C2005-901763-5

1   2   3   4   5   09   08   07   06   05

We acknowledge the support of the Canada Council for the Arts and the Ontario Arts Council for our publishing program. We also acknowledge the financial support of the Government of Canada through the Book Publishing Industry Development Program and The Association for the Export of Canadian Books, and the Government of Ontario through the Ontario Book Publishers Tax Credit program, and the Ontario Media Development Corporation'.

www.dundurn.com

Dundurn Press	Gazelle Book Services Limited	Dundurn Press
8 Market Street, Suite 200	White Cross Mills	2250 Military Road
Toronto, Ontario, Canada	Hightown, Lancaster, England	Tonawanda NY
M5E 1M6	LA1 4X5	U.S.A. 14150

TO THE RESCUE!

TABLE OF CONTENTS

ACKNOWLEDGEMENTS

My special thanks to Tim MacFarlane of Abbotsford, British Columbia, the cofounder and president of the Canadian Amphibious Search Team, without whom this book would not exist. From a young age, Tim wanted to engage in risky, challenging events so that he could feel fully alive and know what was important in life. As he matured, he took risks entirely for the purpose of helping other people.

In 2004, after many years of service, Tim took leave from his position as rescue specialist and captain of the Canadian Coast Guard's dive team on the west coast. Long has he understood the need for people to achieve closure to tragic events; he knows that those members of the Royal Canadian Mounted Police whose mandate it is to recover bodies are constrained by time and cost, so in 1991 he launched his private organization, the Canadian Amphibious Search Team, to fill this terrible need — the recovering of the dead and returning them to their families.

For him, and for all the members of his teams on both the west coast and in Manitoba; for those of you in the pages of this book — and all others who are not, but who should be — I have utmost admiration and respect.

My special thanks to all of you who told me your stories, and in doing so revisited old pain and heartache. In this regard, thanks particularly to:

Rodger and Karen Rinker of Alberta;
Jack and Kathy Flaig of Richmond, British Columbia;
Delmer and Rita Quewezance of Estevan, Saskatchewan;
the Muchaw family of Houston, Texas, especially Ginger Stephens;
Bill and Matthew Hopps of California;
and Debbie Stewart of Lac La Hache, British Columbia.

It has given me much pleasure to write these stories and I feel my life has been enriched through my contact with all of you.

Thanks also to my husband, Tony Matthews, who helped me with all the technical details of preparing this manuscript. And thanks to all the staff at the Dundurn Group, and to Tony Hawke especially; it was a wonderful experience to work with you on this book.

INTRODUCTION

"We live, as we dream — alone." Occasionally, the inner isolation each of us knows is alleviated by chance — perhaps in the aftermath of a cataclysmic event, when rescuer and rescued meet and find that it is bridged for a time, perhaps for all time.

This book of true stories is about ordinary people caught up in extraordinary events: a ski accident, a missing child, a fall overboard, a slip off a mountain, sea rescues — dramas that take place in the wilds of snowbound Labrador, in lonely Chilliwack, on a frozen lake high in the Sierra Nevadas, in the heart of a big city and on the coast of California. It is about the lives of rescuers — adrenaline junkies, yes — who search for life's meaning while engaging in deeds of heroism and compassion. It is about the aftermath of rescue for both rescuer and rescued.

Many rescuers are reluctant to tell their stories. They say that what we call heroism is just something they do. But how many of us, even with the appropriate skills, are willing to dive under ice in black and dirty rivers to search for a body? Or to be lowered onto an ice platform high on a mountainside, knowing that we could easily fall to our own certain death? Or dangle on the end of a rope attached to a helicopter at 12,000 feet?

Penetrate frozen forests in Labrador deep in the heart of winter to search for those lost within them? These are the things rescuers say:

"I want to give back."

"If you have special skills and don't use them to benefit others, you're selfish."

"You have to help — it could be you, your friend…"

"You feel huge compassion … you have to help."

"You have a job to do, and you do just do it."

"When you've risked yourself to save someone, it's almost like you've given life."

Search-and-rescue work involves facing not only risk, but sacrifice: of time, energy, money, and emotional equilibrium. Physical exhaustion and nightmares are frequent companions.

But the rewards are many: there is joy in the act of giving, and in the saving of life. The pitting of oneself against long odds to overcome danger carries with it a sense of achievement. There is the finding of purpose in life, and the adding of meaning to it. One finds fellowship with others who share the same vision, passion, ideals and values, and enjoys their camaraderie. Bonding runs very deep among those who share pain, suffering, danger — and success. Sometimes, rescuer and rescued form lifelong friendships. For many, search-and-rescue work is an all-consuming passion.

Search and rescue in Canada is under the jurisdiction of the Royal Canadian Mounted Police (RCMP) in every province except Quebec and Ontario and is conducted according to formal police services agreements. RCMP search commanders assume overall on-site authority for the organization and management of the actual search, using proven management procedures. Initial responses often include police and civilian dog teams, and police helicopters equipped with forward-looking infrared. Trained volunteer rescue teams are brought to the search site — volunteers with specific skills that include ice rescue, avalanche, helicopter long line, white water, underwater. The assistance of human trackers, too, are sometimes requested. In prolonged searches, other volunteer teams, conducting open- or closed-grid searches, are used, as well as the Civil Air Search and Rescue Association, other provincial agencies, and the Canadian Coast Guard auxiliary.

As a training standard, the RCMP recognizes the Basic and Advanced categories, as well as management search-and-rescue courses based on principles of the United States–based Emergency Response Institute and the National Association for Search and Rescue. Canadian courses which meet those standards include the provincial emergency program (PEP) of British Columbia, and the Emergency Measures Organization (EMO) in the Yukon.

From left: Trevor and brother Brandon with their dog, Tessy, in a hunting cabin.

AN UNFINISHED LIFE
Richmond, British Columbia

Brief were my days among you... — Kahlil Gibran

Kathy Flaig stood in the living room of her home, her son Trevor's school report card in her hand. Her mind buzzed, unable to understand it: he was failing, or close to failing, some of his academic subjects, but acing everything else: A-plus for all his woodworking, electrical and electronic subjects. A-plus for sports. A great kid, liked by everybody, a wise teenager... She read this with pride, but still, here were these poor scores in English, history — such an intelligent boy: how could it be?

Kathy heard him now, in the front yard with his father, talking — always talking, asking his interminable questions, wanting to know how and why things worked. Determined, in fact, to know the why of everything. So why were some of these grades so poor? She looked up, and there was her son gazing out at her from his portrait on the living room wall. She saw in this photograph, taken last year in Grade 12, the keen and inquiring eyes, and his sensitive and thoughtful expression. A wise lad for his age, people said.

Kathy stood before the picture and looked now at Trevor's hands: so clever, he could fix anything he touched. He will eventually do something great with them, she decided; be skilled at fine woodworking and metal work and fashion beautiful things. Or perhaps an expert mechanic. And he will be one of the world's good Samaritans. Already he was loved by everyone who knew him. And loved especially by the family's big black Lab, Tessy. "Trevor's dog, really," his father said. "He idolizes him."

"A man in a boy's body," her husband, Jack, had once said. "He's my shadow — I don't go anywhere without him." Jack would remember these joking words afterwards, and would forever after associate them with a tragedy that was about to engulf his family.

The front door banged shut. "Hi, Mom!" The bright eyes of her elder son beamed at her. "I gotta leave Dad to the car, 'cos I promised Mrs. Briggs I would help her. I can pick up stuff later from the grocery store on my way home if you like."

"Later" would come very much later. Trevor flew through the door as darkness settled like a blackened shroud over the streets. "Sorry I'm late. I'm cruising along Hawks Avenue, and I found old Mrs. Sutton stranded by the side of the road with a flat tire..."

"And you stopped and changed it for her," Jack slapped him on the back. "You did good, young man. Now come and eat. Your mom's got your dinner in the oven."

"Hey, Dad, duck shooting coming up. You said about going out on Saturday — just the two of us. Still on?"

★

Fishing, boating, now duck hunting; every weekend saw father and son out on the river among the marshes across from Westham Island. They shared a passion for all outdoor sports; the two, with their small, grey dinghy, were a fixture down at the docks. It was there among the lower reaches of the mud-silted Fraser River, among the low-lying, salty marshes where only bird songs and the wind sighing through the grasses could be heard, that the pair were to be found. Summer, fall, winter, the man and his boy pursued the sports they loved best in an environment that wrapped its peaceful solitude around them. Late afternoons and early weekend mornings, the two appeared on the old wooden docks, unloaded their small dinghy into the brown, rippling waters of this wide swath of river, and went duck hunting, boating or fishing. Sometimes the whole family — including Kathy, and Trevor's younger brother, Brandon, came along.

Long afterwards, when she could think about it more freely, Trevor's mother recalled how the back eddies of the Fraser River had been Trevor's playground. "He particularly enjoyed duck shooting, and would be off every weekend from Thanksgiving until the end of January," she said. "It was a big part of Trevor's life, and he loved the whole picture of it." She remembered that Trevor and his dad would drive to the island and huddle all day in a dinghy, half-hidden in fog and mist among the marshes. They might be there with fishing lines, or with rifles for duck hunting, among tree roots, long grass and shallow water. Then they would drive off in their van to a small, rain-soaked hut near the bird sanctuary to warm up, relax and eat after the day's exposure. Beyond the windows of this rough-and-tumble hut lay flat expanses of long grass that wrapped them in silence. Here, in this world, they were all that existed.

★

Tonight, at the dinner table, his father frowned thoughtfully when Trevor asked about a duck shoot. The deep ripple of happiness that accompanied the thought that his teenage son would want his company over that of any of his friends was tempered by regret.

"Saturday — no, can't do it, son," he said. "Try Chuck or Dave — they're always wanting to go out with you."

Friday, November 15 dawned. Just another ordinary day, punctuated for Jack by a phone call from Trevor at noon: this was the boy's custom, to phone his dad every day and ask how he was — and add, "See you at home tonight."

At five in the afternoon, the phone rang. It was Jack's friend Henry, asking if he wanted to come over and help dress a deer. Not long afterwards, Trevor came in the door, heard about the invitation, and said, "Hey, I want to go, too." The two ate a hurried meal and drove to Henry's. Trevor saved the deer's tail to use for tying fishing flies. Later, at home, he stretched the tail onto a board, fixed it with nails, and rubbed it with borax all along the flesh side. Then he carefully cleaned his equipment in preparation for the next day. Kathy had ordered in pizza for a snack, and any of it left over was to be packed for lunch the next day. Trevor phoned Warren about nine in the evening to double-check on the starting time for the next day's hunt. The family said their goodnights at about ten-thirty and went to bed.

★

Saturday, November 16 was to be the last day of young Trevor Flaig's life. Early morning saw him, six days before his eighteenth birthday, driving through the empty streets, along the Steveston Highway, across the one-way wooden bridge to Westham Island, a route he could take in his sleep. Tessy, his faithful black Lab, sat beside him in the front seat. Forty-year-old family friend Dave, who acted as an uncle, accompanied him.* The mist that had hung low over the river was lifting, and a weak sun peeped from the clouds. There was a song in the teenager's heart, for this was his life when he wasn't in school: the outdoor world, the feel of the salty wind in his face, his loyal companion Tessy with him. He helped Dave unload the dinghy from the roof of the van and carry it down the steps to the dock, then wended his way among the ropes that tied the four or five old commercial boats to it. They cast the dinghy out on the tidal water and stepped in with their gear. This was the part to be negotiated carefully, weighted down as they both were with sweaters and heavy coats and long waders up to the knees to protect against the damp chill of November. It was no mean feat to sit exposed to wind and cold for the better part of a day.

No other boat appeared on the water, and a silence enveloped the two as they pushed off from the docks towards the marshes directly across from them. But the peaceful silence soon shattered. A small vessel loomed on the horizon, its motors loud in the still air. It appeared to steer straight towards the two and came to an abrupt stop a few feet distant. Trevor saw that it was a Department of Fisheries and Oceans enforcement vessel. Its young officers yelled across the space of water, "Let's see proof of your hunting licences!"

---

* Dave is a pseudonym, used to protect the person's identity.

Dave and Trevor promptly produced the required certificates. The officers inspected them, handed them back and, without further words, gunned their boat's motors, turned the vessel about abruptly and sped down the river's delta at full throttle.

What happened next remains mired in controversy. The river waters had been quiet and barely rippling when the pair had set out in their small boat. Suddenly, out of nowhere it seemed, a large wave reared itself before the dinghy and rocked it violently. The small boat rapidly began filling with water. Dave told Trevor to jump. Both leapt over the side of the sinking boat and frantically began treading water, Tessy in the water beside them. The would-be duck hunters found themselves swamped in the back eddies of the sea reach, treading water while frantically yelling after the Fisheries vessel.

"You would've thought at least one of the guys in that boat would have looked back," Dave would complain later. Instead, it roared off into the distance, its occupants not heeding, or not hearing, the cries of the doomed hunters.

The universe of water, weeds and weedy marshes was an empty one: no one heard the cries of the two. Their yells echoed across the murky waters of the river and along its lonely shoreline, a man and a teenager entirely alone in a cold and dismal world clinging to an overturned boat. The tide was poised at about the halfway mark, and the man, the boy and his dog were about fifteen to twenty feet from shore.

"Take your coat and waders off!" Dave shouted when he saw the teenager having trouble staying afloat. Trevor did so. He was a strong swimmer and was treading water right alongside his friend. Dave urged him to try to swim back to the docks, and he himself struck out, in all his hunting gear, towards the shore. When Dave last heard him call out, he looked back and saw just one hand, and it was slowly sinking below the water. Dave lay on his back and torpedo-kicked his way toward the marshy shore until he felt his head bump up against it. When he looked back, he saw nothing but an empty sea. At first he lay prone upon the shore, then climbed a little higher, grabbed the decoy bag that drifted towards him a while later, and tied it to him. If he did succumb, he would be found floating. Tessy climbed up beside him. Dave suffered from hypothermia and shock.

Where was Trevor? How could this be? The stories and explanations afterwards were many and contradictory. To this day it remains unclear what fate befell the young Trevor.

Some interminable time passed before Dave saw a boat travelling upstream. He waved frantically. The occupants heard, and used their loudspeaker to shout, "Man overboard!"

In his house above the docks, Mike Bennett ran outside in his housecoat, jumped into his fishing boat, *TBone*, and headed across the six hundred feet of channel water. He pulled Trevor's dog, Tessy, all wet and shivering, and then Dave from the banks and into the boat. He had been searching for Trevor a short while when the crew of the Fisheries vessel roared up the channel, asked what had happened, and began their own search. They issued a search-and-rescue (SAR) call.

★

Jack and Kathy Flaig were enjoying their early Saturday morning alone — Brandon was staying over with a friend.

"Want some coffee, Kath? Our Trevor must have made it before he went out."

"Well, he sure must have been up early," Kathy smiled at the thought of their elder son whipping about the kitchen to make his parents coffee before leaving for his day's outing.

They watched a sports show on television while they drank their coffee. At eight-twenty, the phone rang. Jack answered. It was Mike Bennett, who lived near the docks.

"I just picked up Dave, but Trevor's missing," he said. "Their boat overturned and they were thrown out."

Jack stood motionless, but his mind catapulted in space and time. This was every parent's nightmare, the dreaded phone call, the unspeakable words: There's been an accident... something's happened... I think you should come... I want you to know... I'm so sorry to have to tell you...

"Well, the lad's got to be somewhere, damn it!" Jack spoke with sudden ferocity. It was his immediate and unshakable belief that his son must be alive somewhere. He yelled the news to his wife. They threw on some clothes and jumped into the car, roaring along the quiet streets of

Richmond to the island and to the docks at the small commercial fishery, arriving there within fifteen to twenty minutes. Jack refused to allow the thought to creep into his mind that his beloved son might not be alive, might not be "somewhere," might not ever again exist except as a memory — as photos on a wall, in an album, a laughing voice fading slowly over time.

As he drove furiously past a dull landscape of November grasses and trees silent and still in the chill of the early-morning air, his heart pounded heavily in his chest. An odd, dizzy sensation spread upwards, but he paid it no attention. The long, low line of the island seemed never to end.

He and Kathy raced down the steps and onto the creaking wooden docks where a few men had gathered, and where Dave lay huddled in blankets. Tessy, wet and bedraggled, jumped all over them. The brown river waters lapped quietly against the docks. There was Dave, but where was Trevor? The dizziness spread and Jack held onto a railing for support. If Trevor wasn't on shore anywhere, he must be — "No, no, no!" he shouted. "Who's looking for him? Why isn't anyone searching?"

"We found Trevor's waders — down there," Mike said, pointing to the reedy shore not far from the docks.

"Where is he, damn it?" Jack shouted at Dave. "You swam to shore. Trevor's young, and a strong swimmer, so where is he?"

"It was a sudden big wave—" one man began explaining.

"It was the wake of some boat," said another.

Wake? What wake? What boat? Jack looked out on the peaceful river, devoid of vessels, except for one that was racing towards them at this moment from the opposite shore, and he knew that it was the beginning of an interminable nightmare — one that has yet to end. In the distance he saw a group of kayakers, and knew then that the water had been calm when Dave and Trevor launched their boat. Kayakers would not be out on rough waters.

The Canadian Coast Guard's hovercraft vessel skimmed across the surface of the river and roared to a controlled crash stop right before the docks. Rescue staff had learned of the accident minutes before and had raced to the scene. It was nine o'clock.

"Where is the wave? How could this happen? Why, why, *why?*" The situation was incomprehensible to the frantic father.

When Dave eventually spoke, he described how a huge wave had suddenly swept in and overturned their boat. "'Jump out!' I yelled at Trevor as our boat rapidly began to sink." Both did so, treading water within arm's length of each other. Dave recalled striking out for shore, weighed down heavily by his hunter's clothes.

Did he look back for Trevor? Did he have any idea why the boy did not make it alongside him? These details and all others associated with this tragic event remain disputed. But questions about what had happened would have to wait: the urgent task at the moment was to find Trevor's body. There was no hope now that he would be found alive. Divers from the Royal Canadian Mounted Police and the Coast Guard staff aboard the hovercraft had begun a methodical search in the muddy waters of the Fraser. While it was not the mandate of the Coast Guard to recover bodies, the crew stood by to offer any help they could.

Jack and Kathy stood on the docks that chilly morning, deep in shock and denial. As they watched the activity, the search for their son, they were not yet to know how their whole universe was about to be turned upside down, tossed up in the air and scattered. Suddenly Jack could stand it no longer. Taking Tessy with him, he launched his other dinghy and, together with Henry Parker, began a search of his own.

The two men searched until darkness fell, then Jack and Kathy Flaig drove home in the dark, silent in their shared disbelief and misery. Kathy seemed burdened by additional anxiety that she struggled to express. As they reached the corner of Highway 99 and the Steveston Highway, she turned to her husband of twenty years.

"Jack, you wouldn't do anything stupid and…you know…do something to yourself, would you? Would you?" The words were spoken softly, gently, as though to a child. She rested her hand lightly on his arm, tears slipping down her cheeks as she looked at his profile.

"You mean, take my own life? No," he said. "But… I might die of a broken heart." They were words that would later seem prophetic.

Jack returned that night at midnight with Tessy to search for his son at low tide. A local fisherman offered the loan of his boat, which had several spotlights attached.

"Each time I spotted a log or clump of dirt, my heart skipped a beat," the desperate father said.

★

Tim MacFarlane, a rescue specialist for the Canadian Coast Guard, strode about aboard the hovercraft feeling frustrated. It was a feeling that would surface again and again over the ensuing days; it is not the mandate of the Coast Guard to recover bodies, so he knew he could not help in the search for Trevor Flaig. Divers from the RCMP searched the river, following a grid pattern, for the remainder of that Saturday as the tide receded. Eventually, they found a shotgun. But by ten that evening they had called off the search, saying they had done all they could within their time and cost constraints.

November 18 dawned. Jack continued to search, sometimes with his son, Brandon, and Trevor's dog, Tessy, and sometimes alone. Kathy returned to her part-time job as a florist at the local supermarket. Flowers … full of beauty, of perfume, blooming briefly, then dying. Flowers for funerals. Still, it helped to be busy, to be around other people. It was something to do.

Jack and Brandon made a silent pair, each locked in his own cycle of pain and misery. One day, Jack looked up as a vessel approached. It was the Coast Guard's hovercraft. The front hatch popped open and a clean-shaven head appeared. Its owner asked Jack if he had lost a bilge and manual pump. Their eyes locked. Jack would learn more about this man MacFarlane in the days ahead.

The Flaigs went through the motions of everyday living, except for Jack's daily trips to the river. He was seen from the banks when the tide was low, a lone figure with his dog, patiently searching the water. He awoke each morning from a soft pit of exhaustion. Instead of rising through the remnants of sleep into the half-wakeful state that is a prelude to full consciousness in his old, exuberant fashion, he fought himself out of his habitually poor sleep and thrust himself into a world that had a dull ache to it. Every day it was the same.

Increasingly he experienced tightness in his chest, and a recurrence of the strange dizziness he had felt on that fateful day of his son's disappearance. But beyond this, there stubbornly remained the belief that Trevor would just come walking in the door. It seemed impossible that he could have drowned. Incredible. Just not plausible. A much older man weighted down by all his hunting gear had made it the short distance to shore, while a fit, strong teenager who had pulled his waders off had not. Why? *Why?*

Jack continued to get up each morning and go to the river to trawl with a line and a hook — up and down, up and down, back and forth across the wide mouth of the river, and along its length. Kathy maintained a normal routine as best she could, but she worried about her husband, and about Brandon, who increasingly retreated into himself, and about Tessy, who skulked about with mournful eyes and slept in Trevor's empty bedroom.

A thought ran through Jack's mind: if his son's body did indeed lay somewhere in the river, it must be found before the river could begin its work of disintegrating a corpse that had long surrendered to it. If you don't find a body right away, then don't find it — that's what Jack believed. Jack also wondered how he could ever come to this place again — sail it, fish, hunt in the marshes — knowing that his son's body lay rotting within its depths. How could Brandon come here, the younger brother who loved all the things Trevor had loved and who had once haunted the same places? As he trawled the river in the days after the accident, Jack could scarcely bear the thought that he might wrestle his own flesh and blood from its muddy bottom. But he never ceased his efforts. One day rolled into another, and another, as Jack continued his lonely, tragic mission. At home, Kathy — stalwart, stoic — quietly went through the motions of everyday living. Her anxieties were for her husband and her son Brandon. Tessy slept in Trevor's bedroom and sat by the front door as though believing that, if he were patient enough, his young master would once again come whistling through it, play with him, take him in the boat, go for walks. Would life ever be the same?

Unbeknownst to Jack and Kathy Flaig, the Coast Guard's Tim MacFarlane, as owner and director of a private search organization called the Canadian Amphibious Search Team (CAST), had not forgotten the family's plight. He understood something of their desperation at not being able to find and bury their son; a situation like this was the very reason he had been driven to create his private search group: to find and recover a missing person, so that a family could know where their loved one was and bring closure to the tragic event. And since MacFarlane had children of his own, he was able to comprehend the family's living nightmare.

"I couldn't stand it, that these people were trying to fish up their son's body from the river by themselves, not finding him, not being able to bury him," MacFarlane said. "I had to try and help. There was something else: what had happened did not make sense, and what the family had been told officially made it even less so. They believed that nobody was telling them the truth — they believed that the Department of Fisheries and Oceans were protecting themselves from a possible lawsuit by concealing the actions of their crew aboard the Fisheries vessel, by lying about all the details."

MacFarlane and his CAST team studied maps of the area, as well as the tides, and went out one evening at midnight — when the tide was at its absolute lowest — to conduct a shore search. Within fifteen minutes they had found and recovered Trevor's body. MacFarlane called the RCMP and informed them of the discovery. At four that morning, Jack and Kathy were awakened by a knock on their door. On their doorstep, illuminated only by the dim light of the street lamp, stood two Delta Police officers. They informed the parents gravely that their son's body had been found.

It was only afterwards that the Flaigs learned the identity of the group that had actually located him.

The massive memorial service in Richmond, attended by more than seven hundred people, provided one kind of resolution for the Flaigs. Parents, grandparents and younger brother knew their beloved teenager would never again come walking through the door or go fishing, boating or duck hunting. Would never become an expert metalworker or mechanic, or be of assistance to all the people in the neighbourhood, whether young or old or in between. But at least they knew where he was. Their little old young man, the teenager who lived his life in a hurry as though aware that he had little of it left, kept journals, as if to say to the world, "I was here. This is how you can remember me." This teenager who had dreamed of reincarnation, of returning to Earth as an eagle who would soar above it, free, would never make good his mission in life: to grow up and make a difference.

There was unfinished business for the Flaig family; it had to do with the nature of the accident, with what had actually happened to cause this mishap, with all the lies they felt they had been told in the aftermath. Jack felt that his family had been given many inconsistent — and to them, improbable — statements. In answer to his insistent questions, representatives of the Delta police force, the Ministry of the Environment, and the Department of Fisheries and Oceans gave him contradictory information about the time of the accident and about the visit and conduct of the Fisheries enforcement staff. Dave himself later retracted his earlier testimony and offered another.

The Flaigs just wanted to know what had happened. They were a family who based their whole approach to life on truth, honesty and integrity, and they just wanted — and needed — to know the truth about their son's accident. To receive acknowledgement of responsibility if appropriate, and an apology. Only then could there be a letting go, a release of a toxic brew of anger and cynicism, of distrust in authority figures and in all public institutions. Only then could there be closure of another kind and the beginning of a process of healing.

Jack's frustration with the web of lies and inconsistencies about the accident mounted with the passage of time. He decided to launch a lawsuit, but without monetary value. His was a crusade only for the truth, and an apology.

All this time, Jack knew something was happening within himself, and his body. "This pain in my arm, my shoulder, and in my chest… I think it's a broken heart." What he really thought was that his shortness of breath, his lack of energy, the pain that burned up into his arm and shoulder, was part of the anger at the never-finished business of Trevor's death. He firmly believed that Trevor's accident had been the result of the carelessness of the crew of the Department of Fisheries and Oceans boat that had turned about after inspecting the fishing licences and raced off at full throttle, creating the large wake that capsized Trevor's dinghy. That they had not heard, or ignored, the cries for help from the two in the water. And afterwards, had spun a web of lies about it.

Jack Flaig was a man with a code of honour that demanded that he tell the truth always, regardless of the consequences. He could not understand why others could not.

One June day, almost two and a half years to the day of his son's death, Jack suffered pains in his left arm and shoulder. He had previously dislocated his shoulder, and thought this might be related to that injury. But the pain persisted all day, as did a shortness of breath. Jack supposed it was a minor attack, and he stayed in bed all weekend. "I felt like shit," he said. He went to work on Monday, but knew that something was up. "I guessed it was the cold air that brought on the shortness of breath," he said, "so I decided to go home, and see my doctor the next day."

After an examination, Jack's doctor told him he had probably suffered a minor heart attack and advised him to go home and rest, to return on Thursday. On this visit, the doctor confirmed that a heart attack had indeed taken place. He advised his patient to rest, either at home or in hospital, while he waited to see a cardiologist. Jack chose to go home.

Not long after supper on Sunday, June 20 — Father's Day — Kathy went off to visit her father while Jack watched a soccer game on television. Suddenly he felt himself unable to breathe. He lay down on the floor. Nothing helped, and he was rushed to hospital. No treatment was instituted on Monday, and Jack checked himself out of the hospital. But the shortness of breath returned, along with crushing chest pain. Another emergency trip to the hospital, and Kathy was told her husband was not expected to live. An angiogram showed that the left ventricle of his heart had ruptured and there was bleeding in his chest. Within four hours, open-heart surgery had been performed to repair an aneurysm. The consequent adrenaline rush injured his pancreas, which would subsequently contribute to severe diabetes and hypertension. Jack became a candidate for a heart transplant, but none was available, so a patch was stitched over the rupture instead. He is considered to be only the second person ever to walk out of that hospital alive after such surgery. Afterwards, he would joke about how he had warned Kathy that he might die of a broken heart.

Jack slowly recovered physically, but he did not resume any kind of a normal life. With his loss searing through him, and moving slowly in a pain-filled haze, he assembled a shrine to his son. He gathered Trevor's hunting and fishing trophies, photographs, an anvil he had fashioned, and his wallet, car keys, graduation cap, coffee mug and other memorabilia from the boy's bedroom, then built a shelf on the living-room wall on which to place them. Increasingly he could be found seated before this altar, his eyes fixed on mementos of a life that had been abruptly snuffed out before it had even begun.

Kathy felt perturbed, then increasingly worried, as Jack passed the days slumped before this shrine, showing little interest in anything other than his dead son and the physical remnants of his life. She cajoled, pleaded and remonstrated, to no avail. He largely ignored his wife and son, his friends, and all the elements of the life he had once enjoyed.

"My own feeling was that these things — your grief and pain, the regret, all the memories of your child and how you tied his shoelaces, helped him with his homework — they exist within your own heart; you have to get on with life," Kathy said. "One day, I was in the kitchen with a broom in my hand, sweeping the floor. Something in me snapped. I threw the broom down and yelled at Jack. 'I've had it! I can't take this anymore,' I said. I picked up the broom and threw it across the floor. I started crying and yelling. Then I said, 'Jack, get out! Just get out. It's too much. I haven't got a husband and Brandon hasn't got a father. You're no use to us, so just pack your things and go!'"

A long silence ensued. Then Jack looked up, stunned and unmoving.

"Go on. You're no use to anybody. I don't care where you go, I just don't want you here."

"You want me to leave?" Jack got up slowly, looked about him as one bemused. He gathered a few clothes and other possessions in silence, packed them in a bag and walked, as if in a trance, out the door. He climbed into his truck and drove away.

"I felt relief at first," Kathy said. "But then I thought, 'Oh, what have I done? What have I done?'"

Jack spent the night in his truck, went to work the next day, then phoned his wife from his office. "Can we meet for coffee tonight and talk?" he asked. Kathy agreed, but on the condition that Jack make two lists: one of all the things that he considered good about himself, and the other listing the bad things. She would do the same. She asked for commitment from him about all the things he would change about himself, like "cut the lawns, be a good father to Brandon, a husband to me, get therapy," Kathy said. "I felt we should work together through this. In the beginning we promised for better or for worse… can't get any worse … We should try, as we promised."

They met and talked. Jack produced his lists. He promised his wife everything except the part about seeking therapy — this he refused categorically to do. They agreed that he should come home. In the following days, Kathy, with the pretext of wishing to repaint the living-room walls, dismantled the shrine, puttied the holes in the walls and began painting. Jack said nothing, but kept his promises to his wife and son. The family worked together slowly through all the pain, including all of Brandon's difficulties in the aftermath of his brother's death.

Jack Flaig, a man once innocent of cynicism or distrust of people and public institutions, remains angry and bitter at the lies he felt he was told, and the cover-ups. He does not know, and will never know, exactly how or why his son died. Only one person, Tim MacFarlane, and his organization known as CAST, has inspired him, saved him from total despair. MacFarlane, dive captain at Richmond's Coast Guard Base, and owner of the Canadian Amphibious Search Team, cared enough to quietly search and find his son. Cared enough to talk and listen to him, encourage him to hang on. To this day he cares enough to keep in touch.

Jack Flaig at the Fraser River delta.

Mike Muchaw.

TOWARDS A TERRIBLE HORIZON
Teton County, Wyoming, and Houston, Texas

No stranger are you among us, nor a guest, but a son, and dearly beloved. — Kahlil Gibran

Ray Shriver leaned against the doorway of his house, gazing out at the fresh morning — at the Teton Mountains rising above Snake River Park and a mist lying low over the valleys. He thought then of his childhood home in the flatlands of Kansas, and his heart quickened with pleasure that he had chosen this place for his home. His eyes drank in the soft colours of the cottonwood, the willow and the blue spruce trees that followed the line of Trail Creek. He knew that if he were to take his dog, Kita, for a training session there, or simply for a run by the river, he would find many of the one hundred species of wildflowers in bloom; that among the sagebrush he would find larkspur, harebells and stonecrop, tiny and perfect, their fragile beauty hidden among towering mountains and a primeval forest.

The ringing of the phone interrupted his musings. Across the wire came Sergeant Gaylen Merrell's voice from the sheriff's office in Teton County, Wyoming. "Ray, we need you and your dog. A man's gone missing around these parts — his family's not heard from him in a month. I'm thinking how Kita could well lead us to him — or to his corpse."

"Of course. I'll come at once." Adrenaline flooded Ray's body, and then a familiar feeling — a sort of edginess — began bubbling up somewhere inside him. As Ray looked around for Kita, his mind ranged over the countless hours he'd spent exercising and training her to search for people and objects in this rugged, mountainous state. His thoughts flitted back to that day when he'd claimed her as his own, the German shepherd puppy he would train and use in the service of search and rescue (SAR). How deep the bonds between them, he thought, developed through intensive training together, during the times they'd hiked and swum in mountains and streams and had suffered alongside each other in searches that took them over harsh terrain in severe weather conditions. The bonds had further deepened by their sharing of the long winter nights.

He lingered for a moment longer, his tall, lean frame silhouetted against distant Mount Oliver. *Once we were warriors, now we're robots*, he thought as he drove the eighteen miles from his home to the sheriff's office in Jackson. *We sit at desks all day, go home, flop on the couch, park ourselves at a computer. Life's pretty boring, really — no challenge to it anymore. Too bad, because that's what we're born to do: to use our bodies.* He smiled as he thought of his own adventures: the ski trips, the climbing expeditions, the river-running. To him they were necessary challenges. In addition, after work and on weekends he volunteered his time, the skills he had honed, and the use of his dog in the service of SAR. To do so meant everything to him: whenever a SAR call came, it was as though a gauntlet had been thrown down and his sense of everyday reality ceased to exist — the mission, for as long as it lasted, consumed his entire world.

Clouds hung like shrouds over the mountains and the air felt cool and damp. Little traffic rumbled along the roads and highways at this early hour. Ray wondered how many search-and-rescue volunteers would be available. His mind turned to the case the sheriff had outlined: a middle-aged man who had not been heard from for at least a month. A man no one had missed, it seemed, because no call had come until now. What sort of a fellow was this, and what was his life like? Why was he wandering around this lonely place, out of contact with the rest of the world? Perhaps it had begun to close in around him. Dimly, Ray considered what he might find, given a man missing for about a month, the cool weather, the hungry wildlife, and the rivers peaking with meltwater.

★

In a small three-bedroom bungalow in the suburbs of Houston, Texas, a beautiful baby boy, the first of seven children, was born to delighted and proud parents Don and Lena Muchaw — "a real sweet little boy, he was," his mother said. The devout Catholic couple christened him Michael Terry, cherished him, loved him, took him to church regularly, and to weekly Mass. They raised him in a home full of love.

Not quite two years later, his sister Virginia (Ginger) was born, a sister who would be to him the closest friend and confidante he could ever have. Mike and Ginger shared a bedroom, and for seven years they remained the only two children. Then, over the next eight years, another four were born: Douglas, Crystal, Holly and Heather. Finally, six years after Heather, Ben, the last Muchaw son, was born.

Don Muchaw was strict but fair, holding each of his children accountable for their actions to ensure they grew up to become responsible people. Honesty and integrity were the family's watchwords.

"You know, I knew there was something different about Mike when Ginger came along," Lena Muchaw confided. She stood in the den, looking up at the portrait of her son that stood propped on a bookshelf. Green-flecked eyes looked back at her from a thin, angular face, his teenage expression a curious mixture of humility and defiance. "Ginger was just twenty-two months younger, but I could see the contrast right away. It's hard, really, to explain what I mean.

"He struggled always at school," Lena said, explaining that the nuns were very strict and pushed the children to achieve, but that however hard Mike worked, he didn't quite make it. He struggled to meet others' expectations and felt bad about himself when he failed. He began to lose confidence, and some behaviour problems followed. The one thing he did well was to excel at sports, particularly baseball.

Ginger later described how she too felt she must always look out for her older brother and protect him. For her, in later years, it became her mission to save her brother from himself.

"We were childhood playmates, then teenage friends," she said. "Throughout later life, we maintained constant contact, in spite of all the problems and difficulties I had in tracking him down — because of his near-nomadic life, and all the tangents related to his drug addictions."

The tragedy of this young man's life was yet to unfold. Those with fanciful notions might say that he was doomed from the moment of his birth, not having the innate strength to refrain from habits he knew were destroying him. Others might say he was doomed from the day he took his first drag on a marijuana cigarette. He got hooked, and could not say no.

"I felt I was too soft with him," Lena Muchaw said long afterwards. "My son used me and I knew it, but all I wanted was for him to know that I would always be there for him and always love him. His father was much stricter; he wanted his boy to be responsible for his actions."

On a fateful Fourth of July, 1973, Mike attended a party while in college.

"Something bad happened at that party, and he was different after," said his father. "He didn't know truth from fiction, right from wrong — just clumsy with the truth, he was. After that, we had trouble with him. He took some bad drugs at that party, and it hooked him." Gradually, almost imperceptibly, Michael Muchaw changed into someone his parents and siblings didn't like. At college, his use of marijuana continued, and eventually he progressed to cocaine.

"He attended college for one full year, then Don had to go and get him from the trailer we'd purchased for him and bring him home," said Lena. "He bailed out. He was failing his grades, and we thought he was into this dope-taking thing, but we weren't sure because he never levelled with us. I'm afraid he was one big disappointment after another, our firstborn son."

"He didn't have it in him to say no to drugs," his father said laconically.

With continued use of harder drugs came the process of alienation from his family: the profound disappointment, the anger and loss of contact, except for Ginger. The younger children were told the truth: that their oldest brother was taking drugs and was not welcome in the house. His fate served as an example for the children, who learned that drugs are not your friends. All the while, his parents never quit trying to help him, three times sending him to facilities for rehabilitation. Not once did he co-operate; he wasn't prepared to give up his habits which, at the same time that they made him feel good about himself, consumed him with guilt for the pain he knew he was causing his family.

After dropping out of college, Mike worked offshore for McClelland Engineering. He married Marci, and eventually two daughters, Lisa and Nicole, were born. Sometime after the birth of son Jerry, Marci, no longer willing to tolerate her husband's drug habits and behaviour, packed up the children and moved back to California.

"Here was a man haunted by what he did to others, especially at losing his own family," said his mother with a deep sigh. "He felt such a failure, so empty."

"Yes, and I loved him; I tried to save his soul, wanted desperately to help him," Ginger said. "I never did quit trying — and my husband, too. We tried to integrate him back with the rest of the family, who were very angry with him all these years for the many things he did. Like taking the only valuable things we had — my mother's diamond earrings and the ring given her by her mother — then pawning them to pay for his drugs. A saxophone, too, and my clarinet.

"We had little money in the family all our growing up years, but Mike kept asking for it, all to pay for his drugs. It was very hard for us, going through his worst times with him. Once, he phoned every half-hour all through the night because he was frightened by his hallucinations. Another time we visited him in jail… He hurt us real bad."

"But he did try in his last years," Lena was anxious to add. "In the end we knew he was there for us: he came to our fiftieth wedding anniversary, and he read aloud the scriptures — he wanted our forgiveness. We saw that he was full of guilt and anxiety, acting differently, and estranged from us in his final weeks and months.

"Towards Easter weekend, he'd pulled away from our family. He knew things were not right, and we knew, but we didn't know what — only that he longed to get back to Jackson. The time wasn't right for him to go there, the weather not warm enough, but we saw how he pined to go. We watched as he became thin, and pale and anxious. One day — the Monday following Easter Sunday — he came to us to say he'd made a decision to go back to Jackson! He didn't say it, but he didn't want us to know about the things that were happening to him. But God knew. And God was with him at the end."

Mike called Ginger and asked if he could come and say goodbye before he headed out. "Of course," she said. "I'm home today." Michael Muchaw came for one last visit.

On May 21, 2002, Ginger, having not heard from her brother in almost a month, contacted the Teton County sheriff's office to issue a missing persons report. And so began an investigation into the last days of this unfortunate man — a drifter, a drug abuser, a man who no one wanted to employ, who had exhausted the good wishes and abilities of church groups and social and family services agencies.

★

Sergeant Merrell sat in his office in the sheriff's department that day in May, in the eye of a whirlwind of activity. A call to dispatch had come in from a Ginger Stephens from Richmond, Texas. She wished to make an official report of a missing person — "my brother, Mike Muchaw," she had said.

"Deputy Mark Priest took the cold missing persons report, followed up information he received, and forwarded it to the investigative division," said Sergeant Merrell. "Then Ginger Stephens called dispatch again, and was referred to me." Merrell would usually assign a case like this to a deputy, "but with this second call, I felt a heightened sense of urgency and decided to take it and run with it myself."

He began with Ginger Stephens and her parents' statements that Mike had left Houston on April 16 to travel to Jackson. The last time Ginger had spoken to him in person had been that afternoon, when he came to her Richmond home to say goodbye in person. She remembers giving him all the money she had in the house, packing him sandwiches, snacks, and bottled water for the long drive to Jackson, and then kissing him goodbye. "He called me — collect — every morning, between six-thirty and seven. Sometimes twice a day. But there hadn't been a call for almost a month," she said, adding that she had already phoned the mission and been told he had left there on April 23, saying he intended to live in his truck near the Snake River.

Merrell learned that Muchaw had, over the years, wandered around Houston, Salt Lake City and various parts of Wyoming — most recently, Jackson, in Teton County. His pattern had been to work at various construction jobs during the summers, always returning to Texas to spend the fall and winter with Ginger and her husband, James. While there, he worked for his cousin Frank, who owned a construction company and who had also become a very good friend to Mike.

As Merrell sat pondering the case, he recalled the time about two weeks earlier when he and Deputy David Hodges had tagged an abandoned pickup truck by the side of Highway 191 at milepost 162. It had Wyoming licence plates registered to Michael Muchaw. The two had taken a short walk to the Hoback River from the truck to see if anyone had set up camp in the area, but found no signs of human activity.

Deputy Ben Adams reported that he had contacted Mike Muchaw very early on the morning of April 22 to make sure he was all right. Muchaw told him he had been let go from Evans Construction and was feeling pretty bummed out about it. At five o'clock that same morning, Adams contacted Muchaw again, offering to help him with his truck, which had run out of gas on South Highway 89 near High School Road. The two pushed it to a Mini Mart so that Muchaw could refuel. Adams saw the truck again on May 7, parked on Highway 191. He stopped to check it out and found it to be abandoned. Muchaw's parents would later say that the truck was the only thing in the world their son owned, and it would be very odd for him to leave it abandoned on the highway.

Bishop Gayle Matson in Idaho Falls had given Mike a phone card to call his family as well as three nights' lodging at Motel West in Idaho Falls.

Carl Oksanen of Orville Mission knew Mike, knew that he was having trouble with his truck, and, wanting to help this pale and hungry man, invited him to Bubba's Bar-B-Que for dinner on April 24. He looked across the table at a sallow-faced man with a haunted expression who refused to look him in the eye. He had thin brown hair and a scruffy beard; he hunched in his chair, motionless except for the constant plucking of his beard, and had little to say. Carl had supposed that Mike would be ravenous, but he ate little. Carl got up from the table after the meal and went about ordering the part that Muchaw would need to get his truck running, and arranged to pay for it. Muchaw looked at him, expressed his thanks, and walked away to his truck with a slow, loping gait. After that, he seemed to disappear from the earth: neither Carl nor anyone else heard from him again. It was sometime afterward that Director Doug Meyer in the sheriff's office learned that Muchaw had moved out of Orville Mission on April 21 to live in his truck.

Sergeant Merrell spoke with Larry Lamb, Muchaw's supervisor at Evans Construction. Lamb said that Muchaw had walked off the job site and did not show up again until April of 2002 — one year later — to ask for his job back. Lamb felt bad about not rehiring him, but said Muchaw had proven himself an unreliable employee whom he could not afford to have on staff. Merrell ran a check on Muchaw's criminal record and found out that the missing man had been in the penitentiary in Utah on a drug-related offence. He learned that Mike had a history with drugs; that he liked to wander and was loath to stay in one place for very long; that he was a very friendly man who enjoyed talking to strangers — a man very much attached to his family in Houston, about whom he often spoke, telephoning his sister Ginger collect once or twice each day to tell her he was okay.

Merrell found out that Muchaw had been a frequent user of the local temporary employment agencies. He was not a dependable employee; he often didn't show up for work, and frequently complained he was sick, that he had been injured on the job — a litany of excuses that, to the staff who had tried so hard to place him, seemed to have no end. "But he did have some ties with the community," Merrell explained. "There was his work, as sporadic as it was, his accommodation at the mission in the town, the fact that he was known by many people in the community — it all meant he was considered to be a regular member of the community."

Sergeants Merrell and Moss searched the truck that had been retrieved from the highway. Their search verified that it was indeed regis- tered to Michael Muchaw, but they found no other useful information, other than that it had been locked, with no keys in the ignition.

Back in his office, the sergeant sat, head in hands, considering the possibilities. Here was an unfortunate human being who had come to the end of the line: the construction sites refused anymore to hire him; Roy Meyer at the Orville Mission could no longer help him and could no longer afford to support him with accommodation and meals; Family Services would no longer cover his prescription drugs. His truck had become his home, and even this accommodation was tenuous: the police or the forest and park rangers would make him move him along no matter where he parked it. Life was closing in on him. What would he do? Where would he go? He was adrift somewhere — cold, hungry and cut off from all contact. It did not look good.

The sergeant made his decision: he would call out Jackson's volunteer search-and-rescue team. It was still possible that Muchaw would also be found alive — it happened often in missing persons cases. Either way, the case would be closed.

Doug Meyer, hired under the sheriff's office in the position of SAR co-ordinator, also understood the need for closure. He set about to help co-ordinate the search effort, gathering five other board members to study maps of all possible areas where the missing man might be. Each spot was then rated as high, medium or low probability. Twenty or more volunteers would enter the areas deemed most promising, searching them and then reporting back on the probability of detection.

"If the area is treed, ten people go into a quarter-square-mile area where we think the probability of detection is 30 per cent," Doug explained. "Others searching in the open rate their area at 50 per cent. We keep recalculating the percentages for probability of detection and eventually we come up with areas where the probability is that he is not there. We abandon those areas and move on to another."

On that Saturday morning, twenty-four search-and-rescue members ranging from small businessmen to engineers, doctors, lawyers, nurses and construction workers spread themselves out, ten feet apart, to comb the scrubby, flat land around milepost 162 on Highway 191. Janet Wilts, from Grand Teton National Park and the only other local person who owned a search dog, rafted the river with her dog, Commanche, while Ray Shriver searched the steep hillsides on the north side of the highway and river with Kita. Low clouds flitted fitfully across a grey sky and the air was cool. The group found nothing, and saw that the area was undisturbed. They then extended their search north of the highway toward the mountains and well into the trees. Ray thought that Muchaw might have gone antler hunting. "Horns are worth money, and transients often sell them," he said. Meanwhile, Janet continued to searched the river in a spider boat.* No clues were found that Muchaw had been this way.

The mobilization of the SAR team prompted articles about the missing man in the local papers the next morning, May 30. Immediately the sheriff's office received a call from a man who said he had been kayaking on the Hoback River and had seen a half-dressed man wandering about the banks on the far side.

"He wore only a brown jacket — he didn't seem to have anything underneath," the caller said. "He had boots on — but they were unlaced. He wandered about on the bench† on the south shore of the river. I thought it a bit odd at the time."

Sergeant Merrell and Ray Shriver met with the kayaker — one of many who leave their workplace at the end of a day and head for the river to fish, kayak or boat until dusk. Together they drove to the spot where the near-naked man had been sighted. Merrell showed Muchaw's photo to the kayaker, who immediately recognized him.

"Okay. Now we better get busy and search the south side of the river," said the captain.

"Why would he have crossed the river?" a volunteer asked. "At this time of year, runoff is at its peak. He could easily get swept away or could freeze. Maybe he was confused, remembering other times he had so easily waded across it."

"If we see someone camping out, living out of their cars, we keep note of it, and move them on after a time," explained Merrell. "Then these people try to find other areas where they think they will not be found and forced to move on. Muchaw had probably done this — crossed the river, intending to set up camp on the other side. There, he would be less visible to the forest rangers and wouldn't be hassled so easily by them or their deputies."

---

* Spider boats are cata-rafts, consisting of two parallel tubes (pointed on the ends) with a netted aluminum framework over and between them. They are typically about sixteen feet long and sit two feet above the water. They are very manoeuvrable and handle rapids well. The boats have no motors.
† A flat lip of land or rock preceding the drop to the river below.

On that first day of searching, all that was found was a baseball cap lying on rough ground close to where the abandoned truck had been parked. The volunteers retreated home, knowing they would not give up until they found this unfortunate man.

★

Sergeant Merrell gazed through the window of his office, to the timberline that hugged the foothills of the Grand Teton Mountains. What now? He thought over the day's search, recalled all the dedicated volunteers who had combed the landscape. The image of Ray Shriver lingered. Ray was one of the original members of Jackson County's volunteer SAR group, and a board member. He had been responsible for all SAR training over all the years — and he had Kita, his search dog! Kita had been specifically trained to sniff out cadavers and had been used on this kind of mission before. The sergeant would appeal to him specifically to help in this case. Merrell picked up the phone.

"Of course, Kita and I will do everthing we can to help." Ray answered the sergeant's call. "I'd like to suggest we ask Janet Wilts at Grand Teton National Park to come out with us again — and, well, I think it's best if we don't call the other SAR members, Gaylen. You can guess what we'll find — if we find him at all. We both know it won't be a pretty sight. The guy's been missing over a month now; there's the weather, the wildlife—"

"I know, I thought of that too…"

Shriver, Wilts and their dogs met and immediately began searching the other side of the Hoback River, combing its banks and hillsides to the timberline — slow and exacting work under a now-scorching sun. They reached the edge of the forest about half a mile below the spot where the kayaker had seen the half-dressed man, an area almost directly across from the spot where Mike Muchaw had left his truck. One hour passed, and another. The task was monotonous and tiring, the landscape dull and drab: scrub, sagebrush and tussock to the river's edge. Close to the tree line, Ray suddenly spotted a splash of colour — a single bright bloom in a grey landscape. He rushed towards it. There, among the scrub and brush at the edge of the forest, he saw a pile of neatly folded clothes: swimsuit, towel, jeans, underwear, T-shirt and long-sleeved shirt. He

The Hoback River in Teton County, Wyoming.

shouted, and Janet immediately joined him. Anxiously they searched the pockets of the jeans for identification. They found a set of car keys — and a wallet! A pregnant silence ensued. Here lay the clothing of the lonely figure the kayaker had seen wandering on the riverbank. They must be close to finding Mike Muchaw, as these objects belonged to him. The man himself — or his body — could not be far distant.

Deep down, search-and-rescue workers dread such a breakthrough. Ray knew that the searchers would eventually come across Muchaw's body — indeed, that *he* would most likely be the one to do so because of Kita's help. Today, however, as night fell, they would be spared what they now knew they were bound to find.

The search was resumed the following Saturday, June 1, led by Ray, who accompanied Gaylen Merrell and Lloyd Funk from the sheriff's office to the spot where the clothing had been found. Ray refused to call other SAR members, aiming to spare them what he was sure would be the sight of the corpse of a long-dead man. They crossed the river a mile or more upstream, west of the Spotted Horse Ranch, over a bridge that led them onto private property. They dropped back to the river, and to the bench above the spot where the clothes had been found. While the investigators searched it, and the areas adjacent to where Muchaw had last been seen wandering, Ray walked downstream to check out the river eddies to see if Muchaw, or any part of him, had been caught among the debris.

He tramped along the edge of the river, whose waters coursed swiftly and ran high within their banks. Kita ran back and forth, from the bench to the slopes above, disappearing every few moments among the sagebrush about a quarter of a mile downriver from the spot where the clothes had been found. Dusk began settling over the landscape and the air was cool. The group was considering calling it a day when the wind shifted. A brief few minutes passed, and then a series of short, sharp barks punctuated the tranquil river scene. Ray's heart sank with the knowledge that his dog had discovered a human body — the very thing she had been trained intensively to do. He climbed up the riverbank and followed Kita, who ran about in circles and continued barking. There, lying among the scrubby growth of the upper banks of the river, Ray saw a human body — or what was left of it — curled up in a fetal position, dismembered and disintegrated both by wildlife and the elements. The various parts of him lay scattered among the scrubby foreshore in a lonely spot near a river and a timberline he had intended to call home.

Ray turned away and hiked back to tell the others that he had found the missing man. He was sent back to the sheriff's office to notify Sheriff Zimmer and coroner Robert Campbell.

★

The last whereabouts of Mike Muchaw became a crime scene: photographs were taken, as were measurements and notes. Ray watched, then took his dog Kita and walked slowly away. This was the natural world: one animal preying upon another and another, he knew that. But all the same, he felt profoundly disturbed.

"The finding of a body is always shocking and disturbing, but this was much worse: the body had been dismembered by a variety of animals, among them coyotes, ravens, magpies, bobcats, mountain lions," Sergeant Merrell explained afterwards. "We've lost SAR members over situations like this. We debrief and offer counselling, but sometimes it's too shocking. I myself try not to get involved personally; try to treat it as a case — it helps."

Merrell made the phone call to the family — always a difficult task, even in this case when its members expected bad news. "I'm sorry to have to tell you… the bad news is that your son and brother is dead… but we have found his body. You can bury him and move on with your lives…" He explained that Mike had died of hypothermia* after crossing a river raging with melting snow — that he had simply curled up and gone to sleep.

★

After taking the phone call, Ginger contacted all her siblings and they agreed to gather at their parents' home so that they could be together to give them the news. They waited a considerable time, and eventually Don

---

* Subnormal body temperature. Muchaw's loss of body heat was exacerbated because he was wet and buffeted by wind. In later stages, the victim feels hot, thus explaining why he began removing his clothes.

and Lena Muchaw returned from a funeral service and Mass at their church. Don Muchaw opened the sliding glass doors, saw his entire family gathered, waiting for him, and sat down heavily in his wingback chair.

"Dad, they found Mike... He... he's no longer with us." Ginger paused, then added quickly, "He had his little Bible with him. He's at peace now. He's up there with God, Dad. You don't have to worry about him anymore."

Silence filled the room. Don slumped in his chair, his head in his hands. The five brothers and sisters who had been too young to know their eldest brother very well glanced at each other, then at their parents, aching for them. Ginger felt desolate, grief-stricken — both for herself and for her parents.

Lena was the first to break the silence. "A few weeks ago, a strange thing happened to me," she said. "I knew Mike was dead. I knew the moment when he died. Remember a while back — the Sunday after Good Friday, it was. I had fallen and broken some ribs, or bruised them, when I was helping your father move a couch and patio furniture on Good Friday. I had gone upstairs on Sunday afternoon to lie down in the middle bedroom to rest; I was just drifting off to sleep when I felt the bed start to shake. I thought it was you, Don, trying to wake me. I sat up, alarmed. 'What is it? What is it?' I said, and opened my eyes. It wasn't Don I saw, but Mike. His soul was being lifted to heaven. I called out, 'Mike, Mike... come back!'

"'No, Mom, I have to go.' That's what he said. I saw the Holy Spirit come, and then the Father. Mike was lifted up in their arms — and his soul, too. I could even see what he was wearing: a little orange golf shirt tucked into blue jeans. Oh, he looked so happy. I knew then that he'd gone — gone from us."

"Mom, I knew it too!" said Ginger. "That very same night — Sunday — I woke up, sat straight up in my bed and said to James, 'Mike's in trouble, he's in the water!'"

"Ginger, don't worry about him. He'll be okay," James had said.

"'No, Mike's in trouble. It's to do with water — it's about the water — that's all I know.' I didn't have any vision... just these words came out of my mouth. James said, 'We're going to find him. Don't you worry.' I just knew Mike was in the water somewhere. I don't know how I knew that — it just came to me.

"Doors were closing for Mike — I knew that," she continued. "I wouldn't ever know when he would call to say he was in trouble. I got to the point where I wouldn't give him money anymore, but I would always give him a roof over his head. He used to tell me how he awoke every morning with demons in his head — how he had to fight them all the time. I never told…" She looked around at the family. "I knew how he struggled; one day I went in to wake him up for work — you know, when he worked for Frankie. He looked so small and frail in that bed, so tiny, and very thin at the end. I know he brought a lot of trouble to us all, but I always forgave him. I never quit loving him."

Tony and Dolly, Lena's brother and sister-in-law, offered to drive the family to Jackson in their large Ford Excursion. Dolly bustled about, preparing food, fresh fruit and drinks for them to take on the drive, which would take two long, hard days. The interminable, and largely silent, journey took them through the West Texas plains, but they saw little of them because of severe thunderstorms — *appropriate to our mood*, Ginger thought. Through the foothills of the Rockies in northeastern New Mexico, through a scenic Colorado that they did not see as they travelled through the night. The family reached high desert in southeastern Wyoming, and eventually the rivers, hills, forests and distant mountains of Teton County. Each member tried to cope with this new idea that their troublesome son and brother was no longer alive. A thorn that had long been embedded deep in their collective subconscious had been removed, replaced with a dull pain that would endure forever. Had Mike suffered? Had his death been painful or prolonged? Whatever he had done, he now no longer existed and could no longer be helped. But he was theirs; he had been born in hope and innocence. He had been offered love and opportunities, like all of them. He had not been able to cope with life's demands — he'd never seemed able to help himself. He had died an early, and lonely, death. Was it his fault? Theirs? Could any of them have done more? The torment remained.

The family finally arrived at the sheriff's office in Jackson on a beautiful day, warm but crisp. The town of Jackson appeared serene and quiet, bathed in a soft sunlight that burnished buildings, trees, mountains, rivers and valleys below in shades of gold and amber.

As the disconsolate group crossed the grassy slope to enter the sheriff's building, "We immediately understood Mike's love and passion for this gorgeous, God-given country," Ginger said. At the same moment as they arrived, Ray Shriver was approaching, with Kita at his side. He realized at once who this family was, and introduced himself and his dog. At last, face to face — the searcher and the family of the dead man came together on the grassy foreground, under a bright sun and a sky that arced blue above them. Lena looked at the dog, and the hard pain of suffering in her face softened. When she learned about the discovery of her son's effects, and eventually of his body, she sank into the luxuriant green grass, hands folded in her lap, tears streaming down her face. Kita moved to her, sat at her feet, and licked the tears off her face as they fell. He then nuzzled close, as though to say, "I'm sorry for your grief and want to comfort you."

"Hi, I'm Mike's mother… I'm Mike's mother." Lena said the words with unfathomable sorrow. Ray led the family indoors, to the office of Sergeant Merrell, who greeted them kindly and led them into the office of Sheriff Zimmer.

The family was driven to the spot where Mike had spent his last days, to the place where he had planned to live out of his truck. They stood first on the riverbank, then moved to the timberline, and finally wandered about the river's scrubby foreshore. The highway was empty of traffic, and only the calls of wildlife and birdsong and the rippling of the river disturbed their silent pilgrimage. The wind sighed in the trees, and blue sky stretched wide above them, the snowcapped peaks of the Teton Mountain range glinted in the sun. The family saw that the place where Mike had died was both wild and beautiful. Gaylen Merrell stood by, quiet and respectful. The family asked if they could see Mike's truck — go through it to see if they could find any clues as to his behaviour near the end of his life.

"He died from the feet up — I just know it," Ginger said. "I knew Mike would die an early and tragic death. One thing I'm relieved about is it wasn't because of drugs. He was clean, you know, in his final years, or so we believed. These last ones had been good for Mike, and for the family — we shared a lot of great times together."

Mike Muchaw's body was eventually cremated, and his family took the ashes home with them. "Mike is finally home. We know where he is.

He is at peace," they said afterwards. They recovered Mike's little Bible, which he had kept with him at all times, and this comforted them. As tragic as his life had been all the way through, they believed that he had God with him till the very end, believed he had died a dignified death, and it gave them solace. His ashes are stored in an urn on a bookshelf in his parent's family room to this day; son and brother has been returned to the bosom of his family, at last.

"The poor man, he struggled to try to do the right thing. He caused great heartache and displeasure, he broke all the rules, he wasn't welcome in the house when he wasn't 'clean.' But all he wanted was to be home with his family," said Ginger in epitaph.

"We knew he crawled out of that river and onto the bank for us, so we could have his body back," said Lena. "We're telling this story about our son as a message for other parents, and for all people. We're not here just to cry, but to send this message. Our son has left a footprint in our hearts."

Ray has maintained contact with Mike Muchaw's family. They remain grateful to him for what he did, and hold tremendous respect for the unsparing efforts he made and for his kind, compassionate manner. They also hold deep respect for Sergeant Merrell, and all members of the SAR team. To show their gratitude, they had a plaque made for Ray. He also received a letter of commendation from the Sheriff for his dedication to SAR efforts.

★

For Ray Shriver, finding Mike Muchaw's body was not simply the closing of the case of a missing man. Images of death and mutilation, and of a family's suffering, swept over him in waves. He kept seeing the remnants of this human being, and for a long time thereafter he felt haunted by the final end to which Muchaw had come. He had seen people broken up and burned, but not dismembered — not until now. In all the years he had been involved in local search and rescue, this recovery was the most shocking. The nightmares and insomnia drove him to seek counselling. He felt a kinship with this man Muchaw, relating in some ways to his drug habit and refusal to quit, to his inability to do those things that enable people to successfully be part of a family, a work force and a community.

Ray had himself once lived the life of a hippie and rebel. When he was young, he had refused to cut his long hair, had become caught up in drag racing and cars, and generally found himself in trouble. At nineteen, his driving licence was taken away for recklessness and speeding. He bothered little with schoolwork and received poor grades, but, like Mike Muchaw, he enjoyed sports — for him it was wrestling and football. With supreme effort, he had turned his life in a different direction, becoming a hard-working, successful man. He served as a soldier in the Vietnam War, and returned to marry and father two sons. He educated himself, then obtained a good job with an environmental engineering firm in Teton County. His job gives him jurisdiction over grading, designing small septic systems in rural areas, and analyzing various natural-resource issues such as wetlands, hazardous slopes and water quality.

"This is a special place," he explained. "It needs to be protected. I would like to prevent any further development if I can — keep it 'green.' I feel that it's my mission to protect this part of the earth. I love what I do and feel it is important and worthwhile work."

In addition to his work, Ray has selflessly offered his time and expertise as a member and training director for the Teton County volunteer search-and-rescue organization. But throughout all his successful efforts at creating a life for himself, he has never forgotten those early years.

"I realized at some point that I must comply and play the game society demands," he said. "I saw I was not getting anywhere, and knew I had to face reality. But it's very hard to actually pull it together. You do — I did — because I knew I had to." He did what Mike Muchaw had forever been unable to do.

"But early on, I did fail in many things," he said humbly. "My marriage — I should never have married. It constrained me when I wanted to go on weekend skiing trips, month-long climbing expeditions… I was away from home, learning to rock climb Grand Teton Mountain — I climbed it many times. I learned to rappel, to belay… I have to say that when my sons were small I couldn't relate to them. But now they accompany me — river running, climbing and skiing. During a ski trip with them in 1991, we got caught in an avalanche and nearly perished." This rescue — his own, and that of his sons — was the beginning of his interest in search and rescue.

At around the time of Ray's avalanche misadventure, Doug Meyer was working as a ski-lift operator. He had firsthand knowledge of the accidents that occurred on the ski slopes. No SAR system existed at that time in Jackson; the sheriff and his deputies were, in addition to their law-enforcement duties, solely responsible for search, rescue and recovery. But the sheriff had neither the time nor the staff to devote to search and rescue. Meanwhile, people were increasingly participating in technical, and potentially hazardous, outdoor adventure. Ever nastier mishaps were occurring.

Ray had become friends with Sheriff Roger Millward. The two skied together while their wives knitted and wove. One day, the sheriff called Ray. "We potentially have a big problem on our hands," he said. "The place is growing. Ugly accidents are happening. We don't have the manpower, the expertise or the equipment to do much about it. We need volunteers to train and form a search-and-rescue organization."

"Count me in," said Ray without a moment's hesitation. This was the beginning of a huge effort that was to consume all of his spare time, but not one moment of it did he begrudge.

"This is a wonderful community," he said. "I wanted to give something back. It's a small town where most people know most others, and I wanted to help anyone in need. About that time, two separate avalanches occurred and killed the people on the slopes. That's when Sheriff Millward called Doug Meyer about starting an avalanche rescue team; that's how the SAR team got started."

Advertisements were placed for volunteers. To the astonishment of the sheriff, two hundred and fifty people applied. Each, like Ray, expressed a general desire to give to their community and help people in jeopardy. All the applicants were screened, and thirty were accepted. None had had any SAR training, other than backcountry survival skills and expertise in skiing, kayaking and climbing.

A training program was designed with help from Alan Merrell, a man who had been on a SAR team in Nevada, as well as three commercial SAR operations: Rescue 3, NASAR and CMC. Ray's military background also proved helpful. Costs were borne by the county, aided by private donations. Training took one year to complete. It included land navigation, high angle rope rescue (climbing), cave and swiftwater rescue and first aid. Radio communications skills were added, together with helicopter operations —

how to enter and exit and work around them — wilderness survival skills, and how to pack horses and ride them. In addition, those with expertise in blood-borne pathogens were involved. Donations came in all the time to help defray costs. Since 1993 more than two hundred missions of various kinds have been completed. In 1998 rescues using search dogs were begun.

"The training of volunteers is intensive," said Doug Meyers. "We have about sixty SAR cases a year: some plane crashes, high-angle river rescues, whitewater rafting, kayaking, cave rescues, climbing, swiftwater, lost persons — not many, but they are the most difficult of all searches, about three a year. Even though it's not really that easy to get lost here in this county. Missing persons is mostly about injured people and lost hikers. Muchaw's case was unusual."

Doug spoke about how well SAR is supported in Teton County. It costs $800 to buy personal gear for each SAR volunteer — a cost usually paid by local charities and nonprofit business groups, but only if a member completes two-thirds of the training and engages in 50 per cent of the callouts. Government funding from the county is added. The organization has loose ties to the sheriff's office — loose, because the group likes to be free to make its own decisions. The sheriff, from the beginning, has been 100 per cent supportive of SAR efforts.

"Volunteers want to give back to the community, and to show compassion. Lots of people here are outdoor enthusiasts and understand that others, too, are driven to play in the outdoors, to seek challenges. It could be them — they must help. And of course, they love their place. I've made a lot of the mistakes these people make who get into trouble, so I understand and sympathize — it could have been me. I've been there, done that."

Doug tries not to get involved emotionally with the people he rescues or searches for. "So often the person is not alive, and this is very draining if you get involved, or even if you don't. I guess about a third of all calls are for recovery."

Ray Shriver agrees. He has been personally involved in more than thirty fatalities during the time he has been doing SAR work. Mike Muchaw's case was the most difficult and draining of all, but he is not deterred. He has spent eleven years as a founding member of the board of directors, and has been responsible for all training programs during that time. He remains the only dog handler on the team. Each day after work, he is outdoors for an hour or more, playing with or training his dog. Weekends are more of the same, but in the company of other dog handlers.

"In rural communities, volunteer SAR workers make big sacrifices," he said. "Some of the work, and some situations volunteers find themselves in, can be horrible, gut-wrenching and ugly. But unless volunteers do it, no one does. But it also provides challenges. It offers the rewards of being able to show compassion, to do humanitarian things for other people. You know, we're all in this [life] together; we have to help each other."

Today, Ray lives in a south-facing log cabin that looks across to Mount Oliver, a classic limestone pyramid rising 9,500 feet up into the clouds, snowcapped for all but two months of the year. From his windows he can see Game Creek and Moose Creek Drainage. Depending on the position of sun and cloud cover, the mountains can loom close or appear to be more distant. His home, near the Idaho-Wyoming border at the upper end of a high mountain valley, sits 6,450 feet above sea level in the middle of an old twenty-acre hay meadow, surrounded by trees and flowering bushes: chokecherries, aspen and sagebrush five feet high.

"I do have neighbours, but not close ones," he said. "I came here from the flat plains of Kansas, feeling I needed a wilder, less civilized place to live — like mountains and valleys and rivers and forests. I wanted the lifestyle of the West because I love the outdoor world, and I need its challenges."

WHAT WILL I BE WHEN I GROW UP?
Lynn Canyon, British Columbia

Don't regret the things you've done, just the things you haven't. — Murdoch Falconer

Lynn Canyon, just to the north of Vancouver, is Brad Falconer's office. He stands, on this warm day in late August, looking above and about him at the giant red cedars, the hemlock and the fir trees that crowd the park's slopes; he listens to the roaring of the waters as they twist through their narrow canyon a hundred or more feet below. A subtle change has occurred in the colour of the leaves; the air feels different, he thinks. Ah, but how soon the earth begins to change, how brief its summer flowering. He notes that fewer people come to visit the park each day. This late afternoon, he's been on duty since noon and things have been quiet. A few strollers linger on the shady paths; a scattering of local kids yell to each other and laugh as they clatter back and forth across the suspension bridge. Brad sees them most days after school and during the weekends. In fact, he practically watches them grow up. Here's this tough kid Kyle, running in and out the park as if it were his own backyard.

Brad relaxes for a few moments in the doorway of the ranger's adminis-trative building that sits on a rise not far from the park's entrance. He's a very tall young man whose slight frame belies the muscular strength hidden with-in. The sun shines on a face suffused with innocence, sensitivity and warmth.

He remarks to himself how nice it is to have a moment's respite after a hectic summer of strange incidents.

Brad Falconer in Lynn Canyon, British Columbia.

"This is what I'm supposed to do in this life," he thinks contentedly, proud of all the skills he gained at a young age so that now, in his thirties, he's fully qualified to walk in and get this job as forest ranger. But not only that: he is also a member of the Canadian Amphibious Search Team

(CAST). CAST has become the part of his life that consumes all his waking moments outside of work hours, the part that has reached into his dreams, absorbed his emotional and physical energies and given shape, purpose and meaning to his life.

He has followed a strange and tortuous path to get to this place. After high school, there was motocross racing for Honda, then the music store. Meanwhile, there were the first-aid courses and rescue training that have qualified him for this current job in the northern idyll that he considers Lynn Canyon to be. And it was that training that prepared him to become a member of the unique elite search-and-recovery organization known simply as CAST.

In the dappled warmth of a sun that occasionally pierces the canopy of leaves, Brad stands thinking, remembering all the broken bones and concussions he suffered while motocross racing. He remembers his job at A&B Sound — ten whole years of it. He'd loved bluegrass, hip-hop, country, classical — heck, the whole gamut — but as one year slid into another, and another, he gradually became aware of how much he disliked office politics and being crowded by other people. Given his introspective nature, it was little wonder his spare time was filled with the pursuit of solitary sports: mountain and rock climbing, cycling and skiing. He realized, with some surprise, how much he liked being alone, being responsible for his own fate. To live or die was up to him, and no one else.

One day in the music store, something strange happened to him. Up and down the cramped aisles he walked, music droning overhead all the while, when a sudden feeling of oppression seized him. His first impulse was to blame the absence of fresh air in the building, as well as sunlight and the breezes that stirred the trees and the aroma of the outdoor world that he loved so much. Every day was the same, as he walked between the endless, tightly packed rows of gleaming merchandise and the stock room. He stood poised before a row of neatly packaged CDs, feeling a roaring in his head. He shook it, then stood as one paralyzed. Then came his moment of epiphany: here he was, doing work that was safe, predictable and nothing if not boring. Then he pictured himself: a loner, independent, preferring to work by himself. A man who loved physical challenges. Until this day, he had lived without any real knowledge of these characteristics about himself.

When he finally regained the ability to move, his first act was to walk out the door and drive home. He'd gone to work as one person and come home another.

"There are no challenges to what I'm doing," he told his wife when he got home. "I get up and go to work indoors, just to move around a bunch of CDs. I go home, then back the next day, to do it all over again. That's what I do."

His young, blonde spouse, Kelly, stared at him in amazement. She was stunned into silence. He looked at her intensely and said, "You know, it seems to me I'm not really living my life, but just going through it." He paused, then added: "I don't feel really alive. I'm not making any mark in life. It doesn't mean anything. This is no way to live." His habitually kind and gentle expression transformed into a troubled frown.

In his mind that evening, he saw his grandfather leaning over him, blue eyes twinkling as he rocked back and forth in his chair on the front porch of his home.

"Well, my boy, from where I stand, I see that you gotta have a photo album of your life to look back on. Just so you know you've done everything you wanted to do. And here's something else: don't regret what you've done, just the things you haven't. When you're old, you don't get to do things over. Make your life count, and do things you're proud of."

★

Brad was lost in this reverie, the sun shining on his face, still seeing his grandfather's face when he became aware of a stillness in the park. It was shattered almost immediately by a loud shout. Brad was on his feet in a split second, looking into the face of a kid called Kyle S. who stared back at him, a few feet distant, his eyes like huge saucers.

"Wanna know something? I just found a body — I tripped over it, way down there… Oh man, I think I just stood on a dead guy."

Brad was stunned. He moved, grabbed the kid's hand and said, "You better come and show me where." The boy led the lanky forest ranger, stooping through the trees and down a shadowy trail deep into the park, a twisting track a few hundred metres off the main trail. It was a no-man's-land, a dank and canopied place, a spot where few people ventured. Overhanging hemlocks cast permanent shade over the rough-hewn path that rarely registered the thump of human feet.

"What were you doing down here?" Brad asked the kid.

"It's a shortcut to our swimming hole," Kyle answered, surprised, as if Brad ought to know these things.

Brad prepared himself for what he thought he would find: a body most likely in a state of decomposition. Probably a suicide, he thought. A fitting place to choose to end one's life: a quiet, peaceful, beautiful place — but creepy, too, with heavy, tangled undergrowth. He wrinkled his nose at the dank earth all about him, the stillness of the cloistered air. Abruptly, among straggling branches and ferns at the foot of a giant red cedar, the man and the boy came upon a shape on the dirt path — a skeleton in clothing, the twisted form of what had once been a man. Brad stood and stared, then stooped and carefully turned the face toward him, looking for signs of its owner's identity. The boy's instant cry echoed his own as they both recognized Tim Watson, a middle-aged man who had lived close to the park, his house actually backing onto it. Brad remembered how he had first seen the man wandering many months ago, lonely and despondent, along the various paths and trails of the park — more frequently since his teenage son had been caught repeatedly breaking into the ranger's office. Brad had felt curious about him then, wondered what solace he had been seeking, what answers he thought he might find in this near-wilderness. It seemed to him as he stared at the corpse that Watson had deliberately chosen a beautiful, and secret, place, one he knew well, to be the spot upon which he would end his tortured life.

If only to distract himself from the immediate task at hand, Falconer turned to Kyle and suggested, "How about, in the future, you stay on the main trails? Then you won't meet up with dead bodies. Come on, we better get back to the office."

Dave Irvine, Brad's fellow ranger, immediately phoned the Royal Canadian Mounted Police to inform them of the discovery.

As it turned out, Kyle did not heed the ranger's advice. Just one week later he ran into the office with news that he had found another body in a remote corner of the park.

"There are bodies that have probably lain in secluded spots in this park for eons," Dave said. "You have to admit, it's a quiet and dignified spot to end your days if you're so inclined."

Brad and his colleagues had been hired, not to take care of the forests or to be involved in conservation, but to provide medical assistance and perform rescue work. He and his fellow rangers responded to medical emergencies and assisted the fire department with rescues. Their jurisdiction encompassed 250 hectares of mountainous forests and a river that coursed through a rocky gorge. It was named Lynn Canyon and dedicated as a provincial park in 1991. All too quickly it became a haven for gangs of young people selling and doing drugs. As a result, the park was sometimes dubbed Killer Canyon, and not only because people chose to die here.

"It was like the Wild West," Dave said. "People knew it was policed very little by the RCMP, so it was a good place to go and party, get drunk, do stupid things. Hells Angels used it, too, and bodies were dropped here. Then the local kids would come in after school and on weekends and do bizarre things — you know, show off. They'd go cliff jumping and swimming in the canyon, not realizing that the water came from high up in the mountains — melting snow and glacial runoff — and there was no sun creeping through to warm it up. The kids saw others jumping into the rapids on a dare, so they imitated, not understanding that conditions can change. They'd swim up a channel to explore, but get too cold to swim back, and then they were in trouble from hypothermia. Some hit rocks when they jumped. Others went kayaking, got drunk and fooled around. It's like, 'Hey, I'm seventeen and haven't been killed yet.'"

After Brad had found his first body in the park, Dave told him, "You'll get used to it. Plenty have been dumped here over the years; plenty more will do it, and some will always do themselves in accidentally."

A year passed, then two. Sometimes Brad would catch glimpses of the future stretching out before him, see himself as an older man, still striding the leafy pathways of the canyon. Then another image hovered: he was older yet again, bent a little as he walked the pathways of this treed and canopied paradise; an old man still stumbling over dead bodies. He came to view the park in the same way as he'd thought about the music store, as a constant reputation of the same routine. Faint stirrings arose within him of the desire for something more, the need for new challenges. Every so often he thought about the members of CAST, the Canadian Amphibious Search Team. He, Brad, might be a loner, but he'd taken a liking to the fellows in this organization. Perhaps he'd been a little too committed to the life of a hermit; maybe he needed to be around others like himself. The questions persisted as time passed.

And such thoughts were not far below the surface when Brad, as a member of Rescue 3 International,* attended a special meeting to which members of CAST had been invited.

"Crazy … guys who dive in zero visibility, in swiftwater currents … who do all kinds of insane crap!" These were the ways in which members of Rescue 3 International described CAST members. It was an image belied by the way they presented themselves at the meeting — they were dressed formally and behaved respectfully. They didn't seem interested in uniforms or slogans. By the end of the meeting, Brad felt like running after them and saying, "I want to be part of your organization."

★

Brad Falconer did eventually join CAST, but not before he had survived a torturous physical and mental trial.

"We need to see what you can do," Tim MacFarlane, the group's founder and president, told him bluntly on a day that was to be forever etched in his memory. "If you have what it takes, if you have the right stuff, if you can fit in, we'll consider having you a member of CAST."

Need to see what he could do … if he had the right stuff … Brad felt anxious as he approached the defining day. Tim and his group's co-founder, Jim Garrett, commanded the contestants: each was to perform under-overs — the swimming of laps one way underwater, returning on the surface. This was to be followed by bobs — breath-holding under sixteen feet of water. While they were below the surface, candidates were to unscrew nuts and bolts from a plate that lay on the pool's bottom. Then they were to tread water for one hour.

---

*An organization that provides training in swift-water rescue as well as ground, boat, water, and high-angle search and rescue.

Next came the team-building exercise. *Team-building? Teams? Oh, boy,* thought Brad. *But I'm pretty good at all this stuff, and how tough can it be?* And so he encouraged himself. This "stuff" involved a team of eight people, each of them treading water for half an hour while they supported a twenty-four-pound dive belt. A team leader had to be identified and supported in the water as he disassembled the belt and passed out the weights. Once this was accomplished, other team members were required to pass the weights around and keep them afloat. If a weight was dropped inadvertently, a team member had to swim to the bottom to retrieve it. Anyone accidentally touching the side of the pool was considered "drowned" and could no longer assist the others. The exercise was taxing — brutal, some said — and a few hopefuls deliberately touched the side of the pool in order to "drown" themselves. Others simply swam away. The tasks for the remaining members were made all the more difficult.

"You don't have to like it. You just have to do it," Tim said then. It was a mantra he would often repeat.

The seeming trackless eternity of that half-hour eventually passed. The belt got reassembled, but as it was being passed up to Tim, it dropped and fell to the bottom of the pool. Brad swam down to retrieve it, but found it too heavy to carry to the surface alone. Two other members helped him, and together they carried it up and out of the pool.

Brad was considered to have the "right stuff," and he became a member of CAST, but not before he endured its founder's famous pep talk.

"Most of you have a mental idea about what you think are your limits," MacFarlane said, "but it's just something you've set up in your minds… We've been called wannabes — little boys pretending to be men — but we already do it. We're not little kids playing a game. I mean, some of us have been in Afghanistan as soldiers; others as ski patrol, as search and rescue and divers. There's a lot of skill among us, and none of us do this for fun. We do it because it matters to us. A person has got to have a mission, some reason for being on this earth, a purpose for their life.

"CAST is the solution when all else fails. It's about attitudes — about how you go after your personal best. If you become part of this group, you become part of a family; you're closer to us than any blood

Tim MacFarlane, founder and director of the Canadian Amphibious Search Team.

brothers. Whatever you achieve, we'll be sharing it with you — and your pain and difficulties, too. We work together as brothers, for others. We bring closure to grieving families so they can get on with their lives."

As his exposure to the various CAST members increased, Brad got the impression it was a society made up of an elite, select few, all of whom were expert in the various components of search and rescue and had been rigorously trained. Silent, like panthers in the wild, they knew what they were doing, and it was not important that others knew.

Only the team-building part gave Brad pause. His sense of independence was such that he had taken many courses in advanced first-aid, become a paramedic, in order to care for himself and others if the need ever arose. Yet Brad understood now that something greater than his pleasure in his own company could be gained: this thing about bonding and camaraderie … his mind reeled. Deep in his bones, he wanted this; it was the beginning of a personal odyssey that would alter how he saw the world, alter how he interacted with it.

Once accepted into CAST, Brad was given a pep talk by Tim MacFarlane, who was by this point a figure who loomed in his mind as a kind of beneficent godfather. It was a talk he was never to forget. "The road is long and not easy," MacFarlane counselled. "It can be dangerous. Do you want to walk it?"

"I felt a bit like a kid," he confessed afterwards.

How soon Brad was to be tested in his capacity as a member of CAST. How soon he would be thrust into the cruel realities of the world out there.

★

They had cried themselves out. Now, exhausted, cold and wet, the teenagers headed for their vehicles parked near the old wooden bridge, silent as an army approaching its enemy. Twelve of them had come; eleven were going home. Only Jay remained with the police and ambulance attendants — Jay, who would carry within him an inner agony, like an albatross around his neck, for the rest of his days. He had been fooling around — daredevil stuff, hanging over the edge of the cliff — and had fallen into the raging waters below. His buddy, without thinking, had jumped right in after him. Jay had struggled to shore, but his friend disappeared in a fury of white water and drowned in the rocky gorge.

All had searched frantically. Some became hysterical. Darkness had begun to creep through the trees when local rescue teams arrived. The would-be adventurers, all so young, lean and supple, now moved as if imbued with the dull pain of the elderly, weighted down with a new comprehension of their mortality because of one life snuffed out, drowned and washed away somewhere; not even a body to take home.

The strobe lights of police vehicles and ambulances now illuminated the woods that crowded the lonely spot near Liumchen Creek, the place where the young people had set up camp with such joy and abandon just two days earlier. Volunteer rescuers worked under the direction of the Chilliwack Provincial Emergency Program (PEP) and the RCMP's ground and water-based groups arrived very soon after news of the accident was learned.

The dense undergrowth snapped under the feet of a dozen or more search-and-rescue workers. Rain dripped down the collars of the local groups who organized themselves under the province's emergency program and huddled to discuss search protocols and methods. Members of the RCMP had already fanned out through the trees and towards the banks of the creek. The retreating line of teenagers had been questioned by police, and since there was nothing further they could do they were advised to go home. They gathered their tents and equipment, loaded their vehicles in near silence, and were gone.

★

Tim MacFarlane, the founder of CAST, heard on the radio that a teenage boy had drowned in Liumchen Creek, near Chilliwack, and that he had been part of a high school graduation party that took the form of a camping trip in this remote area. One boy had fallen into the freezing waters of the creek, while another jumped in to save him. The first climbed out, but the would-be rescuer drowned. The RCMP and local search-and-rescue teams were searching for the body. So far, they'd had no luck.

Tim phoned the police to offer the help of his team.

"No, thanks," he was told. In spite of the rebuff, he decided to scout around anyway. He contacted team members John Merrett, Roy Klohn and Brad Falconer. Together they drove to Chilliwack to see what they could do to help — unobtrusively.

The van belonging to the Canadian Amphibious Search Team sped toward the scene along a highway that ran like a ribbon down the middle of a fertile farming area. Cattle grazed the flat land spread along a valley bottom, all green to the rocky outcrops of mountains. Farmhouses squatted, bathed gently in the late afternoon sun — a placid pastoral scene out of sync with the mood of the men. Fields soon gave way to encroaching mountain ranges, and the valley narrowed. In places, the rock face seemed to hang right over them, sharp and cruel. Closer still to Chilliwack, the bush spread densely to the roadsides. The van now entered an old logging road and crossed a wooden bridge that stretched across the creek. It lay concealed in a steep valley, an old wilderness area that had once been a forestry campsite. On the brightest day the spot would still be dark, with its overhanging trees and undergrowth that crept close to the muddy clearing the teenagers had chosen as the place to pitch their tents.

Brad Falconer asked in wonder, "Why would these kids choose such a place for their camping trip?"

"Easy for them to get to," John Merrett answered. "Big enough for several tents, and isolated enough. It's about fifteen to twenty minutes' drive from the main road, close to the Chilliwack River. When you're seventeen, you're not all that selective."

"Ugh, I could think of almost anyplace better than this," another said. They drove close to the one open area where many other vehicles were parked, and all about them hung a dripping green world: trees descended to the creek's edge, whispering above them, and the dark stained rock face that formed the creek's boundaries menaced on either side. Below them, creek waters swirled. *How fast the moods of the atmosphere can change*, thought Brad, remembering the pale sunshine bathing the farmland earlier.

The members of CAST spilled out of their van, their boots squelching the mud underfoot. They approached SAR crews from

Chilliwack to ask if anything had yet been found, what areas had already been searched, and what further plans, if any, they had. A discussion ensued. CAST members offered suggestions, but were ignored. It seemed to Brad that these other crews wanted no part of the CAST people, interpreting their offer of assistance as interference.

"These other groups just don't want us around," Jim Garrett said to the new recruits. "It's common; we expect it. We just say, 'Fine, we're happy if you guys are successful and there's closure for the family.'"

"No one's found the boy, or any part of him," MacFarlane said. "Here's what's to be done, *quietly* — the rest of them don't have to know what we're doing. If the body's not anyplace it was thought to be, not anyplace that's already been searched, then we have to study the flow of the stream and the currents — yeah, I know it's been done, but we have to do it again. Find the obstacles that have not been accounted for. What about the waterfalls — has anyone looked under them, on either side of them?" His eyes were piercing as they ranged over each of them in turn. "We have to find this guy; none of us can begin to imagine what this must be like for the family."

Brad looked about at a scene familiar to him, but imbued with a particular clarity. Yes, the trees were the same as his everyday world in Lynn Canyon Park: old red cedars, hemlocks and fir, long dank weeds and underbrush. The same roaring of waters squeezed between the imprisoning walls of a canyon. In the park, he would stride about, a ranger in control, reacting to any emergency, assisting people and controlling situations. In this place, at this moment, there was a familiar urgency, but he was not the one in control. In fact, he was not even wanted.

The afternoon fell upon them in a hurry; the gathering clouds opened and began emptying themselves violently, heaving through the dense foliage onto the men underneath. Tim ran his hand over his clean-shaven head. Jim turned up his collar to deflect the deluge. John stood tall, straight and unflinching as though he were part of the forest itself, seemingly oblivious to the cold and drenching rain. They continued their search of the area: the rock pools beyond the rush of the series of waterfalls, the flow of the stampeding water, all the catchment areas. They combed whatever creek banks were accessible among dead branches and rocky outcrops where a body could be trapped. Two small waterfalls culminated in a large one, their waters then heading swiftly under the bridge and out toward the highway, eventually spreading out to form a wide, shallow creek.

Tim the detective unflaggingly searched for clues that helped explain people's motives and habits, as well as those that helped him comprehend the vicissitudes of the natural world — for instance, the flow of the creek.

"My guess is this is where the body will be," he said, pointing to the base of the large waterfall. "Right here." They stood staring down at the fall where about seventy feet of water thundered into the narrow gorge that stretched just a hundred and fifty yards from one cliff face to the other. Each strained to see through the falling dusk, but the coming darkness foiled any attempt to search. The group made the long journey home in silence, like bloodhounds called off the trail, frustrated.

Crew members returned to Liumchen Creek whenever an opportunity presented itself, offered their help to the local search teams and the RCMP, but were rebuffed once again. Undeterred, they continued, as time allowed, to hike the trails and search the creek, the canyon and waterfalls. Recognizing the need to retrieve the body for the sake of his family, they would not give up.

The summer passed without any sign of a body. The search was called off by the provincial volunteer groups and the RCMP because of time and cost constraints. Not long afterward, Tim received a phone call from the boy's family, asking if CAST would continue to try to find the body. The family would begin raising money to pay the team's costs. CAST now mounted a full-scale search effort, but at the last minute the family said they were not prepared to pay.

During the Labour Day weekend, John Merrett took a group of new CAST recruits to Liumchen Creek and used this tragic drowning as a training exercise in navigation and rope work. A few weeks earlier, John had scouted out the area once more and identified three areas that he wanted to search. The group took with them navigational equipment, rope and all the equipment necessary to conduct a serious search of an isolated and treacherous canyon.

The searchers crowded together at the highest point of the canyon walls. Sheer cliffs fell away, stark and smooth on one side and a steep-sided gully on the other. The rocky gorge below was protected by giant walls that rose at ninety-degree angles from the torrents of water racing out to join the river; it seemed to them an inaccessible abyss.

Attention was focused on the large waterfall, and the area at its base was identified as the likeliest spot where the boy's body might have been trapped. John began training his recruits in the use of ropes and other equipment they would need to scale the canyon's walls, starting at the highest point above the water. A tense half-hour followed as his trainees rappelled down sheer walls of smooth rock.

A shout pierced the air. A recruit had spotted something in the water at the foot of the large waterfall, and it looked like a boy's body stretched over a rock near the side of the canyon.

John pulled out his cell phone to call Tim. "Hey, it looks like we've found the boy's body," he said.

"Well! Okay, great. I'm on my way." An hour and a half later, Tim arrived in the van, soon to be joined by Brad Falconer and Dave Ramsay, his two CAST members experienced in the type of recovery that would be required: swiftwater rescue and rappelling.

★

"It was like this," said Brad Falconer. "I'm driving with my wife to go shopping. I got this message from my boss: 'We've found the boy's body, but we can't get at it. We need you, if you can get here soon.'" Need him? Of course he would come! Regardless of time of day, inconvenience or general fatigue, he would get there.

"I dropped Kelly off at home, picked up my gear, met up with the others and we got there as fast as we could," he said. Each man took with him dry suits, helmets, masks, fins and gloves, throw bags with rope, life jackets, personal flotation devices, a body bag, a stokes litter and a camera.

Tim swung the van into the muddy campground, joining CAST members Dan Hildebrand, Dave Ramsay, Christine Leipscheur and Andy Meecker. The group strode towards the creek that ran close by the camp. They saw how it flowed towards the waterfalls, which were about three hundred metres distant on a steep slope. At the bottom of the last fall lay the boy's body. Tim saw how the first waterfall dropped down ten to fifteen feet, the second a little deeper, and the third thundered about a hundred and fifty feet below. He heard how Meecker, the CAST member described as "the little engine that could" and "the howdy-doody kid who just goes," had stripped to his boxer shorts and begun a climb down the nearly vertical cliff sides. Squirrel-like, he'd reached the cliff bottom and plunged into the icy creek waters to confirm that what they had seen from the top was indeed the boy's body.

John Merrett, Dave Ramsay and Brad Falconer walked along the water's edge and began rappelling down the sides of the canyon to get to the pools at the base of each waterfall and to the pool at the very bottom. The canyon narrowed sharply at this point and the water roared through it. At the base of the big waterfall stood a boulder the size of a large car, and it was there the body had become wedged — jammed between the boulder and the sheer cliff walls, the powerful body of water thundering upon him.

Dave and Brad, the two members of CAST with swiftwater rescue training, entered the water and fought their way under the thunderous falls, searching the base when the water levels had dropped. Each put on a face mask as they approached the mutilated figure of the boy. He lay twisted in a prone position, one arm hooked over his head, his back to the cliff face and his legs folded in front. Half his rib cage was exposed.

"It was a bit risky for us," Dave Ramsay said. "We had to get right under the fall ourselves because there was no way to get behind it; we had to stand under it, and felt it pounding down on us. We were a bit worried too about being washed away by the river currents. We'd rappelled down the canyon walls and swum over to the rock where the body was jammed right under the fall. Our dilemma was: how can we pull him out without causing more disintegration to his body? Also, we had to find a way to work under the thundering water — well, trying to avoid being under it while we extricated the body — and all the while, not letting ourselves get swept away with the flow.

"Anytime you're working in a river, there's danger," he added. "We were worried mostly about the waterfall itself, and about how to get him out from under it where he was pinned, and then all the way up the cliff.

I mean, you can't move rocks, and he was disintegrating. We do try to preserve the body for sake of the family."

Brad stared at the body. "His feet are pointing the wrong the way and are all twisted about," he said. "How awfully painful it must be for him!" He shook himself then. How silly — this poor boy is dead and won't feel any pain in his feet. Afterwards he explained: "You know, I always feel I must introduce myself whenever I meet someone, whether alive or dead; it makes me feel better. I know every person has their own way of reacting and dealing with death, and especially the sudden confrontation with it. Some laugh and crack black jokes, some cry, some turn away, others are very respectful and treat the body as though it were still alive. I believe that the dead person's spirit is still around and must be treated with respect."

Dave, meanwhile, explained that he feels less affected when he has to deal with a long-dead person than with someone only recently deceased. "It's hard when you've just seen the person alive, and then they're dead," he said. "I don't relate so immediately to a long-deceased person, a body hardly recognizable as having once been a person."

Tim, in command of CAST's operations at the cliff's edge, had contacted the RCMP to tell them where the body lay and about the difficulties involved in getting it up the canyon walls.

"Good. Would your team recover the body and bring it out of the canyon?"

"It's going to be a long and costly job," said Tim. "We need to get equipment, my members need their travel costs and time reimbursed. They face difficulty and danger — are you prepared to cover this?" Negotiations for cost recovery continued as Dave and Brad plunged about in water so cold that Brad developed a headache. Eventually the RCMP agreed to reimburse CAST for the costs incurred in recovering the body.

There were also costs that could not be repaid. This was the type of recovery in which a body hunter prays not to have to be involved, the type of body they would rather not find. It struck at their sensibilities — even those who fancied themselves hardened. There were huge logistical problems in retrieving the body, one that belonged to a young man who had attempted to save the life of another. Here lay a hero, his remains disintegrated by time and the effects of rocks and waterfalls.

The CAST members wore masks. Brad climbed a rock and lay prone on it, trying to figure out if the body could be pulled straight up or shifted closer to the bank.

"Pick him up by his rib cage!" shouted John.

"You get down here and do it," Brad muttered behind his mask. While trying to remain respectful of the corpse, he and Andy Meecker slowly dragged the body bag over the young man's head and shoulders, shifting him inch by inch, pulling at his jeans and moving him gently in the water and then into the bag. RCMP officers waited at the top of cliff by their vehicles. As the CAST crew inched him into the body bag, they performed a forensic examination, then, assisted by CAST recruits, carried the body up the cliffs. For some of them, it was the first corpse they had seen. For some, it would be the last.

CAST crew had been twice turned aside from assisting in this search, but they had persevered when other search-and-rescue bodies had long since given up.

Brad Falconer spoke about this recovery some time afterward. "A body maintains an imprint of the person who has just left it," he said, "like the signature of that person. This is why I treat dead people with respect." He does admit that this was one of the least pleasant recoveries with which he has been involved. He spoke of the decomposition and the trauma to the body and said quietly, "It leaves an impression. Individually, these cases don't bother me, but cumulatively I guess they do. One day I might have problems and have to deal with them, who knows? For now, CAST plays a very big role in my life. It is my family, as close as any mother, father, wife and children could be."

CAST members know that many of their experiences may seem lurid, morbid, depressing and unpleasant to most others. Often, they are. But each member knows that what he or she offers is unique and compassionate; no one else provides a service they see as necessary — "When all else fails" is their motto. As well, it gives a sense of purpose to their lives, the opportunity to offer compassion, to challenge themselves to achieve their personal best.

Not least, there is the sense of belonging to a group that that holds common values, the associated bonding that is forged when difficult and sometimes life-threatening events are shared. The benefits cannot be overestimated.

"Some members joke about being wheeled out of a CAST retirement home and sitting out on the deck, sharing memories," Brad says, smiling.

Left to right: Cary Smith, Bill Hopps, Matt Hopps, Don Kinnamon.

AFTER THE DAY, THE LONG NIGHT

Santa Cruz, California

I expected every wave would have swallowed us up, and every single time the ship fell down ... in the trough or hollow of the sea, we should never rise more; and in this agony of mind I made many vows... — Daniel Defoe, 1719

"Hey, Matt, how about a sail? The wind should pick up later today — want to get wet with me?"

"Sure, sounds like fun," said his brother.

"It happened like this," Bill Hopps said. "In two weeks I was to be married to Nadine. Here it was in the middle of Labour Day weekend; warm, sunny, a good wind, and there was our Prindle catamaran on Santa Cruz Beach. I was thinking how the sailing season was almost over, and it made the idea of getting out on the water seem compelling — why not a quick spin beyond the harbour? Take every sailing opportunity you can get, that's what I believed. I picked up the phone to my brother."

That fateful phone call resulted in four adults deciding to make a whole day of it — Bill and Nadine to go for a massage first, then to meet Matt, Darnelle and their five-year-old son Ryan on the beach.

"I got my massage while Bill unloaded the boat and gear on the beach," Nadine said. "Bill decided to cancel his — because of the wind, he said, 'We should hurry up and get out there.' I watched them getting ready; thought of asking if I could go, too, then changed my mind. We said goodbye, and in the blink of an eye they were a speck on the horizon."

Someone watched as Matt and Bill Hopps launched their white-hulled catamaran, watched as they bucked their way out of the harbour in a sea made choppy by strong winds. Cary Smith, the assistant deputy harbour patrol in Santa Cruz, stood in the doorway to the office, shading his eyes from the glare of the midafternoon sun. Today, on this most westerly reaching stretch of the Pacific coast where the edge of the solid world gave way to a watery universe, the ocean heaved restlessly in short, choppy waves — the face of a monster showing its teeth in ruffled white grins. "Windy, yes, but not overwhelmingly, just a typical afternoon breeze, and not dangerous," Cary was to say later. "Santa Cruz itself is sheltered, but beyond the bay you get the ocean swells."

And catamaran sailing is always exhilarating, the Hopps brothers might have added. They might also have said that, while Monterey Bay can serve up the best of the Pacific Ocean, it can also deliver the worst. In spite of this, a hardy fleet of catamaran sailors call it home and think of it as the best place to sail in northern California.

Cary, long after this day and night ended, found himself endlessly replaying his sight of the brothers setting out in their catamaran, white froth breaking against the hull. Saw them as specks in the distance, their boat ultimately becoming indistinguishable from the sea. He wondered idly how often Matt and Bill Hopps had sailed upon the surface of this body of water, dipped into it, flown over it with enormous speed in their trusty Prindle cat — countless times, no doubt. Cary himself enjoyed the view of the land from out in the bay: the sweep of sand and shore, the town's busy-ness, the beauty of its contours against the backdrop of low-rise hills beyond — a perspective to be gained only from a distant, off-shore view.

Bill and Matt, sailors seasoned in the conditions of the Pacific Ocean in Monterey Bay and beyond, would not know that on this day one or both of them were about to be grasped and held in Neptune's cold embrace — that their time on Earth might be snapped short by today's mood of the ocean, and by a freak accident. One minute, they were enjoying the sound of the slick water against their hull; the next, they were being thrashed by gusting winds and giant swells and speeding out of control.

While the brothers flew across the surface of the sea, Nadine, Darnelle and little Ryan, enjoyed themselves on the beach. Santa Cruz

Bay, the quintessential beach and ocean playground and one of the busiest harbours on the coast, hummed with people and vessels of all kinds. Winds had chased off the fog, had dissipated moisture that otherwise would have slung about hills and beach; bright holiday crowds thronged restaurants, shops, wharf and boardwalk, while others lay supine in the sun. Beyond, sailing boats of all classes tossed on their moorings in the brisk wind out in the bay. A day at the beach or aboard a boat on a holiday weekend — this was a rite of passage.

Evening approached. Nadine looked at her watch. She saw sailing boats making their way to shore, but could see no sign of Bill and Matt.

"They really enjoy each other's company," she said, "so I expected them to be the last ones back. But both of us began to worry. It was six-thirty; Darnelle asked what we should do. Give them fifteen more minutes, I said. Then we went to the harbour master's office to get help."

Cary, still standing in the doorway of a three-storey grey building perched at the upper end of the beach, recognized his own state of exhaustion; he had come to the end of his shift as assistant deputy harbour master. On his shoulders, and those of his boss, lay responsibility for search-and-rescue within a thirty-mile radius of Santa Cruz Bay on behalf of San Francisco's Coast Guard. Also within the scope of their duties lay the safety of watercraft that came and went upon the tides, and all those that anchored in the bay. Harbour staff looked after the safety of surfers and maintained general order on the beach, the boardwalk, on the wharf. They even supervised the parking lot. Tonight, Cary felt ready for home and an evening of gazing at the TV. He dawdled, looked out over a beach still in constant motion: warm weather, the last long weekend of the season, and it's usually all on, he thought as he watched people soaking up the evening under the lights that beamed across the water, or frolicking in the warm breeze that blew down from the hills.

Only the harbour itself lay almost devoid of craft — an odd sight. No surf thundered onto the beach to attract the usual crowd of enthusiasts — only choppy waves that thrashed to shore to deter would-be swimmers. Small craft had long since retreated from the buffeting winds, leaving but a few larger vessels, all reefed in.

Now water taxis had begun checking out, and parking authorities shut down to count money. The harbour office itself began closing up for the day, leaving one man to tend the graveyard shift. Tonight, Don would stand on lonely vigil until dawn.

"I'm off," Cary said to Don Kinnamon, deputy harbour master. "Home — football and pizza for me tonight." Cary was often loath to leave at the end of a shift, but today had been long and busy; he sorely needed some space — and rest: he had a long workday ahead of him tomorrow. He glanced once more out the windows and over the holiday scene — still busy except for the bay waters and a near-deserted beach.

Cary piled his long, lanky frame into his car and drove the streets of Santa Cruz to his apartment. On 26th Avenue he stopped to grab an egg roll and some beer at Kong's Market. Finally he drew up in front of the bungalow he shared with a couple of friends.

The silence in the house jumped out at him: his roommates were away somewhere and Cary had the place to himself. As usual on weekends when you're working, everyone else is out having fun, he thought — a momentary sour note — but then he grinned. What could be better for him tonight than the evening he'd planned? He picked up the phone and ordered a pepperoni pizza, then switched on the television to begin watching Chris Berman's Fastest Three Minutes in Sports on ESPN. He cracked open a beer and took his first bite of pizza. Oh, boy, to relax at last. But the ringing of the phone shattered Cary's cocoon.

★

It had been around three in the afternoon when Matt and Bill Hopps headed out of the harbour, each wearing wetsuits and life jackets.

"Looks like we're dressed for getting wet," Bill had said — prophetically, it would seem — as Matt began harnessing himself.

"We just paid up Matt's life insurance," Darnelle had quipped.

The challenge for those who sail catamarans off an ocean beach is to get into deep water quickly so that the rudders can be put down. Otherwise there is no way of steering, and waves can send the cat crashing onto the beach. As soon as the Hopps brothers' boat touched water, it accelerated. Bill popped down the windward rudder, then the leeward one, pulled the sails in, and set them on a close reach — "an exciting one, but comfortable," he said. "It takes a while to get all prepared, set up right, and used to the motion, but this boat moves right along. It's a pretty powerful rig."

Bill and Matt's boat was a smaller version of a Tornado, a high-performance racing catamaran. Bill had purchased it because he wanted the speed and the excitement that go with it — "This cat covers ground very quickly," he said, grinning. At this moment, he began pulling in the sails, but the port rudder kept popping up and he found himself having to keep kicking it back down to get it to lock into its mechanism. "That this was happening was something new," he said. "We're sailing along, and at this point the rudders and tiller extension are connected to themselves and the boat, and the mainsheet and the traveller are both using one interconnected line. Most sailboats have two jib-sheets to trim the sail, but catamarans attach these lines together to create just one long line. One reason for this was so things can't get tangled up."

Abruptly, the rudder came off the back of the boat while the brothers were trying to tack. They had turned back into the wind when one of the lines for the mainsail wrapped itself around the rudder. The boat rolled over and turtled — *Not the end of the world*, Bill thought. *We'll probably be okay; because of the way we spun around we'll be headed for shore, and we can go in and fix the rudder.*

The two young men pulled the boat back upright, but it immediately flipped over again, this time right on top of them. They tried again. Each stood on the hull and held a righting line, pulling together. With the first effort, the boat somersaulted clear over both of them. With the next try, Matt climbed on top of the boat as it came upright, while Bill held the mast, hoping to keep the boat from flipping straight over again once it was righted. His weight would be more or less in the middle of the catamaran and would stabilize it.

It worked. Matt scrambled up on top, but because the rudder was loose on one end, the main sheet got tangled in it. The winds whipped the sails and the boat powered up. Matt stood astride it, trying to untangle the main sheet, but the boat took off. Bill was underneath and being dragged. He hung on tight, even while his face was being smashed about underneath the trampoline. The catamaran raced through the ocean swells at a furious speed and still Bill held on, even as he was flung through seething water — "like a water skier who falls, but doesn't let go of his tow line," he said. His arms ached, his hands and fingers grew numb and stiff. He continued to hang on, pain searing through his consciousness, until finally he could stand it no longer. He let go of the dolphin striker, knowing well that the number one rule on the sea is *Never let go of your boat*. He flung about then to grasp anything else he could. His stiffened hands grabbed a bungee cord, used to tie the trapeze on each side. He grasped this useless object for the next eight hours, not knowing what he would do with it, but it was an object, something tangible — it comforted him.

Once Bill let go, the catamaran took off even faster, and he watched it sail away from him — watched it surf, racing through the angry swells, until, about two hundred yards distant, he saw it flip over and turtle, its mast pointing straight down into the water. Bill knew that one person could not right it alone — what was Matt going to do? Bill panicked for about fifteen seconds, having a sudden image of himself as a tiny figure in the wide open sea, far from the holiday crowd in Santa Cruz Bay, the ocean currents pulling in one direction while high waves washed in another and thundered right over him. Ocean swells came at him from every direction, it seemed, and all the while he was being swept further and further from the cat. He told himself he had to move, and right away, to get to the boat. "I expended a lot of energy trying to reach it," he said. "I felt I had to stay close to it, because I was sure it would be found before I was. But after the first hour, although my eyes burned from trying to pierce the swells, it had gone. I didn't see it again. Then came some dark thoughts: *This is not good, I'm not going to last*. But hey, you don't quit — you don't give up hope — you even laugh. You try to make the most of what you have, in case something does happen.

"I felt happy it was me in the water rather than Matt," he added. "He had a wetsuit on, which would keep him warm for about five hours. My dry suit would last longer. Better that he survive, too, because of his son, Ryan — a dark thought."

Still he swam after the cat. He changed course, was beaten back, got pushed in one direction, then another.

He remembered to raise an arm and wave to his brother to show he was okay.

Bill could not know that Matt had deliberately tried to capsize the boat to try and stop its race across the water and give his brother a chance to swim to it — that he had grabbed the side stay, put his weight out and tipped it. Unfortunately, it spun up into the wind. Waves pushed it so that the mast pointed straight into a wind that hummed up under the sail. Together with its large trampoline, the cat still flew too fast across the waves for Bill to get to it.

I have to get this damned boat to stop! I have to get the mast to point the other way. These were Matt's thoughts. He did it — managed to get the mast up, but it immediately flipped back down the other way. He climbed out on the mast and got it pointing straight down in the water. It took him some time, but eventually he climbed back onto the boat to scan the seas in search of Bill, hoping his brother was close enough to reach him.

With no sign of his brother in the water, and time passing, Matt's thoughts became bleak. Bill was now a speck in the ocean; how could he be found, in the dark? How could he, Matt, live, if his brother died? What more could he do? There must be something — but what? He felt a sudden urge to know the time, remembered he had strapped his wristwatch to the trampoline and wondered how he could retrieve it. He'd have to get in the water and swim underneath. No! If he got it, he'd just be checking the time every two minutes, and feel even worse about its passing. Instead, he'd track time by the sun setting and the stars rising.

Bill, meanwhile, was thinking that in a situation like this, you have to believe that someone saw you flip and that they will raise the alarm and get a rescue organized. "Then, of course, you consider swimming to shore," he said. "I seriously contemplated it, but I knew I was pretty far distant — very far. Time passed and nothing happened. I'm still alone and floating out there. Then I thought, 'Okay, the next window of opportunity will be when Nadine, my fiancée, and Matt's wife, Darnelle, would realize they couldn't see us; that we should be back, or be on our way back. Since we're not, and they can't see us, then they'll go and tell someone.'"

Bill took comfort in the knowledge that he had considerable stamina. He had been in training to run a marathon — he'd run seventeen miles the week before, nine miles two days earlier. *I can hang on,* he thought. A logical man, he understood his chances were pretty slim, but still he tried to find ways to help himself. He took the waves sideways to help keep his head dry and preserve his body heat; he tried to conserve energy, because he knew he would be in the water for a long while. He again considered swimming to shore and tried to determine the direction of the drifts and currents to figure out which way they were taking him.

All the while, he searched the skies for airplanes, and some did fly over, but they kept right on flying. His mind never rested. What did he have that would help? A piece of bungee cord and a life jacket! What would be the time now? Probably late afternoon — about five or six. He felt surprised that he didn't feel cold, but then realized his body was still pumping large amounts of adrenaline. The window where someone would have seen the accident and sent help had come and gone, but the thought remained that someone would surely come — *must* come. Evening crept over the sea as the setting sun's rays flamed in a deepening sky to the west. Bill, a lonesome figure bobbing about like a stick in a turbulent ocean, watched it, his admiration intensified by a creeping thought that this might be the last sunset he would ever see.

But where was the fog? It usually rolled in during early evening, but not tonight. *Amazing, really*, he thought. *I'm out here in the Pacific Ocean admiring a sunset.* Then he got to thinking, *Okay, what might happen now?* Nadine and Darnelle might realize something's up and go for help. Bill held onto this belief until the time, by his best guess, would be around six — the time when most small boats return to shore and people go home. "I knew Nadine would not just jump up and go seek help; she knew I'd be the last person to look for it, knowing I would be embarrassed about things I'd done or forgotten. She knew I always felt silly about little things that went wrong. Now I was trying telepathically to tell her it was okay to get help. Still, nothing happened — but somehow, somewhere inside me, I remained hopeful that help would come."

★

Don Kinnamon, the senior deputy harbour master in Santa Cruz Bay, had worked for eleven and a half hours of his fourteen-hour shift. *Really busy day*, he thought, his right hand propping up his chin as he looked at the reports spread out before him. All the usual stuff: preparing and checking gear and boats, going through checklists of people and equipment, attending to what's on — special events, weather and fishing conditions, yacht races. He and Cary took turns monitoring visiting craft, patrolling the whole facility, parking, the boat launch ramp — anything and everything. There was always something to skewer a day's tasks, he thought. Today, a missing child, a boater in distress, huge crowds on the beach and boardwalk, parking problems, a broken water pipe on J Dock, a medical emergency, a drunk or two, some fireworks — as Cary would say, "Oh, man."

Don knew that the harbour, state and city lifeguards also had their hands full and needed the assistance of harbour personnel. Strong winds had been blowing most of the day, fifteen to thirty-five miles an hour, and by late afternoon the typically crowded bay waters were almost devoid of craft. Only one or two large sailboats remained, all reefed down but tossed about in the swells.

He sat in the harbour master's office, a smallish building that squatted a hundred yards up the beach and the boat launch below. He had been writing reports about the day's incidents, about to lock up to do a patrol, when a knock at the back door startled him. On the step stood two young women, their anxious faces turned up to him.

"My husband and his brother have not returned from a sailing trip. They left at three this afternoon," said Nadine.

Don looked at his watch and frowned. Five hours, in strong winds... these guys were in big trouble. "Why did you leave it so long to tell us?" he asked.

"Oh, we just thought they were having fun, that they might have gone on to another beach — they stay out late sometimes, but they always come home by dusk."

Don't think they're coming home this time, unless we find them and get them back in, Don thought. "Look, come on in and sit down. I gotta make some phone calls... get hold of the Coast Guard up the bay." Don scanned the surveillance cameras that gave a view over a distance on the sea of one mile. No sign of the brothers. "Do you suppose they would drive home?" the women were asked. "Drive home? We had the car keys," said Nadine.

What about the bars on the beach — might they be having a drink? "Two men, one in a dry suit, the other in a wet suit, no money on them and having drinks in a bar? I don't think so," said Nadine.

Don picked up the phone and called Cary Smith. "We've got an overdue Hobie Cat* — are you ready to go for a boat ride?"

"Oh, man…" came the reply. But Cary immediately felt fired up. His roommates were out living it up, his friends were out or away. Here was a chance to get on the water and make a little on a callback. He didn't think this search would take long; other boats were still on the water, and lots of people were still hanging about all over the beach. Most of all, this was a chance for him to be on a rescue with Don. "That's what we live for," Cary would confess afterward. But at this moment he had no idea he was about to embark on the rescue of his young lifetime. He jumped up, switched off the television, and folded his pizza into four quarters and stuffed it into a green bag, then into the pocket of his wet suit. He strode out the front door, got back into his car and returned the way he had so recently come. It was about eight-thirty in the evening.

Cary arrived at the harbour master's office to find two young women there, and Don on the phone, speaking to the Coast Guard in San Francisco. "… boat probably overturned, lost because of the gusting winds," he said. "Hobie Cats are pretty unstable, especially in a wind like we've had all day." Phones were ringing everywhere at once: the Coast Guard's substation in Monterey, twenty-two miles across the bay, was on the line, and so was Coast Guard headquarters in San Francisco. A pan pan (man overboard) call was issued.

Don and Cary prepared to launch their thirty-one-foot rescue boat, a rigid-hulled inflatable Zodiac, while they waited for the night patrolman to arrive. Coast Guard crews gathered at the boat launch, and detailed search plans were discussed. On the periphery, Nadine and Darnelle hovered about, listening, while little Ryan snuggled on his mother's lap. Cary noticed their anxious faces and walked over to them.

"It's okay. We're going to find them. We'll get them back in," he said.

---

* A popular brand of catamaran, often used as generic term for a twin-hulled catamaran designed for day sailing off a beach.

"They're seasoned sailors, you know. They go out all the time," said Nadine. "Cats have good flotation, don't they?"

"Look, we're going out there to do all we can to bring them back safely," Cary said again. "You should think about trying to relax, get some rest… But what you could do is check the beach, check your home and cell phones, just in case they're are trying to call you."

Don explained that the Coast Guard typically sends in two to three of its personnel in one boat to patrol the harbour during busy weekends. This evening, after he had given them the information about the missing brothers, an official search-and-rescue plan was formed. The Coast Guard called personnel who had been in the harbour at the time, while Don phoned 911, then called Brian Foss, the port director, who was once a Coast Guard pilot and director of search and rescue, to ask if he would come in to work the radios.

By nine o'clock, Don and Cary had launched their rescue boat. Around the same time, the Coast Guard sent their own craft: a twenty-four-foot inflatable Zodiac, as well as a forty-seven-foot, self-righting rescue cutter prepared with global positioning system, radar, loran[†] and all other equipment necessary for night searches. Don and Cary were asked to follow a grid pattern that ran parallel to the shore and extended five miles north and south of where they were. The Coast Guard's Zodiac and cutter would work other grids. All the while, a helicopter, also directed by the Coast Guard in San Francisco, prepared to fly to the scene.

★

Dusk spread itself over the ocean. The lingering colours of the sunset faded and died away, and with them, Bill's hopes. In the deepening darkness on the water, he knew he and Matt might never be found. He was drowning — but how could that be? He'd been around water all his life, swimming and boating. No one who lived in Michigan was ever far from water, and Lansing, Michigan, had been his home. But more than just this: his father, his whole family, had sailed; they almost lived on the water. He recalled how he, his parents and two brothers would drive

---

[†] A system of navigation using signal pulses from four radio transmitters.

every weekend to a beach to watch the small boats on Lake Michigan, then to a channel to watch the big boats come and go. He saw himself, a little older now, sailing for whole weekends, first in sixteen-foot boats, then twenty-one, all the way up to a Pearson 30 sloop. Then came the biggest adventure — sailing about six hundred miles up the coast of Michigan when he was fifteen.

His father's face now drifted before him: what a huge influence he had been on the family in developing this love of sailing. All of them self-taught, sailing together as a family, doing all the power squadron courses, the sailing camps. Yes, thanks to his father, a love of water sports had become ingrained and left an indelible impression. His thoughts turned sad as he recalled his father's tragic early death of a heart attack — right in front of them on the family boat. Then came the wonder about an extraordinary event — well, the timing of it: how his father, who had remained a Protestant alongside his Catholic wife all their married years, had con-verted to Catholicism and been baptized, just three days before he died.

After his death, the thirty-foot boat had been sold. The brothers wanted to purchase a catamaran, while Bill preferred a Laser — actually, he wanted two of them so they could race one another! His brothers won out, and Bill found himself sailing Hobie Cats. Now here he was — fallen from one, and drowning in the Pacific Ocean. Such a lonesome place. Once upon a time, he'd thought that cats were not real boats, but after the steep learning curve he'd had to climb, he quickly abandoned such thoughts. So different from other sailing boats, these catamarans. Definitely more exciting than any other craft.

This was what he had done all through high school and college — he'd sailed a Hobie Cat. Had crewed in San Francisco on racing boats and engaged in ocean racing offshore on a J-33. He remembered how, back then, he'd disdained wearing a life jacket — it wasn't considered cool. An accident involving the drowning of a sailor who had not been wearing one changed all that, made Bill extremely safety conscious.

★

"We're going to find your guys," Don called over his shoulder to Nadine and Darnelle as he and his deputy set off in water that had stilled somewhat. The wind had dropped gradually during the evening and the air had become gentle. Don guessed the water temperature to be about 50 degrees Fahrenheit. They moved quickly over water faintly illuminated by twinkling lights from the shore, like a scattering of fallen stars at the edge of the ocean. Water swished against the hull of their boat. The two young men were confident they would soon find the brothers. They assumed the two were clinging to their capsized boat, unable to right it in the strong winds that had prevailed all through the afternoon and early evening. They followed the grid pattern laid out by the Coast Guard. They searched from the shore four miles to the east and west, and to the north and south of the harbour. Intense concentration was required every moment. Although it was a moonless night, scattered lights danced across the water from the land. They tried to accurately chart their position so that they could inform the Coast Guard of their whereabouts — a task made difficult because all they had to work from was a small, ordinary roll-up chart, which forced them to try and estimate their location based on the time and their speed.

The intense search became draining. Deep concentration was exhausting, but emotions ran high. Hope was followed by disappointment, then frustration, but determination continued to drive and sustain them.

In its supervisory role, the Coast Guard frequently communicated with, and directed, the crew in the harbour rescue boat. Members of all search teams had become worried: this rescue attempt was proving tougher than they had anticipated, particularly since the boat they were searching for had a white-painted hull — making it hard to see when overturned on choppy seas because there was little to distinguish it from the wind chop.

Cary and Don searched to the south of the bay, while the Coast Guard concentrated on the areas of Rio Del Mar and Capitola. Around eleven-thirty, the Coast Guard radioed Don and Cary. They understood that the two men from the harbour master's office had worked all day, and must be cold and tired. They did not want to endanger them. The search did not look good, and the men must go home.

"You are released from your search," they said. "You can go back to shore. We're standing down our own Zodiac crew as well, but those in our forty-seven-footer will continue to search."

Don and Cary looked at each other. Are you ready to go home? each asked the other.

"Where are these guys?" one asked in acute frustration. "They left our beach, and have not come back. No way — I, for one, am not going home until they're found."

"Me, too! We've got to get these guys and bring them back in." The two sat in momentary silence, their imaginations dominated by images of two men clinging to an upturned boat, or perhaps floating around somewhere all these hours in an empty sea, not knowing if anyone would come to look for them. They imagine their exhaustion, their hunger and fear. They were local boaters struggling for their lives, approaching death — or already dead. Oh, man…

"Is this is a direct order to stand down, or is it a request?" asked Don of the Coast Guard.

"It's a request, not an order."

"We don't want to return. We want to keep on searching."

A silence ensued, and then came the words, "You have permission."

The two intrepid search-and-rescue workers had to return to shore to check in, refuel and replenish supplies. Don called harbour master Brian Foss. "We want to continue to search," he said.

"Look, I know what you're thinking," came the answer. "You know these two guys are in big trouble out in gusting winds all afternoon and evening, and how can you go home knowing this? I give you permission to go ahead, but I'm concerned for *your* safety, too. You've been working all day and half the night — you know about the danger of extreme fatigue and the making of critical mistakes."

"These guys would haunt us in our sleep — we wouldn't sleep. We have to search until we find them."

Upon their return to the harbour patrol building, Don and Cary found Nadine and Darnelle sitting where they had left them, their pale, worried faces turned up to them. Ryan had been put to sleep in the car. "Daddy and Uncle Bill haven't come back, and Uncle Bill might be in real trouble," Darnelle had told the little boy. "We can't go home yet."

"We've been doing our best," Cary told the anxious women. "I know it's almost midnight and your guys have been in the water now for nine hours. We've come back to refuel and get some warm clothes, but we're going to keep on searching. We promise you we'll do everything we can. At this point, they are not where we thought they'd be, and the search area is a very big one. They're proving hard to see — you know, I think we should prepare for an outcome that might not be good."

People milled about, some approaching Don and Cary to ask if they could do anything to help or to find out if the missing men had somehow made it back to shore. At this point, Don and Cary were prepared to accept anybody's expertise. Just then, a man approached them: Scott Whitehall, the owner of a charter boat called the *Chardonnay II*. He told them how, when he ran charters and headed out of the harbour at a heading of a hundred and thirty degrees, three to four miles out, he saw lots of overturned Hobie Cats. He also mentioned the findings of a Professor Gary Griggs at the University of California, who had studied surface and bottom ocean drifts going back to 1984.

"Yes, I've read these reports," Don said. "The drifts tended to be toward the south. Winds pushed in this direction during spring and summer, then surfaced onshore. Bottom currents pushed in an opposite direction."

Whitehall suggested they use this knowledge and move the search further south, to a hundred and seventy degrees.

Don thought for a moment. "Let's compromise and draw a line at a hundred and sixty degrees," he said finally. "We'll plan a course that will start at the harbour and go out ten miles. Once we get there, we'll come back toward the coast, using parallel lines." And so the rescuers widened their search to approximately six miles offshore. By the time they set out, it was half past midnight. The wind had died, the shadowed moon had completed its journey through the night sky, and the firmament glittered with stars — a beautiful night that bathed the land, belying the drama that was unfolding.

Now that the Coast Guard had officially released Don and Cary, they were free to use their own search methods, taking advantage of local knowledge, tradition and intuition. They felt that the area for which they were now headed would be the most likely spot where the two brothers in their Hobie Cat might have drifted. This was where they had first wanted to search, where their hunch told them they should be, not far from where the Coast Guard's inflatable Zodiac had been searching, and close to the touristy area of Capitola.

Don set the boat's motors to move at two miles per hour and they trawled an empty sea. Time seemed to drag. Suddenly, Don was shaken out of his private thoughts, doubts and worries.

"Hey... I'm smelling all kinds of things to eat — like garlic and onions and other good things," he said, sniffing the air. "Must be coming off the land. Never got a chance to have dinner." The big bear of a man had in fact smelled Cary's pizza.

Cary laughed. "Who's your pal? Who's your pal?" he teased as he stepped below to get his gear bag. In tantalizingly slow motion, he unfolded his wet suit and drew the folded pizza out of a pocket. Still warm! Each man ate a couple of slices and set the remainder aside for the two missing men in case they needed sustenance. Pizza had never tasted so good.

The water remained calm, and birds circled about them. They cruised as slowly as they could, with the windows open, but they were not cold, as each man tried to keep the other's spirits up. "Almost impossible to see," Don complained. This was because, when cold seawater meets warm air and evaporates, the result is condensation. The two men could see reasonably well with their unaided eyes, but when they used their spotlights to widen the area of visibility, the moisture in the air was highlighted and appeared as fog — ironically, reducing their vision. The lights also gave little sense of distance, and the two searchers found them of little help.

"The strobe light we had was reflecting off the water, and because of that, we knew we were getting close to the canyon, because of an up-welling of the water," said Don. "And then there was this — it was crazy, like we were seeing things — the water was brilliant and jumping with colours. We realized there were thousands of jellyfish of every kind of shape and colour there in the water — an unbelievable sight!"

The two were now dead tired, discouraged and depressed about the missing men. They cruised ever more slowly, straining their eyes in the gloom, checking every breaking crest and valley. Each was silent, locked into his own thoughts but hearing the wind whip water up against the side of the hull, hearing the flapping of gulls' wings, and disinterestedly watching them fly about. *Oh, man,* thought Cary, *we're seeing birds instead of shipwrecked men.* "We were in tune with our surroundings — this is what we care about: the natural world, the sea and everything about it. But haunting us every moment was how late it was; how two men are out here drowning, and we can't find them."

Into the gloom, startling the men out of their concentration, came a very bright light. They looked up to see a brilliant star falling from the sky and shooting across their bow. It flashed as it hit the water. "Spectacular!" exclaimed Cary. The two men looked at each other but said nothing. A shooting star — Cary made a wish. "I'll find out later if it comes true," he said. "It was like a sign that every thing was going to work out."

★

Bill was roused out of his pleasant reveries by lights — lights everywhere, but far in the distance, nothing to do with him. Fog had rolled in and he hadn't noticed. It all but obliterated the half-moon in the night sky. The sun must have long since lowered and set. Through the fog he could see the hundreds of lights twinkling from shore. *Santa Cruz — the most gorgeous place on the entire planet*, he thought. *Well, it's peaceful out here, and I always did enjoy nighttime sailing.* Then he saw a bright blue light on the shore — a police light! He guessed it must be about ten-thirty, maybe later. Then he saw a helicopter flying low over the sea — and in a grid search pattern! It hovered over one spot. *Maybe its crew has spotted our boat — and Matt. Why else would they be hovering?* He considered it a good sign that someone was out searching. The helicopter came within a couple hundred yards, then flew off. Bill's spirits reached their very lowest point. The people in the helicopter hadn't seen him, and he believed they weren't coming back.

But what's this? A fishing boat with its racks out? It's coming right for me... oh, no, it's changing direction. I knew they wouldn't see me... like looking for a needle in a haystack.

The water had calmed and the fog continued to roll in; Bill's mind drifted once more. Strange birds came and flew about, then settled. There were five or six hundred of them, maybe more, he estimated. He knew that if he moved, they would all fly off together, and this should create a signal. But the Coast Guard boat was too far away for anyone on board to notice.

Bill grew increasingly exhausted, and cold; he hugged his arms across his chest to keep warm. After a time, he could no longer move the limbs — hypothermia had begun to set in — but he felt a warm energy begin to flow through him. He realized he had better begin to say his goodbyes.

Bill Hopps, a practical, logical person who always looked for solutions to problems, had no solutions now; he was not in control. He told himself that he shouldn't give up, should never quit, but still he said an inward farewell to his dear Nadine, to his two brothers, to his beloved mother.

In the midst of his leave-taking he was struck by a brilliant light that streaked across the sky: a shooting star! Hope flared, as if this were a signal, a symbol. And in so hoping, he drifted into a dreamlike state, his arms still hugging his chest, head scarcely above water — but enough that he could continue breathing. A voice — was that a voice, two voices? No, he had to be dreaming... but there it was — voices, two of them! Bill awoke with a start, and with all the strength he could muster, he hollered. "Help... help... help." In the distance — about two hundred yards, he guessed — he saw a patrol boat with its lights beaming across the water. It headed straight toward him.

Half an hour after sighting the shooting star, Don and Cary thought they heard something: a slight cry, a tiny voice barely audible. Neither man could see anything beyond about twenty-five yards. Don turned off the boat's motors and they sat, straining to listen again. Cary climbed the balustrade, trying to see, to find out, what was out there in the gloom. He thought he heard another boat approaching. Don turned on the radio and tuned in to the Coast Guard Dolphin helicopter. "Two three nine — this is Santa Cruz harbour patrol boat. We think we have a man in the water. Request confirmation and location..."

Thoughts raced through Cary's mind. One man in the water... no boat... What kind of condition would he be in? Don and Cary had assumed they'd find a boat. And how unusual that the Dolphin helicopter would stay out searching for so long. Amazing — it would have had to return to shore to refuel twice. Cary estimated their location to be somewhere between six and seven miles offshore in the middle of the Monterey canyon. The Dolphin now flew over again, past the bow of their boat, then radioed them directly.

"You have a direct hit: one man in the water ten degrees portside, eighty feet in front of you."

"Oh, man," Cary said. "If we'd continued on our course, we would have run right over him." In the near-total blackness of a moonless night on the ocean, the intrepid men in their small boat turned ten degrees, then strained their eyes until they glimpsed a head sticking out of the water. Excitement was intense and adrenaline pumped — they had found one of the missing men — but on the other side of the coin, they wondered what had happened to him and how they were going to get him out. This fellow had been in the water for more than ten hours — they urgently needed to get him the whole way to shore and to medical attention. As they came closer, they caught a glimpse of Bill. "Near impossible to see," said Cary later. "I mean, he was wearing a navy blue life jacket and black wetsuit."

Don positioned the boat in a manner that required Bill to swim only a couple of strokes to reach the lowered swim deck. "Am I hallucinating?" came a faint voice from a ghostly white face, bobbing in water full of multicoloured jellyfish. Don radioed at once that they had found one man while Cary lifted him into the boat.

"Save my brother. Save my brother," the faint voice repeated.

But Cary's main concern was to evaluate the man and get him back to shore. He would have become very cold after all this time in water whose temperature was about 54 degrees Fahrenheit. What to do if he fell unconscious? Cary stared down at the shipwrecked man as he pulled him in. He was limp, like Jell-O, and nearly helpless. He hung one hand slowly over the deck, and the other, then collapsed in prone position, closing his eyes.

"Hey, don't close your eyes! You're with me, you're with me. Open your eyes — we've got you, you're safe! We're going to get your mate. Where's your mate?"

"My brother, my brother, got to find my brother," the exhausted man said.

"Hey, we got to take care of you first."

The stricken man did not utter one more word before he slid into shock.

Cary placed Bill on a seat in the boat's cabin, then threw a blanket over his head. "Hey, don't take this personally, but I got to hug you a bit," he joked. Don gunned the boat back to the harbour. The Coast Guard had decided it was best for the harbour patrol boat to carry Bill back to shore: on the one hand, it would be quicker than using the helicopter for an airlift to a hospital; on the other, it would free the helicopter to continue searching, and thereby cover a much larger than the small boat could manage. Because Bill had been found alone in the water, it stood to reason that the other was with the boat.

★

Nadine and Darnelle jumped up from their huddled position on the beach as the harbour abruptly filled with flashing lights and sirens. First to arrive was a patrol car. The two women ran up to it and asked what was going on.

"Just routine for us to be here," was the reply.

"Then it got crazy," said Nadine. "Fire engines, television crews and paramedics, and crowds wanting to know what happened… Yes! One man rescued, but who was it?"

They soon found out. Bill was retrieved from the arms of his rescuers, placed on a gurney and whisked away in an ambulance. Nadine rode with him, up front. Don and Cary set out once more on the dark ocean waters, altering their course by twenty degrees. The Coast Guard had dropped a data buoy — a buoy equipped with a transmitter — into the sea to get an idea of how much an object might drift, given the wind and ocean currents. They also estimated that a boat would tend to drift more profoundly than a body. Approximately six miles offshore, they reached a point half a mile from where they had found Bill. All the while, the Coast Guard's cutter continued to search in a grid pattern opposite to that of the harbour patrol boat. Suddenly, a message came over the radio from the Coast Guard cutter. "Found a hit! We've got a blip on the radar." The crews of both boats fired up their engines and raced toward the object.

The radar blip revealed a large object. Cary and Don immediately radioed the crew in the forty-seven-foot cutter to tell them they had spotted what appeared to be their target off their bow. The Coast Guard crew immediately broke its search pattern and headed to the area.

About a mile from the spot where Bill Hopps had been plucked from the sea, crew from both boats found an overturned catamaran with one man clinging to it — Bill's brother Matt. He was conscious. His first words were — "My brother — have you found my brother?" When he heard that Bill had been rescued, he seemed to slump, as if relieved.

"You can let go of all your thoughts," he said. "My mind had been hammering me — how to find Bill? When I figured it was about two o'clock — I thought Bill could survive in his dry suit until about that time — I just wanted to jump off the boat. How could I leave my brother? How could I live if I lost him? I kept thinking about how to keep looking for him; about what else to do. Now I could let go."

The Coast Guard cutter reached him first and retrieved him. While it raced him back to shore and a waiting ambulance, the crew radioed the harbour patrol boat to ask that it tow the catamaran back to shore. "Leaving it where it is poses a navigational hazard," they said.

"You guys are killing us," Don said. Later, he explained: "This was no small request. There was a chance we could upright it and tow it much more easily, but it usually takes a guy in the water to be able to do that. At three in the morning, and after all that had happened, after all our efforts and lack of sleep, we weren't up to getting into the water and righting it. We clipped it in and towed it upside down back to the shore. Took us three hours." Daylight was breaking as they arrived in the bay. It was about seven-thirty. "First thing we did was rush off to Dominican Hospital to check on Bill. He was in an airbag and not in good shape. Bags had been fitted all around him to warm his body. Nadine rested her head on the bed at his feet. He was all teary-eyed and kept saying over and over how it was all unbelievable."

"I couldn't hug and thank them enough," said Nadine. "They found Matt to be in better shape, even though he had been clinging to the boat for ten hours."

"Glad we got you, glad you made it," the rescuers said. Bill looked up groggily at them. "Yeah, you guys are unbelievable. I saw you searching in your boats — saw the helicopter. You know, I was out there, thinking about how I was to get married in two weeks, then I thought I would die... I started hallucinating. I kept seeing coloured spots everywhere in the water."

"You weren't hallucinating — those were jellyfish! There were thousands of them.

"Hey, we'd love to see you guys once you're better. Come on down to the harbour office when you're released. We want to know you are okay, and we'd really like to talk to you."

Cary had to work that same day. He drove home, got showered and changed, and arrived back at work at midday.

★

"It was like rising up from the dead and coming back to life." Bill stood at the podium in front of the guests at his wedding to Nadine — just two weeks after the near-shipwreck. "I'm standing here talking to you because of the actions of two men: Cary Smith and Don Kinnamon."

Oh, man, here it comes, Cary said to himself. He and Don had become reluctant wedding guests because they understood that Bill and Matthew wished to express their gratitude, to thank them publicly, but the idea embarrassed them deeply. After all, they had only been doing their job. In the end, they were persuaded to attend because it seemed the right thing to do.

"The reason we are here today is because of these two men," said Bill. Tears welled up in his eyes. "It was unbelievable what they did. They had to know the search was all but hopeless, but they never gave up. It was like looking for needle in a haystack. They were out there most of the night after they had worked all day. They were told to go home; they refused. They said Matt and I had left their shores and they weren't coming home until they had found us and brought us back — they couldn't go home and sleep knowing we were shipwrecked at sea, they said.

"They saved our lives. Rescuers like Don and Cary put their lives in danger to help others and they don't get the credit they deserve. Raise your glasses and toast these two men."

Oh, man, now you've got everyone in tears, thought Cary. "It's like this: if you have a special skill and do not share it, you're selfish. We live and work in a maritime culture. People leave our shores, we have to go get them back. It could be you, could be me. Sticking with it — with your job — is what it's all about."

This was not to be the end of the fulsome thanks for Don and Cary. Bill and Matt's mother stood up then and expressed how grateful she, too, felt that Don and Cary had saved her sons.

"We thought this was all pretty heavy," said Don, "but they all kept saying how grateful they were. In the end we were glad we'd come to the wedding. Afterward we had lunch with the family when they insisted — a good thing, because that's where I met the bridesmaid. She's my partner today, and we have a baby… we called him Dawson in honour of a child who died, whose parents named a light after him — Dawson's Light. We asked if we could use this name."

"It was magical," Nadine said of her wedding. "I got married to my soulmate after I nearly lost him."

Bill Hopps spoke later of the various components of his life, how he had always thought of himself as an intelligent and reasonable man who liked to be in control of the things in his life.

"I studied political science and Chinese history at university. [I was] fascinated by it because it is the opposite of Western thought — an opposing worldview," he said. He also described his physical activities, which included climbing, biking, sailing — especially sailing, in big yachts and small, in rough weather and smooth. He had learned all the tricks, from river sailing to handling Lasers in southern California's Santa Ana winds.

"When I was in San Francisco I moved up to a twenty-five-foot boat and crewed on it," he said. "Then on to a Cal 25, a twenty-five-foot, 1967-vintage, fibreglass craft — great for windy San Francisco Bay. I had to go and buy one myself, but a Cal 29 — big enough to take on the whole ocean! I completely rigged it with autopilot, electronics, the whole works, and sailed it down to Santa Cruz and back. I bought the catamaran at same time as the Cal 29." He paused, then added, "I've seen a lot of the world, and I have to say that Santa Cruz — Monterey Bay — is one of the prettiest places in it.

"There are lessons to be learned from this experience," he continued. "Never underestimate nature — respect it. Of course, I should have had a radio with me, but this really was a freak accident and most likely will not happen again. If I'd had had a radio with me, this would all have been over in an hour."

How many people take radios with them?

"None," he said. "I have all the safety equipment one can have on my big boat. But there is potential for any number of things to go wrong — especially in offshore sailing. I'm well prepared every time I go out because one has to be self-sufficient. On this particular occasion, I was taking out a high-performance cat — you know, out off the beach for a spin, out and back, a fun thing, a few thrills. You don't carry food or a radio, but it's still the ocean; you have to respect its power and size, and be smart. Matt and I intended to go out and glide off the waves, go on a beam reach and drive over the top of swells, get the boat to come out of the water — huge fun. Then we'd go home. We feel we must take advantage of long weekends — and it's great to have someone who wants to get wet with you."

Bill and Nadine Hopps live in Los Gatos. They have been married now for four years, and have a daughter.

Matthew Hopps worked for a computer company and spent much time travelling about, teaching courses — until the birth of his son, Ryan. When he realized he was missing out on his son's childhood, he decided to move from Texas to California for a job that would allow him more time at home.

As deputy harbour master, Cary Smith is responsible for marine safety and all associated affairs. He qualified for this position by graduating in recreation administration and hospitality management, followed by a master's degree in environmental studies. He is president of the California Boating Safety Officers' Association, and a personal watercraft instructor for law enforcement in California.

Don Kinnamon, too, has been in the maritime safety business for the past twenty-five years.

"I have never had a rescue of this magnitude — ever. It just doesn't happen," he said. "And that it should turn out well: the duration, the finding of a person out in the middle of the Pacific alone, without stars or moon, wearing a dark wetsuit and life jacket — and finding him alive! To hear the faint little voice saying, with its last breath, "I'm here… over here… over here. Save my brother, save my brother…"

After this rescue, Cary and Don were awarded the Officer of the Year Award by the California Boating Safety Association for work above and beyond the call of duty. To Cary, what he did was nothing extraordinary: it was his job, what he was trained and paid to do — and he could never do less.

THE END OF AN IDYLL
Lac La Hache, British Columbia

How tedious are the hours I pass in the absence of the beloved of my heart, and how tiresome every scene is. — Susan Sontag

Debbie Stewart stood in the doorway of her house and stretched her arms above her head. She smiled as her eyes took in the view: the ice on the lake below had finally retreated, buds were blossoming... the world was waking up once more with the ritual promise of new life.

On that fateful day, the last of her life as she had known it, she had been roused from bed by a loud knocking on the door. She'd got up, opened it, and there stood Ricky's fishing buddies, Bill and Jay.*

"Of course, the fishing trip — but Ricky's still in bed! Ricky, come on, get up, the guys are here." Her mate threw off the bedclothes, his ever-present smile creasing his cheeks as he moved about with alacrity.

Today was Ricky's day off. He hummed as he prepared for an outing with his near-lifelong friends. The three planned to picnic at a small campsite — his and Debbie's own private spot on a small island. He prepared his lunch, loaded up his truck with beer and spirits and looked over his fishing gear. He relished the thought of rainbow trout broiling on the barbecue and beer and wine on the table by the time Debbie got home at eight.

---

*Bill and Jay are pseudonyms.

"Ready, Ricky? The guys are waiting for you."

"Yeah, babe, I'm ready." Ricky stood on the doorstep. "Bye, babe. Have a great day. See ya later!" A peck on the cheek and he'd gone like a small puff of wind, out the door and into his truck — a slim, lithe man with an incorrigibly cheerful disposition.

Debbie too hummed as she drove to her job at Northwood Lodge, her mind filled with images of another upcoming summer idyll: campsites on an island she considered her and Ricky's private spot, a tent, a campfire, swimming, fishing, eating, drinking and lazing away the off-duty hours.

Debbie's shift this day began at two and ended at eight. Small, swift and capable, she worked wherever she was needed. "Great job for me," she'd said once. "I know so many of the people from the small towns — I see them coming and going from the schools, fairs, bingo halls and tournaments; I meet them in shops, in the community halls... I guess I probably know most people in Lac La Hache — that's our nearest community."

"Deb, give yourself a break for a few minutes. I'll take over." Jackie Hamar, co-owner of the lodge, bustled over to the reception desk. "Go on, you've been at it all afternoon."

An hour and a half to go. Debbie's heart lifted as her thoughts turned to the upcoming evening, to her home among the trees. She and Ricky had purchased a three-bedroom bungalow on a rise overlooking the small lake called Timothy. Private, quiet even though other cabins peeped through the trees — about forty households existed within a four-block radius.

"What does your Ricky do, dearie? What do you do when you're not at the lodge?" an old woman once asked her.

"Well, most people here work in the logging industry, but my Ricky has worked for the Liquor Board for twenty-eight years," Debbie said. "I work at Northwood Lodge for seven months of the year, and in winter I stay home, go for walks, cross-country ski, do some crocheting and ceramics. Ricky and me, we're homebodies. Ricky, he does so love his home."

Indeed he did: when he wasn't working, Ricky would sit for hours enjoying the tranquility of his environment, not doing anything in particular. Summer saw him lolling in a comfortable chair under a birch tree in a spot that overlooked the front yard, affording him spectacular views of the flowerbeds on the slope below the house or the constantly changing colours of the waters of the lake below. The day began with coffee and the newspaper first thing in the morning, then a move over to his chair just to sit. Occasionally he'd bike the local laneways; sometimes he'd watch Debbie work among the flowerbeds — watch the slim lines of her body in motion, the suntanned arms and legs, the arcing of her back as she bent over the blooms. His eyes would follow as she straightened to stand and gaze out over the lake, or to turn to him with a smile. Cup of iced tea, Ricky? Can I get you anything?

"Ricky's probably got some trout cooking. Have yourself a good evening, Deb." Wally Gilfoy, Debbie's boss at the lodge, waved her good-bye. Twilight softened the northern landscape as Debbie drove the gravel road home with a song in her heart. Ricky should be waiting for her, and Amanda and Richard might be home, too. The sun's rays, very low in the sky, cast soft shadows through the trees that danced like bright butterfly wings on the waters of the lake. Debbie drew into the yard. No Ricky yet, but lights were on in the house. That must mean that Richard and Amanda were home. It was now ten minutes after eight.

"Ricky's not home yet?" She felt a surge of disappointment.

"He often doesn't get home until almost dark," Amanda reminded her mother.

Debbie methodically began preparing dinner — too late to fire up the barbecue now. The shrill ringing of the phone a few minutes later interrupted her thoughts. It was Wally Gilfoy at the lodge.

"Debbie, I don't know what's going on, but a woman down at the end of the road said she saw some guy wandering about. He says he needs a boat to get to out to the lake — did you say that Ricky and a couple of friends went out there fishing today?"

"Yes, he's not home yet. Richard and I'll go down and see." At first, Debbie did not connect this call to Ricky's absence. Immediately afterwards, Joseph from a few houses down the road also called to say that a boat was seen upside down on Sneezy Lake, and a man was clinging to it. Not yet perturbed, still not relating this sighting to the fishing trip, Debbie and Richard drove the mile and a half to Sneezy Lake to see what was happening. Around a bend in the road, she braked sharply: a soaking-wet apparition in the person of Bill stood before them.

"Bill! What are you doing... what's happened?" The distraught man tried to explain that he'd walked two miles looking for a boat, that the one he had been in had flipped over, that he had then swum to shore and now he must find a boat to get back to the capsized one in the lake. "Ricky didn't make it... he didn't make it... I saw him go down..." he repeated.

Debbie shrieked. "Oh my God... oh my God..." The blood in her veins ran cold. Her mind raced. She turned the car around and raced home to get her own boat. She had to get out on the water; she must find Ricky. She reached her driveway, and almost immediately, Wally's truck pulled in behind her. In a matter of minutes, he had swung the boat onto his truck. Debbie stood in her driveway, her feelings inchoate before the streaming tears finally came, as well as the loud venting of her fears. Wally, at a loss, hollered to Richard. "Phone Jackie. Tell her it's urgent. I need her down at Ricky Blessin's — there's been an accident. Need someone to be with Debbie."

Wally's wife, Jackie Hamar, arrived from the lodge, and Wally, together with Richard and Bill, drove off with the boat hoisted onto the truck. A near-hysterical Debbie continued to pace about the driveway. "I have to be there, I have to be there... I should be searching for Ricky!"

"Look, why don't we get some blankets and go down to the lake and wait — see what we can do," Jackie said gently.

As the gathering night wrapped itself around them and the lake waters gleamed darkly below, the two women watched as Wally and Richard reached the upturned boat and retrieved Jay from it. Jay kept repeating that Ricky had gone down. No, he couldn't tell what happened, he didn't know. They'd been out to hook a few rainbow trout, Ricky steering, Bill sitting up front and getting his fishing lines ready, Jay in the middle, at the bottom of the boat, eating peanuts. Suddenly the boat jerked and flipped over; Ricky might have sneezed, no one knew what happened.

Debbie called out repeatedly to her mate — "Ricky, Ricky... *Ricky*..." — a thin, desolate voice wailing across the water. Then, abruptly, she stood up. "But anything could have happened to him," she said. "He could have swum to another shore, he could be clinging to a rock, walking around among the trees. We'll find him — of course we will!" It was not to be this evening; in the blackness of night they drove to Debbie's home. Perhaps tomorrow they would find Ricky.

The day after the accident, the Royal Canadian Mounted Police arrived to begin searching the lake for Ricky. Richard and Amanda, together with Debbie's aunt and mother, combed the shores of Sneezy Lake. Various members of the community helped, too, whenever they could in shoreline searches. Hope flickered fitfully in the hearts of all that Ricky might have climbed out and was still alive somewhere.

Bill repeated what Jay had reported: that they had been motoring along, Ricky at the helm of the skiff, when suddenly, without warning and for no reason he could think of, the boat just flipped. The water was freezing cold; the ice had only recently receded from it. Jay had been wearing steel-toed shoes and managed to climb up the sides of the upside-down boat and cling to it. Bill was a good, strong swimmer, he said, and he struck out for a shore that was only about thirty feet distant. "When last I looked, Ricky seemed to be following right behind him," he said. He kept anxiously scanning the shoreline. The next time he looked, Ricky had disappeared, sunk beneath the waters of the lake. There was nothing he could do to save him, he insisted.

The RCMP searched the far end of the lake, rather than the place where the boat had actually capsized, because they believed it must have drifted with the currents. After three days, they told the family that they were sorry, but they had cost and time constraints and could not continue to search.

As long as Ricky's body had not been found, the family maintained hope that he could be alive somewhere, that he would one day come walking through the door. One day gave way to another, and for Debbie, it got scarier as time went by. "I mean, if Ricky had made it out into the bush, he would've succumbed to hypothermia, and so… and so… he'd be dead by now," she said, voice trailing off.

Ricky's family arrived, including his son and daughter — one from Washington state and the other from the east coast. They waited. They searched again and again, and still they waited. Some prayed. Debbie's anguish grew as the days passed; she was in limbo. For her, and for her family, Ricky was no longer alive, but he wasn't dead, either.

★

Wally Gilfoy and Jackie Hamar, the husband-and-wife co-owners of Northwood Lodge, struggled gamely to put on a brave face among their guests and staff, but each felt weighted down by the tragedy and its unfinished business. The pleasure of their day-to-day business was diminished by an event that not only affected them, but cast a dark shadow over the entire community. Frustration grew as the days passed and it seemed that nobody could find the body.

"This is pure hell for Debbie, and the whole community feels it," Jackie said. "This man we all knew and loved so much — he was part of our lives; he belonged to us, too. Such a happy and vital man, he was. He would breeze through the door here and smile at everyone. He cracked jokes, hugged someone, winked at another, laughed as he went out the door again — it gave us all a lift to have him around, made us feel good just to see him come and go. Now here's his body rotting in the bottom of a local lake; we have to get him out and bury him properly."

Debbie Stewart was at home one day, working among the flowerbeds in a desultory way, keenly aware that nobody was sitting in the chair beneath the birch tree. A thought flitted about in her mind that perhaps Ricky was not down there at the bottom of the lake among the fish and mud and weeds. Maybe he had miraculously got out, climbed the banks and wandered about, dazed, for all these weeks afterward. He just couldn't find his way home, she reasoned, and one day he would return.

The phone rang. "Deb, I don't know what you'll think about this," Wally began. "There's this group of people who go searching for people who are lost — or dead. They'll come up here and dive; they'll find Ricky — if he's down there." He told her how he knew of a woman who had lost a brother to a drowning accident a few years earlier. The family had contacted a group called the Canadian Amphibious Search Team — they searched for missing and dead people in their spare time and charged a fee to cover their costs. "It might take some time to get them here because they all have full-time jobs and live around the Vancouver area," he cautioned. "Want me to get a hold of them for you?"

"Oh, yes! Yes, please!" Debbie's reply was immediate. "I don't care what it costs. I'll find a way to pay it—"

"We'll all help raise the money. You know that," Wally said.

"I want Ricky found!" Debbie's voice rose with emotion. "I need to know where he is, and if he's dead, to bury him…" Her voice trailed away. How could she pass Sneezy Lake every day? How could she ever go near it again — sail on it, swim in it — knowing Ricky's body lay somewhere within its depths?

★

Tim MacFarlane spun along the highway from the Coast Guard's hovercraft base in Richmond on his way home to Abbotsford. It was late, and he wondered if he would see the kids before Robin put them to bed. It had been a hard day, and a very long one, too: he should have been home hours ago. His schedule had become much worse since he'd become Coast Guard dive captain; he would remind his family of this once again, but Robin didn't bother to reply anymore. She was intensely proud of her husband, but she had heard it all before.

Dusk had settled late across a full-throated summer landscape: warmth and mellowness hung richly in the air, about the trees, and across the fields.

"Phone for you," Robin said as he walked in the door. Wally Gilfoy from Northwood Lodge was on the phone. His words came to Tim in fragments: "We've heard about you and your team … need help to search for a missing man … we think he drowned … can't find the body." In spite of his fatigue, Tim's heart leaped with a keen sense of purpose: this is something CAST could do. He got on the phone to CAST members he thought might be free to make the long journey up to Lac La Hache, to those certified in underwater diving and swiftwater rescue. Within an hour, he'd assembled his group — Dan Hildebrand, Roy Klohn, John Merrett, Tony Reynolds, Andy Meecker, Kyle Liu, Melanie Robson, Troy Attfield and Greg Ipatowicz — and set a date, time and place to meet.

On Saturday, May 22, at ten in the evening, the group met at Melanie Robson's home in the city of Delta. Most had just completed a work shift. Soon afterward, they were on the highway, in three separate cars loaded with all their equipment, on their way to a remote destination. The seemingly endless journey took them along the valley floors of mountain ranges and vast expanses of an uninhabited wilderness of lakes and trees. They followed the banks of the Fraser and Thompson rivers, north towards the area they were headed to. Along the way, little traffic accompanied or passed them.

Eventually, the road ran alongside open hay fields and large ranch houses, then led to a gravel road lined densely by trees. There was a clearing, then the lodge on the slopes of Timothy Mountain, a short distance from the lake. They arrived at three in the morning. Wally had been waiting up for them. He took them to empty cabins to get some rest, but sleep was to elude most of them over the next three short hours. They rose at six, tired from lack of sleep after the long drive that had followed a long day at work. Now they must prepare for their sombre task.

First on the agenda was a meeting with the widow, the lodge owners and other locals.

"Good people, very good people, I knew that right away," Jackie said, recalling her first impression of the team. "Fit, muscular — and intense. I wondered what they were all about. Like, what were their qualifications? Why did they do this kind of thing? Strange that they should get together in a group to go body hunting — that's what it really is. I was curious about what brought them together; maybe one of them had lost someone close to them — like Deb. Maybe it was a monetary thing that drove them. Then I wondered how they became qualified.

"But they brought with them hope. We'd been feeling let down by the RCMP. We didn't know where to turn next, so we were very grateful that these people existed. I mean, Ricky had to be found; we are a close-knit community, and we all knew that Ricky was there. We all needed closure — not just Deb."

Wally led the group to the spot where they believed Ricky had drowned, where they thought the boat had drifted. CAST members felt confident that one of them would simply drop down the line and find the body on the other side of this narrow lake. Hope surged in the hearts of the whole community that here was a group that would do everything possible to find their beloved Ricky Blessin. While the divers began their sombre task, local people began raising funds to help defray the costs of these body hunters. Hope was in the air. All felt cheered to be doing something productive to help put an end to this miserable episode.

Roy Klohn and Greg Ipatowicz were the first to dive into water that was between seventy-five and eighty feet deep. Their movements disturbed the lake's silty bottom, clouding the water and creating almost zero visibility. Troy Attfield directed Klohn in a jackstay arc search* of the area where Ricky's body was believed to lie. Each time he came up empty, Troy would increase the diameter of the search. All present were surprised that nothing was being found. Troy clambered onto the shore and shook his head: nothing. Randy took his place, followed by Greg, then Andy Meecker.

The group searched intensively all that day, until about three in the afternoon, when the sun's warmth began to wane. The crew packed up and prepared for the long drive home. Even though some had already taken a day off work, they knew they had no choice but to return the following day.

Debbie insisted that they come to her house for a home-cooked meal. The body hunters reluctantly agreed, understanding her wish to show gratitude. They stood awkwardly about her living room, looking down the slope of the hill to the lake as she plied them with food and drink. Tim MacFarlane ran his hand over his shaven head; with his large brown eyes brimming with compassion, he made her a promise.

"Listen: we'll find Mr. Blessin's body, we'll find him for you. We'll be back at the very next opportunity to search again. We'll keep coming until we find him. We'll not give up." The group of exhausted and frustrated young people arrived home in Vancouver about ten that night — "a pretty wacked couple of days," Roy Klohn commented.

---

*In a jackstay search, a team member — the tender — remains on the shore, holding one end of a line, while a diver takes the other end with him/her to the bottom of the body of water. The tender feeds the line to the diver in segments, a technique enabling the diver to systematically cover a prescribed area — think of a compass, with the person on shore as the needle and the diver as the pencil, tracing an arc across the bottom of the lake. After the diver completes a pass, his/her partner on shore pays out a bit more line, thereby broadening the search.

One Friday night a week later, eight members of CAST — this time, MacFarlane, Klohn, Attfield, Meecker, Hildebrand, Reynolds, Merrett and Sean Stevenson — returned to Lac La Hache to resume their search. Family and friends of Ricky Blessin, anticipating their arrival, burst into applause at the sight of their heroes, and a festive atmosphere pervaded.

"Go get him, guys," some said, and applause resounded.

"It meant a lot to me — their warmth, their enthusiasm and belief in us," Roy said afterwards. Wally and Jackie had offered to put the group up in cabins, but instead they departed to set up camp at the lake and try to get some fitful sleep before dawn broke over the water.

For this second search, they had brought with them a side scanner,* hoping to pick up hotspots from the bottom of the lake. Hopes were high. Each diver remained beneath the chilly surface of the lake for between thirty and forty minutes before his air supply ran low and he had to resurface. Intense frustration was felt when each hotspot proved to be nothing more than a log, rock or other bit of lake debris.

While CAST members continued searching, Debbie had hired a private organization that owned and operated sonar equipment meant to detect objects underwater. This group worked with the CAST crew for the entire day, eventually covering the whole lake. No body was detected — only some logs.

"Their sonar equipment went right over the body," Roy would say afterwards. "It picked up an object, we dropped a line, and guess what? We came up with a log! They had equipment that did not detect the body, even though it was going right over him."

At the end of the day, their search had turned up nothing: no body, no fishing tackle, nor any other bits of equipment or clothing. The community hopes were dashed once again. Keen frustration was felt among CAST's crew, too. They decided to camp out at the beachhead that night, but before long their camp was disturbed by the arrival of Debbie and other locals bearing food and drink prepared for them.

---

* A piece of equipment shaped like a torpedo that rides above the water's surface, its undersurface fitted with sensors and cameras to detect objects underwater. The upper surface has a screen on which images can be monitored.

Almost before dawn the group was up and searching before it was time to head back to Vancouver, and home. No evidence had been found that Ricky Blessin lay at the bottom of the lake.

"We'll be back. We will find him," Tim insisted to one and all. He looked at Debbie, the young woman with a cloud of dark hair and big blue eyes who liked to smile, with compassion, but she was not smiling now. He hugged her, invited her to call anytime if she wanted to talk, if he could be of help. Then the grave young men were into their convoy of cars and on the road. Disconsolate, Debbie, the lodge owners and the entire community of Lac La Hache returned to their usual lives.

Two weeks later, a third attempt was made to find the drowned man. This time, the crew consisted of Tim MacFarlane, Roy Klohn, Brad Falconer, Troy Attfield, Sean Stevenson, Andy Meecker and Tony Reynolds.

"Any chance of a boat?" Tim asked Wally. "I'd like to take one or both of the men who were in the boat with Ricky, try to get them to pinpoint for me where exactly they saw him before he went down."

Roy Klohn and Rhett Miller — recovery diving.

A boat was procured. Tim took the two survivors of the boating accident, one at a time, with him onto the lake.

"Would you show me exactly where you last saw Ricky? Try and remember where you were when the accident happened... look at the shoreline — can you line anything up?" Each man indicated the same spot, near the far end of the lake, where intensive searches had already been made. Tim, surprised and discouraged, organized the divers to search this area once more in a circular pattern. In pairs the men dived, surfaced, dived, surfaced and dived again. Each time they came up with nothing.

"I mean, this is a small lake. The body's got to be down here somewhere!" Tim's voice echoed the frustration felt by all. "Let's just forget where this man's body is *supposed* to be and search the entire lake."

Near the end of the afternoon, the CAST crew knew it needed to be on the road back to Vancouver. Roy, fast running out of air, was about to surface when his hands grasped something — fishing tackle! He was underwater, fifty yards from shore, at the opposite end of the lake from where Ricky's body was supposed to be. This was the first find of any kind, and it suggested to CAST members that they were getting close. Roy surfaced with the fishing gear and a marker was dropped. Another diver took his place and circled the area where the rod had been found until he, too, ran out of air.

The intensive search that followed Roy's find yielded nothing. Darkness forced the crew to abandon its efforts.

But only temporarily. Four weeks after they had first begun to look for Ricky's body, CAST's crew returned once again, this time carrying home-built sleds that were occasionally used to skim the bottom of a body of water. These sleds were made of clear Plexiglas in the shape of an airplane — each had wings attached to its sides that, when compressed, would lift it up and over an object that loomed — a log, rock or debris. Each diver or operator donned a dry suit, goggles and fins, fitted himself with a headlamp in front that would enable them to see two to three feet ahead, and had themselves attached to the crew in the boat above by a communication line. Each was then towed across the bottom of the lake, feet dragging the bottom where the water remained shallow. The surface boat had a twenty-five-horsepower motor and moved slowly.

"A very effective way of underwater searching," Roy said. "It's fantastic: no effort was required on our part; we had on our harnesses and lay prone on the sleds, attached to the front of the boat that pulled us. It's pretty far out, but also dark and isolating down there. You get locked into your own private world, cut off from all other life. You're at the bottom of the lake, wanting badly to find this body, but you're sort of dreading it, too. I mean, it was very black down there, and you had to keep up intense concentration. But because we were being towed, we could totally concentrate on the search."

When the crew first began this day, they enjoyed good visibility; the sun was shining and the water was just twenty-five feet deep. Divers first circled around the boat launch, the area where the marker had been dropped. Eventually the whole lake was swept.

"The guy with the side scanner was working, too," Roy said. "We were in parallel track, being moved slowly along the bottom of the lake. It was an awesome experience; each of us was locked in our own little world. I felt excited and elated. If we were to find anything, we would give four tugs on the communication line."

On the second pass, they found their quarry: Tony Reynolds saw Ricky Blessin's body just one hundred and fifty feet from the launch — far from the area where the two survivors, and indeed, the entire community, had believed the body to be. Tony felt exhilarated. He gave four tugs on the communication line. This was his first search-and-rescue case and he had made the find.

"Great, Tony," Tim called to him. "I want you to stay down there with the body. It won't be more than half an hour — just while I contact the RCMP and the coroner, and until we get ready to bring the body to the surface." Tony looked at the body lying peacefully on the bottom of the lake, a body that had once been a man: Ricky Blessin lay facedown among weeds and rocks and silt. He wore a tank top and a pair of shorts… no shoes or socks. Reynolds turned his back on the pale bloated body and waited. Is this what CAST work was about? Ah… a diver — at last!

Andy Meecker arrived with a body bag and the two men struggled to get Ricky's remains into it. Fortunately for both men, but especially for the new recruit, the body — which had been at the bottom of the lake for five weeks — was well preserved because of the coldness of the water and the lack of factors such as rocks, waterfalls and marine life.

The news that her Ricky had been found was conveyed to Debbie, and then to Wally and Jackie at the lodge. Debbie cried, her tears an expression of complicated feelings: sorrow that she now had to accept the brutal fact that her Ricky was dead, that she could no longer fantasize that he was somewhere else and would one day come walking in the door, mixed with relief that she now knew where he was. This was closure, the ending to the uncertainty and to the feeling of her life being on hold. The entire community cried and rejoiced along with her, heaping food and praise on CAST's members and offering them the finest hospitality of which they were capable. Debbie, bursting with gratitude, insisted they come to her home so she could express her own personal thanks. She cooked and baked and set out an abundance of food and refreshments for them all.

The body hunters stood about her living room, quiet and respectful, and more than a bit uncomfortable at the position in which they found themselves. Their custom was to do their recovery work and immediately go home — not to remain to accept thanks or other hospitality.

Today, they had achieved their goal, and to them this was reward enough. It had been a particularly difficult search for many reasons: the inaccurate information given about the body's location, the failures of the side scanner equipment and the efforts of the RCMP and local people in their searches.

"I think we should also remember the efforts of Scott Peake from Central Fraser Valley Region," said Tim, after Debbie's speech of thanks. "He came all this way to help us out."

Debbie looked at the broad-shouldered man with the clean-shaven head and said, "Tim MacFarlane, you're just the greatest. I don't know how I would have got through it all without you — talking to me, explaining things, getting information for me. We all love you — all of you — you're a team like we never saw."

"This was five weeks of pure hell," Debbie said in summary. "But we were helped by these CAST people; I — we — will never be the same because of knowing them. All of us found them very caring, skilled and knowledgeable. So gentle, too. They told me they would find Ricky's body for me so I could put all this to rest and get on with my life. They took the time to drive all this distance at any spare moment. They sat with me when I cried and poured out all my grief. I never expected such compassionate people. All of them have full-time jobs and families, yet they still found time to do this for me and my family."

Her sentiments were enthusiastically shared by others, including lodge owners Wally and Jackie.

"The outstanding thing about these people they all seemed to share, was caring and deep respect — for Debbie, for all of us. For Ricky's body — they called him Mr. Blessin," Jackie said. "It was like they were on a personal quest when they went out to find him… like he was a brother to them. So very dedicated… It was moving, really."

"We wanted them to stay at the lodge for free," said Wally. "But they set up camp at the lake. We knew they needed money, even if just to pay their expenses, but they never named an amount — just pay us what you can as donations, they said."

This is the story, too, of the series of small communities that surround Hundred Mile House that came together and worked as one. It seemed there was not a person in the entire area of trees and lakes and cottages and parks and houses that was not involved in fundraising, cooking, grieving and conducting their own searches of the lake and its environs.

★

Debbie Stewart still loves everything about the place where she had lived with her Ricky, and where she now lives alone — when her adult children are not around. All its memories are precious to her.

"I still miss Ricky acutely most days," she said. "We had a wonderful relationship and a wonderful life. But I have come to have peace about the way he died: I mean, he loved water, being on it and near it, and he once said that when he died, he would like it to be by drowning. I believe that he simply died from the feet up, until he went to sleep — that he was very peaceful about it, that his thoughts would have been full of his family. He would be sorry, but he would know that God had chosen him to leave the world at this time. He would be telling all of us that he loved us very much."

Left to right: Peder Ourum, Doug Wood, Hugh Ackroyd, and John Wilcox.

TO FALL OFF A MOUNTAIN
Squamish, British Columbia

When you reach the mountain top, then shall you begin to climb. — Kahlil Gibran

Two men make a spur-of-the-moment decision to go climbing, to scale the walls of Mount Dione in the Tantalus Mountains north of Vancouver. James Campbell and Gordon Littleton,* experienced mountaineers both, have long dreamed of conquering these ranges. September is well underway, but the weather forecasts promise warm, sunny days for the weekend ahead, and images of these peaks haunt the two men, who have become consumed by the irresistible urge to scale their heights.

The two men head for Squamish, a picturesque little town perched at the edge of the Sea-to-Sky Highway between Vancouver and Whistler. Known to the Indians as "mother of the wind," it is a renowned destination for climbers from the four corners of North America — and from far-off places around the world.

Each man scrambles to prepare before setting off for this ambitious climb — a new route for them. Their plan is to accomplish a technical alpine rock route up to the peak of Mount Dione, high above the treeline.

---

* James Campbell and Gordon Littleton are pseudonyms used to protect the identity of the climbers in this story.

It's a climb that will require rope, ice axe, crampons, rock and ice gear, and much skill and experience, and it is to culminate in a campout on the summit, followed by a retreat from their perch the next day. After this, the agenda will call for a long and difficult trek to Lake Lovelywater and a rendezvous with the helicopter pilot the next morning.

September 17 sees the two men boarding a chartered helicopter to fly up the mountain. James presses his thin, hungry face close to the window. The stocky Gordon stares out as one mesmerized. They see the Stawamus Chief, the town's granite monolith and crowning jewel, standing aloof in the sunshine at the head of Howe Sound. Both men look at it in awe, thinking all the while about the incredible range of climbs it offers — more than four hundred routes. They know that these long free climbs to the top are the only places in North America where people can scale such spectacular granite walls — aside from the infamous towers of Yosemite.

Today, the views from the helicopter are of spectacular old-growth forests, expansive mountain ranges and impressive waterfalls, with the Chief at the heart of it all — a majestic mountaineer's playground. *A great place for all types of climbers,* James thinks. Images from the window appear to him picture perfect: a cobalt-blue sky, brilliant sun, smooth aprons of snow and a line of footprints tracking up to a windless summit — a climber's paradise.

The helicopter hovers over a lonely snowcapped crest, searching for a spot to land. The two men drop down into the snow with all their equipment at the place where they will begin their climb.

"See you at the pickup spot at Lake Lovelywater, day after next," calls the pilot as his blades begin spinning for takeoff.

The two leave their gear at Red Tit Hut on the col, or small pass, between Serratus and Dione mountains, then set out to climb a route up Mount Dione. The elevation is close to 6,700 feet. The air feels warm and mellow; sunrays glance off the granite walls to glint fresh and soft on the remnants of old winter snow. They climb all day, reaching the summit at nightfall. This first night is spent on a ledge, partly sheltered by an overhanging rocky lip. The night temperature dips, and a chill wind blows from the north. Both men are a bit the worse for wear in the morning, particularly Gordon, who has forgotten to bring all his water and feels somewhat dehydrated because of it.

The two now prepare for a series of rappels down near-vertical rock, a manoeuvre that will bring them to the glaciated snow below — hard snow that never melts because it is forever hidden from the sun in heavily shaded, north-facing valleys. Each in turn descends the fifty-metre rope to the next station, then retrieves the rope by pulling on it through the anchor.

"We prefer to make use of natural anchors if any are available," James has said. "Like a rocky horn protrusion, a tree trunk or an ice bollard. But — no trees up here, so that's no option." Manmade anchors take many forms: for instance, a short piece of rope or webbing may be secured to a rock to form a loop; or a tapered piece of aluminum, connected to a wire loop, may be wedged into a crack so that it bears weight. Other possibilities include a piton — a thin, wedge-shaped metal blade that is hammered into a thin crack — or an ice bollard. Cheap, but time-consuming, ice bollards are built by chiselling a large ring in the ice or hard snow, leaving a post in the centre, around which to place the middle of a rope. The softer the snow, the larger the bollard that is required. Manmade anchors are reusable, so climbers take care not to leave them behind.

James makes his last descent of approximately one hundred feet and lands on a bridged ice mushroom* that is supported over the bergschrund.† Gordon prepares to rappel down after him. But what's going on? Why is he doing that? James sees Gordon traverse out and step sideways off the rock, watches him place his feet on the steep snow slope in the gully, then take the manmade protection from the rock. He supposes that Gordon plans to fashion an ice bollard for himself. Somehow in this process, Gordon falls, and his fall is unprotected. James watches in horror as his body tumbles seventy feet down the mountainside, watches him go into a free fall for the last thirty feet, land close to where James is standing. He grabs his friend to prevent him from falling further into the bergschrund.

---

* "Mushrooms" are so called because of the shape of the platform. In this case, the bridge consisted of unsupported snow.
† A crevasse or gap at the junction of a steep upper slope with a glacier or neve, where the top of a glacier pulls away from the rock face.

James stands, momentarily immobilized. He notices, irrelevantly, that the sun has risen higher, diminishing the shadows cast across the rugged mountain slopes. It is around eleven in the morning and his friend and climbing partner is lying unconscious on a precarious ice platform high up in the mountains. Neither climber has a radio or cell phone with him, and the stolid walls of the mountain ranges seem devoid of other human life. With a plummeting sensation in his heart, James knows it will take six to eight hours for him to hike to the helicopter meeting spot — where their meeting is not scheduled to take place for twenty-four hours. He stares out over a cold, impersonal universe of snow and granite, knowing that his only option is to stay beside his unconscious friend — stay, and try to keep them both warm.

★

Like James and Gordon, Val Fraser and Peder Ourom could not not resist the allure of the mountains during this stretch of unusually fine weather. Longtime climbing partners, together they set off on an overnight climb to scale the peaks of Mount Dione. Skilled and experienced, they have come to Squamish prepared to tackle some of North America's most challenging vertical cliffs. On the same day and at the same time, they happen to be scaling a slope adjacent to the peak on which James and Gordon are climbing.

"I get to the top of the notch about eleven-thirty," Val says. "As I climb, I hear noises in the background — rock falls, I think. Has to be, because of the unstable perches I've been climbing on. Over it is the noise of heli-logging across the valley. Then I think I hear voices — no, not possible — I look across to the base of the snow gully, and I see two people!"

Val stands and stares; an eerie silence fills the void, and then the shouting begins: a yell from one of the climbers that the other is badly injured and can't move. *Oh, dear God.* She calls out to Peder, and both of them shout across to the other party: "What can we do? Do you have a cell phone? We have one... We'll be down to you as fast as we can get there." While their voices bounce across imperturbable granite and shadowed valleys, tiny, waiflike Val begins constructing bomber anchors to try to secure her safety and Peder's. Meanwhile, Peder yanks out his cell phone to dial 911 for help. He dials over and over, but cannot get a signal.

"No service — damn!" After a frustrating half-hour, he finally succeeds in getting a call relayed through to Victoria, on Vancouver Island. He tells the operator that a climber has become injured on the Tantalus Range above Squamish and needs a helicopter rescue. The 911 operator refuses to take this information, responding that she will transfer him to another centre. Then the connection is lost. Furious, Peder dials his wife, Louisa. Fantastic — she's at home!

"Louisa, listen: this is urgent. There's been an accident. A climber up here's in big trouble and could lose his life." He gives her all the information and asks that she relay it to the Royal Canadian Mounted Police. "Call me back, soon as possible."

Val and Peder make the difficult decision to abandon their own gear in order to make a series of rappels down to the snow slope through treacherous loose rock to get to the injured climber. They are on a mission; gear can be replaced.

"We're at a scary spot and in a great deal of danger if we are to knock anything down on ourselves," Val says. "Every step we take is critical, and has to be taken slowly. Peder gets to the bottom first. Then I rap[pel], careful not to knock any rocks on him. He pulls me down with one hand while he talks on the phone with the other. Next we have to get across the bergschrund at the bottom."

While Peder is on the phone, Val attempts to retrieve the ropes, but one is stuck in the moat. "Oh, damn," she says.

Peder manages to climb up to where Gordon lies, introduces himself and makes an assessment of the site and of the whole situation. James greets him with an expression of profound relief. Val remains in the magic zone where cellular phone calls are still feasible. Peder scales back down to Val, and the two devise a plan of action: they will try to get all their gear up to the accident site, where it might provide additional padding and warmth for the victim. They will then try to find a way to secure all four of them on top of the ice mushroom while they wait for help. Peder's wife Louisa calls back to report that she has done as requested and asked for a helicopter longline rescue service (HFRS).

Together Val and Peder build an anchor with an ice axe and ice screw. They tie one rope in, and Val fastens herself onto its end and jumps onto the mushroom. It holds, but it's very thin and might break off and plunge her all the way down into the bergschrund. Her blood chills at the thought. But now she's on the ice mushroom and greeting James and Gordon. The victim lies twisted on the snow, a little bloodied, but conscious and able to respond to questions. Val immediately places rope, a backpack, jacket and fleece-lined shirt under him for padding. The injured man looks up at her, puzzled. Who is this stranger who seems to have appeared out of the great snowy void? Both his hands are wet and cold. Val struggles to get them into James' gloves — "like trying to dress a big child," she comments.

"Val, we need the radio," Peder says then, and he promptly begins scaling down the ice mushroom to the camp site to retrieve it.

The rescue platform remains precarious, and more needs to be done to secure it. The three uninjured climbers agree that the ice anchor has to be backed up to the rock on one side of the bergschrund, and to the glacier on the other, to prevent any of them from falling off. In silence, they work to fashion an anchor on the top surface of the mushroom. Once accomplished, they will all be secured to something if they are to slip.

The job is done, but immediately there is a thump — and then another and another. Part of the mushroom gives way, and a profusion of white spray flies up all about them. A stricken silence ensues from the three. Each glances at the others, understanding their thoughts: that the whole area on which they are perched might collapse at any moment. In silence they search for other anchors among the solid rock on one side and the glacier on the other, so that they can back up their existing anchors.

Once accomplished, Val turns to talk to Gordon while she performs a check of his vital signs. She asks his name, age and where he's from. At this point, "Gordon is conscious but in a great deal of pain," she says. "He's cold and complains about his legs. We pad him with ropes and our backpacks, a jacket and a fleece shirt. He has a broken nose and his eyes are beginning to swell, but there are no signs of other bruising and bleeding." Val turns her attention to James. To her calculating eye he seems to be okay — perhaps mildly in shock, but able to function. There remains nothing further to do. The group on the ice mushroom wait for what seems to them an interminable time. "It's like time has become stuck. It doesn't move, nothing moves," Val says. "Then we hear a chopper! Oh… but it seems not to see us, and it flies right past."

★

Brad Thompson stands on his back porch on a quiet street in Squamish, chatting with Nathan Dubeck, his friend and search-and-rescue (SAR) colleague. The sun arcs over the mountains. It is noon on a beautiful Saturday, and the two are discussing the possibility of their families getting together for dinner that evening. A sound pierces the air then, to shatter the peaceful scene in Brad's secluded garden: both their pagers emit a summons, and each knows what it means.

"Injured climber on the Tantalus Range," comes the voice of the area co-ordinator for the Royal Canadian Mounted Police. "Will all SAR members report immediately to Warehouse Number 5."

"There goes dinner," one says to the other, and they lock eyes. "Okay, what do you want to be?" These are not little boys playing a game: a quick decision has to be made about who will assume what role in this rescue. Each man holds the same positions: deputy co-ordinator and search manager for the town's volunteer search-and-rescue team. Each takes his turn in these positions, under the direction of the RCMP. The most onerous duty falls to the deputy co-ordinator, whose responsibility it is to orchestrate all aspects of the search effort.

Brad calls the RCMP for details while Nathan phones to see what helicopter company is available. "A call to a rescue — as opposed to a search — creates a much more immediate adrenaline rush," he says. "Time is critical because of probable severe injuries that can become more life-threatening as time passes. You have to put yourself into a rescue mode, cast your mind over all the training you've been through and all the methodical steps you've taken. You have to try and visualize how things should unfold in the first ten minutes after the call. It's an awesome responsibility: you've got to be worrying not only about saving lives, but also about the cost — you're held accountable for this, too."

Brad's adrenaline pumps as he scrambles to find pen and paper to record details. He phones all the SAR members, asking them to report to number 5 Progress Way immediately for a rescue mission on Tantalus Range. "Yes, I will be responding to this," he tells the SAR operator. His mind races: there is no quick way to get to the accident scene on foot: a river has to be crossed, which can take hours. The fastest way is by helicopter. Fortunately, the weather is clear and cool and bathed in bright sunshine.

When Nathan hears of a man falling down a mountainside while climbing, it revives memories of his own fall off Brohm Ridge on Mount Garibaldi, and these are invariably followed by images of his coming to the rescue of the young Paul Hopkins after his fall off the same ridge — images of a teenager lying half-dead at the bottom of the mountain, cruelly mutilated. These have haunted him over the years, but they rush back now to crowd his mind, until he resolutely banishes them.

On this same day and time, John Willcox is up early. His life has become busy since the birth of his second child, and he likes to be up at daybreak to get a start on organizing events. Sun streams through the east-facing windows when he opens the blinds to look outside. The day has dawned with breathtaking clarity. John stands for a moment before the living-room windows, gazing up at the mountains. The sky stretches above the ranges like a giant blue canvas; the sunlight glistens on old snow that clings to the peaks — he can also see remnants hidden in the valleys. This is surely a day to be up there, with no other soul around. The mountain peaks always seem to beckon John: *Come up… come on up.*

Willcox recalls the time some years earlier when he had made the decision to move to Squamish. It had been simply because the town stood halfway between Whistler, where he worked as a ski patroller — ten whole years, he thinks in surprise — and his home in North Vancouver, where he worked as a third-level paramedic. Eventually he began to appreciate the opportunities available here: mountain climbing, snowmobiling, kayaking, skiing and windsurfing — it was an outdoor paradise. Remote it might be, but the town is celebrated by many as the recreational capital of the world. He has come to love the mountains of granite and limestone that reach up into the heavens and brood over the tiny figures that scurry about at their feet. He knows that some people find them menacing and oppressive, but to others they are awe-inspiring, like gods of antiquity soaring upwards to communicate with celestial life.

John is startled out of his reverie by the screech of his pager. The message: "Area co-ordinator, call the RCMP dispatch re: injured climber on Tantalus Range."

The Tantalus Range was named after the ancient Lydian king and son of Zeus, whose name is also at the root of the verb *to tantalize*. And the mountains do tantalize the viewer to come on up. It is one of John's favourite spots around Squamish — both the park and the vast, empty alpine environment. He hasn't been up in a while — not since before the birth of his second child, he realizes in surprise. Life has become busy. But it's not just that: to climb that range requires a great deal of planning and effort. It involves crossing the Squamish River, slogging up a steep, heavily treed trail — with an elevation gain of more than a hundred feet — then continuing on for more than three and a half hours to reach Lake Lovelywater. Only then does the technical climb begin. Of course, for those who have the means, there is always the choice of a five-minute helicopter ride to the top — the choice made by James and Gordon.

The second page comes minutes later. "All available SAR members please attend Number 5 Warehouse for an injured climber." John's pulse quickens and he feels a rush of adrenaline. He turns to his wife and begins, "Honey, it's an urgent call—"

"I know, I heard the word 'injured,'" she says. "Of course you must go. I can manage on my own."

John races along the quiet streets of the town to the highway toward Brackendale, onto Progress Way, and into the Squamish Industrial Park. He stops in front of number 5, the building that serves as the search-and-rescue unit's headquarters and houses their equipment: the command van, rescue vehicle, boat, communications equipment, maps, radio, oxygen tanks, stretcher, rope, head lamps and all the first-aid supplies. Brad Thompson is already there, acting as co-ordinator, and has already placed a call to three helicopter companies. The first to respond will be given the assignment. Blacktusk Helicopters comes through first, and its staff is hired.

Vehicles squeal to a stop outside the warehouse, and members of the volunteer search team stride in to hear the words, "seriously injured climber... helicopter flight rescue system needed. It's urgent."

"I've requested a longline rescue," Brad says. He has the authority to do it, and his judgment is trusted. It's a request that is not made lightly, as it involves many highly trained people and a lot of money. Brad begins the lengthy process of assembling the required equipment. To save time, a near-by cul-de-sac is secured as a helipad. Now he has to choose from among the group those he will authorize to fly to the area to do an assessment. John Willcox is one of them, without question: his advanced training and experience make him *the* choice as a paramedic. Then, who to make a res-cue plan, who to assess the patient — this is what the injured climber will now be called. Who to report all the details, as they are made known, to the SAR manager? The responsibilities and decisions to be made seem almost overwhelming to him as he moves swiftly through his tasks.

Half past noon: the sun is high above the mountains. The air is cool and clear, unlike the many September days when winds blow noisily along the canyons like a raucous jester of the ranges. The team members who are to fly confirm with the pilot the reported location of the acci-dent, and the group as a whole discusses the possible whereabouts of other volunteer search-and-rescue workers to provide backup if needed.

"Perry is somewhere out of the country on a training exercise," some-one says. "John's on holiday... Chris is teaching a course down east..."

"Among us there is a high level of skill, experience and expertise," John explains. "But it comes at a price: many of us are not always avail-able — we're teaching, working, climbing, guiding clients, or out there recreating ourselves. Three of us are here, two are up the mountain with the patient, and we get others: from North Vancouver, and from Whistler, fifty kilometres to the north — a group that has a mutual-aid team trained and equipped for helicopter flight rescues. They are ready to come and help us — great, fantastic!"

The helicopter takes off with Doug Woods, Hugh Ackroyd and John Willcox on board, and is soon eight thousand feet above sea level, on the west side of Mount Dione. The crew is tense and anxious. They are rap-idly approaching a silent and primeval world high above the earth, a place where big dreams are fulfilled, sometimes dashed; where life is occasionally tragically snuffed out.

High up on the mountainside, James does everything he can to protect and sustain his friend and climbing partner. His anxiety increases as the time passes. Beside him, Val and Peder work tirelessly to secure the ice platform that holds them, but still it seems precarious. They are tied to an ice block, but they have no idea how long it will stay in place. Both are anxious, and they, too, must wait — how very hard in such a helpless position. But they are aware of how difficult it can often be to muster volunteer rescue workers from work, family and other obligations.

Then they hear it! The chopper flies right past them, then circles about and returns, searching for a place to land.

"We are at your three o'clock, approximately one kilometre out." Peder Ourom's voice breaks through the chatter on the helicopter's radio. He recommends that the crew approach a small saddle, one-quarter of a kilometre distant, as a spot for a hot unload.* The pilot tries to get as close as he safely can without affecting the people huddled on the perilous ice shelf. He places both skids on the snow, but continues to hold power, blades turning, until the crew deplanes and unloads its gear.

"I'll circle above you and relay information to the SAR command," the pilot says, as Hugh Ackroyd, Doug Wood and John Willcox tumble out of the aircraft. Val's heart jumps with pleasure and relief. She smiles at Gordon and says, "Hey, a great bunch of guys has just arrived to help you. Soon we'll all be out of here and this will seem like just a bad dream.

"They have a bunch of gear, but I don't see a litter among it all," she says. "I'm confused about this... I see John's medical pack, his tech pack, and a rope pack or two... weird."

Peder hikes down to greet the chopper's crew and to offer to help carry their medical equipment and rope rescue packs.†

"As the boys are traversing the snow slope below us, our ice mushroom rumbles and cracks all around us," says Val later. "Then a huge horseshoe of the snow collapses and falls into the void of the bergschrund. It feels like an earthquake or an avalanche... it's one of the strangest and wildest

---

* Disembarking from a chopper while its engines are still running, its blades still turning.
† Packs complete with rope and all the necessary hardware to make various anchors, mechanical advantage raises, and controlled heavy lowers.

things I've ever experienced. The ice mushroom collapses right where I've been sitting for the past hour, and Gordon is lying inches from its edge. Suddenly I feel overcome with a huge adrenaline rush. My arms and legs shake for ten minutes."

The men below also hear the *whumph* of the collapse as two sides of the ice mushroom where Val and James are standing break away near Gordon's feet. Those on the platform are petrified until they remember they're all tied into the ice anchor that Val rigged up. The trouble is that their perch is now only about ten feet by twelve, and getting smaller all the time. "I wonder how all of us can fit onto it — how John is going to work on the patient," someone says. "How's he going to get up there to do it, anyway?"

Peder, Hugh and Doug have gone on ahead and climbed up to the ice platform. Each works frantically to build better anchors on either side of the mushroom: three snow pickets on the snow slope, and two ice screws and an axe in the wall above now support a rope strung across as a Tyrolean. If more pieces continue to break off, at least all of them will not be lost.

They all connect themselves to the rope in case the mushroom collapses even more. It provides Doug with a belay, too, to help John get onto the ice mushroom. Val still has an ice axe in the mushroom, and she moves it over to the stem and hammers it in — "I figure it won't hurt to be attached to a couple of things," she says.

Peder and Hugh Ackroyd push ahead to examine the stability of the area where the rescuers will have to work. Doug Wood and John Willcox come after them. Together they decide that the ice axe anchor must be backed up to the rock on one side of the bergschrund, and then to the ice glacier on the other. This is done in short order, and Val prepares to belay.* John simultaneously goes up the ten feet to help. With two ice axes, a boost and a knee hold, he is on top.

"The approach I make to the patient will be no different from the way I attend all my patients," John says. "But — I have to confess that in this environment, and without my partner, I feel I'm not keeping pace; I'm finding it very slow."

---

* To control the amount of slack in the lead climber's rope, making it possible to stop a climber's fall if it should happen.

John's patient is conscious, but distracted by pain. The paramedic makes the following report:

> A head-to-toe examination around a helmet, past zippers and multiple layers of Gore-Tex, all poly-restricted by a climbing harness tethered to our common anchor, reveals a restless, pale, thirty-nine-year-old male with a broken and bloodied nose. He complains of thoracic, back and pelvic pain.

Willcox feels pressured to get treatment started, but he is first obligated to obtain, and report back, a set of baseline vital signs. Val is trying to open his pack to get him the blood-pressure cuff and stethoscope. But she can't find the zipper. There is severe frustration at the seconds passing — and at Gordon's constantly moving about, making it impossible for John to get the blood-pressure cuff on him. He peels back the layers of clothes sufficiently to apply the blood-pressure cuff, but the operation is very awkward and difficult.

"I can't feel his pulse, either at wrist or groin, but he must have one," John says to Val. "I mean, he's talking to me, and the artery in his neck is palpable at a rate of 104." After two attempts, John finds himself arm-wrestling his patient to straighten his arm so as to obtain a blood-pressure reading.

"Please, please try to keep still," Val begs, but Gordon has become restless. He tries to sit up, but this is his last rally of energy before he again lapses back into unconsciousness. John gives him a trapezius squeeze, but gets no response.

"He's stopped breathing!" John says this under his breath to Val and James as he yanks an airway out of his pack. He places the oral airway and quickly assembles the bag valve mask.

"It went in easily," Val says. "Not a good sign."

John fights to maintain a seal on the gaunt face of his patient. He feels for his carotid pulse — present, but probably not for long. He turns to Val. "Ventilate him. Bag him, please!" he says. "He's bleeding internally, but he has held out through the golden hour."

It is now six minutes after two in the afternoon, three and a half hours after Gordon's fall. His veins are flat, but John thinks that with a lucky stab he can get an IV started. He manages to insert an eighteen-gauge needle to begin a rapid infusion of the one-litre bag of normal saline he carries in his pack. James holds the bag and Val checks regularly to ensure that Gordon still has a pulse. Hugh relays radio communication both ways while Peder and Doug continually assess the stability of the area, ready to tweak their plan if the working platform should collapse further. One more rescuer and a stretcher has to be added to an already crowded spot.

John recognizes that his patient's condition is worsening: his pupils are dilated and he will require ventilatory support when he is transported. He makes preparations to intubate. Sometimes awkward under ideal conditions, up here it will be nearly impossible: bright sun reflects off the snow and John can't see anything past Gordon's teeth. Someone throws a jacket over his head and shoulders to block the glare. Now he can use the light from the laryngoscope, and after suctioning, and four attempts, he finally manages to pass the tube through Gordon's vocal cords and into his trachea.

Young tiny Val remains supporting John as he tries to sustain Gordon, but in the end, there is little either can do but wait. Each stares out across an impersonal vista of jagged peaks, remote and imperturbable in the light of the group of puny mortals scrambling to sustain their lives. And all about, the impersonal, cold white world stands perfectly still.

Then they hear it! Each looks up, relief flooding their faces. Whistler-Blackcomb Helicopter's A Star circles above them. Hope at last for the man who lies before them on this ice bollard. They are relieved for themselves that their ordeal — one that will later seem unimaginable — is soon to be over.

The chopper flies over, then radios that it is off to "burn some fuel." After conducting a reconnaissance of the rescue scene, the Blackcomb pilot searches for the nearest flat spot to reconfigure. He finds one just one kilometre to the south. The crew — Daryl Kincaid, Brad Sills and Binty Massey — studies all the variables, including winds, weather, weights, elevation and proximity to the rock, as it prepares for the long-line rescue. The group on the ice platform is unaware that the Whistler SAR team has acquired the necessary equipment and training for this type of rescue just one year before; that, while their services have been

requested four times since, each occasion has resulted in a no-go decision. This one has come close to being yet another no-go when the
Whistler SAR members hear on the radio that the paramedic at the site
has begun cardiopulmonary resuscitation. This is to be their first actual
longline rescue.

The mood at the foot of the mountains is equally tense: a jumble of
people running and calling, trucks pulling in and out, phones ringing —
the scene might seem chaotic to a passer-by, but order does prevail under
the calm direction of Brad Thompson and Nathan Dubeck. At brief
moments, Nathan's mind flips back to another time, another place, but
the story is always the same: he's falling off a mountain, the stuff of his
recurring nightmares. In a brief lull in the activity, he's back there once
more. He's a late teenager — just a boy, really. Anytime he has a spare
moment away from school and other chores, he's off with his friends to
the lofty playground high above the world to criss-cross the alpine slopes
in exhilaration. They know there are risks on the steep icy slopes, but
their challenge is just this: not to slip right off the mountain.

"Fabulous views of Mount Garibaldi on the way up," Nathan will
tell you, when asked to explain his passion for this sport. "Off to the side
is Brohm Ridge, and once you're there you have a beautiful view all the
way across Howe Sound, down into the town and up into the valleys.
Everyone knows it's a spectacular place to ride: not risky, really, although
the Ridge is five thousand feet above sea level and falls away very steeply
on either side. It just means you don't want to fall over its edges."

★

But that's just what happened: one day, at midafternoon, a machine
roared up alongside Nathan.

"A sled's gone over the side," its owner said abruptly. "Can't see
what's happened to the rider."

Someone's fallen off the ridge! Nathan had immediately revved his snowmobile and raced it along the north ridgeline. Others followed. Nathan
stopped, leaned forward on his machine to try to get a look. Nothing: a
rocky outcrop blocked anything below out of sight. As if in slow motion,
he stepped off his snowmobile and moved toward the edge of the cliff.

"I put my feet down, and immediately they began sliding toward the edge of the ridge," he says. "I tried frantically to pull back, to grab something — anything — but next thing I'm slipping right over the edge. I can't believe it. I'm sliding, faster all the time, and suddenly I see this small rock sticking out of the ice. I try to grab it as I go flying…"

The nightmare continued: he bounced over walls of ice, slid on his stomach headfirst down the mountain. A windblown line of rocks reared up… he did something resembling a push-up to clear them, all the while picking up speed. He came ever closer to the edge of the ridge, flew right off the rocky rim and began another, more nightmarish fall. Like a rock hurtling into space, the teenager fell all the way into a valley along the north side of the long ridge.

★

The memory of the sensation of falling, and the sheer, immobilizing horror of it, overtake Nathan for a brief few moments before he shakes himself free of it.

★

Up on the mountain, Val and John repeatedly look for a pulse in Gordon's neck. They find none. At thirty-two minutes after two in the afternoon, John starts compressions, knowing that they will not help start a heart without blood, but he has no other options.

"Where's the chopper gone? Why is it taking so long?" The voices are fretful, even though all understand the time it takes to organize a rescue of this kind. Finally, the helicopter pilot's voice comes on the air. "Listen. Before we fly in, we need to know: Does the paramedic wish to escort the patient in flight?"

"Yes."

James has taken over chest compressions while John prepares to place the patient in a stiff-neck collar and an orange, cocoon-like wrap, readying him to be placed in the clamshell stretcher for the airlift. James has to temporarily stop cardiac compressions and bagging. Wait… something's not right. Gordon is about to be moved, he's being pulled tight, but he's not moving. He's still tied in! James frantically unties a bunch of cords from the anchor and the double fisherman's knot to which the patient is attached through his harness. He yells for a knife, but no one can find one. Val reaches over, struggles and unties the knot. John prepares his pack to be slung below him off his harness, then puts on a jacket for the short flight.

Tension permeates the air as Daryl Kincaid from the Whistler SAR team is lowered with awesome precision onto the ice platform right beside them. He dangles from a one-hundred-foot line below the chopper, the stretcher attached horizontally at his waist. He is immediately secured to the web of safety lines before he unclips himself from the long line. He stares uneasily about him as he is briefed on the plan to move Gordon into the aerial-rescue platform, also known as a Bauman bag. Peder, Doug and Hugh wait anxiously below: all these people are perched on a precious ice platform that might break away at any time. Knowing this, they limit their movements to those parts of it that are known to be well supported.

Within a few minutes Gordon is secured in the Bauman bag stretcher, Daryl on one side and John on the other. John shortens the utility strap that connects the screamer suit harness* to the master-point ring of the aerial rescue platform. "This places me higher, with my knees pivoting at the edge of the clamshell," John explains. "I've never needed to perform CPR during any of my six previous longline rescues. This is tough." The quiet understatement of a self-deprecating man. But by positioning himself in this way, and with a one-foot extension tube between the bag and valve of his bag valve mask, he is able to rock forward to compress with one hand, then flip his other hand over to squeeze the bag to ventilate.

Daryl, John and Gordon are all unclipped, waiting for the free line to come in. Daryl grabs the line clip, and in an instant it seems they are off in the air. At the same time, Val and Peder try to get James off the mushroom in case it collapses; Val exhales a sigh of relief that the wash from the hovering chopper doesn't send a cascade of rocks their way.

---

* A "screamer suit" is a large, diaper-like enclosure with a pair of armholes. Rings are attached to each of the three corners, and these connect to a single caribiner that is attached either to the master carabiner on the rescuer's harness or to the fixed helicopter rescue line. It fits a person of any size, is easy to use, and is considered foolproof.

It's just a short hop over in the 'copter; the group is deposited less than fifty metres from the helicopter that waits to receive Gordon and take him on the fifteen-minute flight to the Squamish hospital. Back on the ice mushroom, the remaining group starts to clean up the tangled mess of ropes and anchors.

"Val, I want you off the mushroom immediately," Peder says firmly.

It takes her only about ten seconds to get ready to get off the platform. Doug Wood lowers her from its lip. Meanwhile, Hugh is taking care of James. It's a very emotional time. Each gives the others a hug. Val looks then at James and worries that he's "losing it" as he begins to blame himself for everything.

"He didn't have his water bottle... he hadn't slept well... didn't feel so good when he set out..."

"None of it is your fault!" exclaims Val. "It just happened — an accident, James. It was simply an accident."

"But he was dehydrated," James says, his lean face twisting with emotion. "I mean, the guy drank one litre of water yesterday. I didn't know he'd forgotten his water bottle. I should have asked, I should have checked." He slumps and Val reaches over and touches his arm.

The remainder of the rescue team from Whistler has the crew members disconnect themselves and move to the waiting helicopter. Less than a minute's break in CPR occurs while this takes place.

During transport to the hospital, John notices that the IV was empty, that the oxygen has run out. With a heavy heart, he feels that their best chance has come too late for Gordon.

The helicopter lands at the hospital and the group is met by waiting ambulance and doctor. While transferring the patient to the ambulance stretcher, they speak rapidly, in hushed tones.

"Outcome rather bleak, I'd say," says one. "Guess we'll find out soon enough."

Once the heart monitor is connected, it shows a flat line. When the placement of the leads is rechecked, it is discovered that one was off; when it's replaced, the patient's heart rhythm is detected.

"I can feel a pulse!" exclaims the second doctor. "Keep bagging — can we get him out of all this stuff? Gordon is removed from the stretcher, wrap, harness, boots and his multiple layers of clothing. A second IV is started. His blood pressure is ninety over forty. Rewarming commences, catheters are placed and tests ordered.

All the while, the SAR command constantly updates all the appropriate agencies so that a smooth and timely hand-off takes place each step of the way. Because of this expert communication, an Advanced Life-Support Airvac crew stands by at the Squamish hospital, waiting to transfer Gordon to Vancouver General Hospital, site of the Lower Mainland's major trauma centre.

★

At SAR headquarters, Nathan and Brad hear the news and know it isn't good, that all their efforts to co-ordinate a complicated rescue may not, in the end, result in a live rescue. "It's over," Brad says now. "We did our best." Both remember another time when they worked together to try to find and save the life of a young man who had fallen off the mountain.

★

Brad sees himself again, stumbling out of bed in the early morning, the sky as dark as his thoughts as he whispered to his wife: "I'm needed urgently to organize a search of the Brohm Highlands for two boys who were lost snowmobiling. Call you later." Then he was gone into a cold winter's morning, his vehicle groaning as he turned the ignition key. As he raced toward the ridge along streets that were still silent, the lack of sound struck him as ominous.

He thought fleetingly about Brohm Ridge. Did he sometimes wonder about these ancient volcanic cores that had been exposed during the last ice ages, their lava flowing out to the sea — about the presumptions of mere mortals who scaled their peaks and played about on the wintry slopes high above the rest of the world? In winter, it was a little-visited white wonderland, but always there were those who ignored the pitfalls. His blood ran cold as he thought of the possibilities for the two boys. He spurred his vehicle faster.

★

Gordon arrives at the Squamish hospital at three in the afternoon; an hour has elapsed, and he is now breathing on his own. No one is more surprised than John. But his sense of exhilaration is short-lived: the young man dies three days later. His injuries included a lacerated bladder and kidney, and a fractured pelvis. The lack of blood and oxygen to the brain also resulted in significant damage.

The entire rescue effort has been an emotional roller-coaster ride for all those involved; the rescuers' emotions have fluctuated in lockstep with Gordon's condition. One constant is the widespread, profound admiration shown toward John Willcox, who had risked his life for another.

John denies that he is brave; he maintains that he had simply done the very best he could under the circumstances. The difficulties had been enormous. The rescue effort had gone well in all its details, but the obstacles had been nearly insurmountable. Hopes had been high, but in the end a young man's life had been lost. He knew that when the helicopter showed up, its crew had not been prepared for the myriad tasks required to get Gordon off the ice platform; that they themselves had had to arrange all the details of getting him onto the ice block and belayed. Within fifteen to twenty minutes, Gordon had gone into cardiac arrest, and CPR was required throughout the remainder of the preparations for getting him onto the stretcher and into the helicopter.

"The more rescues I participate in, the more I learn that people who get lost and injured are often not careless and foolish," he said. "They've been caught by a series of small errors that accumulate in an event — I've made some of them myself."

The entire experience was one that would also haunt Brad Thompson. For many years he has been the deputy program co-ordinator for the town of Squamish and a certified SAR manager. He has acted as a training officer, SAR co-ordinator and communications officer. "But it's all too much," he said. "This was a particularly difficult rescue attempt — very stressful."

Why does he assume all this responsibility, live with this stress and trauma?

"There are considerable rewards," he says. "Each of us knows we did a good job and we don't look for recognition on the outside. We bond through these shared experiences, and it feels good to offer your expertise."

Daryl Kincaid, search manager for the Whistler SAR team and a ski guide there, talks about this rescue after the fact: "When you receive a call to respond in a high alpine environment, in rock and ice, you always take more equipment than you think you will need — a full HFRS kit, an additional rope-rescue kit, a twenty-four-hour personal pack for each rescuer, and backup medical kit. You have to be prepared for anything.

"Dave Brolin, as pilot, added a litre of extra fuel, as we did not know how much flying time would be involved — that's why we had to burn some of it off before we could land. The greatest responsibility with a longline rescue always lies with the helicopter pilot, and this one was tough: Dave had to hover at altitude, deposit a live load — me — on a small block of ice while winds gusted, while his rotor blades spun very close to the mountain sides. He exercised superb skill and judgment."

James, meanwhile, is devastated: he has never lost a partner in all of his twenty years of climbing. He had sat beside his friend, waiting powerlessly for what seemed an eternity for help to arrive, while his friend succumbed to his mortal injuries. Not wanting this accident to affect him or to slow him down, his response is to go climbing again right away.

★

This attempted rescue has entered local lore and legend — a good rescue with a bad outcome, a very challenging rescue and a first for the Whistler team. No dry run for them.

Longline rescue is used when there are no other means of removing an injured person from inaccessible terrain, when a helicopter cannot be shut down while the patient is loaded on board. Both doors are removed or snapped back; a special nylon rope — a belly band — is placed through the open doors around the floor of the helicopter. This belly band has a releasable latch located on the floor at the spotter's feet, and it is also connected to the helicopter's pilot-controlled releasable hook by a nylon strap called the Y lanyard. This gives two points of attachment to the helicopter. In the event of an emergency, the pilot tells the spotter to release the belly band, and the total weight of the rescue long line is then transferred to the helicopter's hook. The pilot can then release the hook

— electrically or manually — at an appropriate moment, and those attached to the long line are placed on the ground before the line is released. It is arranged this way because of the risks: of equipment being snagged in rocks or trees, of loss of power, or the need for the pilot to make an emergency crash landing.

Imagine a two-hundred-foot rope with a stretcher at the end of it, the patient secured inside. On each side hangs a rescuer, feet dangling but hands relatively free, rigged up so that he can compress the chest, then switch over to squeeze the bag and ventilate the lifeless patient.

Images of trapeze artists come to mind — someone performing delicate manoeuvres while suspended at the end of a rope, with no safety net. Certain death awaits if one were to fall.

★

The town of Squamish bears a special burden because of its reputation as a rock climber's paradise: volunteers are needed who are willing to give much time and effort to maintain their expertise, and to train others; to organize, procure and look after expensive equipment. Demands are made on the town for funds, and then more funds to enable sophisticated rescue efforts, such as this one, to happen.

Some call climbers "rock jocks." The stereotype is of a wiry, spidery, long-limbed figure, anonymous outside the climbing world. Few seek publicity, media coverage or sponsors; most just want a hard, clean climb, then to climb and climb again. There are those who scoff, who write climbing off as a selfish game, pointless and undignified. But a climb is a journey, one more complex — and with more inherent risk — than the average glory hunter is willing to assume. Externally, of course, there's the world of long shadows and self-exile, of snow and shattered black rock. But it's also an inner journey for most.

"It's a cycle of passion and drama, all of it pointing to a personal truth: 'How far can I go? How much should I push?'" says John Merrett, co-founder of the Canadian Amphibious Search Team, and a climber. "Your limits are not what you think. You ask, 'Was I scared?' Yes — scared silly.

"You rely only on yourself and your own fortitude," says Merrett. "You embrace obstacles rather than avoid them."

Another climber says, "A serious commitment to climbing exacts a terrible price: losing a friend, and another and another. But you can't live without it."

"In this sport, you realize how easily death can occur, how fast," says Merrett. "You see someone who has been rock climbing with you, then you are called to retrieve his body when he falls to his death. You haven't faced death so intimately before — it could be you. It makes you think about life — yours, and all others. It increases awareness of the risks in what you're doing. But [the risk] is calculated: if you know how to do the equations, you're all right. You know there are risks to everything.

"Doing these things — scuba diving, rock climbing — it focuses you and is your challenge," he adds. "It gives a different view of another life that is not available unless you do them. Yes, it's a lot of work to prepare and clean up afterwards, but the rewards are huge. Take climbing: a rock is a rock — it doesn't change. But it is the things you do that make the difference. If you're not able to do a climb, it's because of *you*, not the rock.

"It's different in other sports, where you have to rely on others. Here it is just you. You have two hours to climb this rock that's four hundred feet high. You decide not to put anchors in the rock at intervals of five feet because it takes so much time. Instead, you put them in at ten or more feet, and you take a calculated risk."

Stretcher rescue, Lake Lovelywater.

The Rinker family and their children.

EVERYBODY'S CHILD
Sunchild Native Reserve, Alberta

[Joy and sorrow] are inseparable. Together they come, and when one sits alone with you at your board, remember that the other is asleep upon your bed. — Kahlil Gibran

Karen Rinker lay in bed with her youngest child, Jesse, talking to him. Early-morning sunlight filtered through her window, bringing the promise of spring at last to the still-dormant wilderness where the mission compound stood.

"Daddy and Jenny are away in the United States," she murmured to her baby. "But soon they'll be home. Jesse, tell me, how old are you? What is your name?"

"Jesse... two," the small boy piped. She smiled and hugged him. It was a special time, and the memories would stick with her through all the pain associated with the tragic events to come. "I can hear little Jesse's voice saying, 'Jesse... two... two,'" Karen said. "It meant so much to my heart."

The child and his mother were in and out of the small mission school all that morning, as Karen prepared classes for her older children, Seth, Joshua and Reuben, as well a boy from the Sunchild Native reserve. Jesse ran back and forth across the yard and in and out of the school, a happy, busy little boy. Near the end of classes, he climbed the steps to the door of the school, hovering there.

"Mommy's still in school, Jesse. I'll be a little bit longer yet. You play out here, okay?"

The toddler, dressed in blue jeans with the happy-kid tag still attached, a sweater with deer running across the front and little red boots, looked up at his mother, then smiled and ran off towards the swing that hung between two trees.

The children tumbled out of school to play about the yard. Karen followed. She saw Jesse playing happily by the swing and began cleaning up the grounds around the school. When the sky darkened and large raindrops spattered, she looked up to call him inside. The swing stood empty. She glanced quickly all around, but saw that he was nowhere in the yard. She looked around a second time, but the yard and playground remained empty; no sign of her youngest child. Funny — he was there a moment ago. Perhaps he'd climbed the steps and trudged indoors all the way up to the bedrooms. Karen sprinted upstairs and searched them. No Jesse.

"My mind said, 'Okay, where was the last place I saw him? Yes, over by the swing.'" She ran back outdoors, then walked slowly, deliberately, toward the two trees. The swing moved slightly in the breeze, empty. A sense of dread overtook her, manifesting itself in the form of pressure in her chest and forehead. Oh, but of course! He'll be playing over in the schoolhouse. But it, too, stood silent and empty. It was then that Karen realized that her toddler was lost.

The events that immediately followed became a blur, blotted out by pain, by the beginning of a nightmare that would all but consume Karen, her husband and her four remaining children. But at this moment the mission compound on the Sunchild Native reserve became that dreaded scene: one filled with police and police dogs, neighbours and, inevitably, the media.

★

Rodger Rinker had gone on a mission to the United States with his eldest daughter, Jenny. He wanted to raise money for the alternative school program he'd started just seven months earlier, known as Accelerated Christian Education. At the very moment that his baby went missing he was on his way home, stopping overnight on a farm in Iowa. He sat in the kitchen with Ruth Morris, his hostess, telling her about his dreams for his school.

"Our local government schools have not offered a good education," he said. "If we'd sent our kids to one, they might not have learned to read. Things will change, but at the moment,* many Native children don't come to school because their parents believe education to be a bad thing — the kids might lose their culture and belief systems because of it. We want to offer a good education to our own, and to Native children, with Karen as teacher. It's a low-budget school — we get only mission donations from the church to fund it, but I'd say already it's a huge success."

During supper, the phone rang — for Rodger. He took it and listened to the voice of his wife saying something about Jesse missing, that no one could find him… the police were there… but she sounded positive. "It's not dark yet. I'm sure he'll be found," she said.

Rodger thought, *This is major. This is serious. We live on the edge of a vast wilderness. You can stand and look out from the house in any direction for hundreds of miles and you'll see very little.* He got up and walked out of the house and down the road in the dark, a cloud of depression beginning to form over him. Deeply disturbed, he returned and went to bed, but not to sleep. Ruth sat up all night in her chair by the phone.

Rodger and Jenny flew out the next morning from Sioux Falls, reaching Rocky Mountain House by late evening. This was the place where they purchased all their supplies, the town closest to their home on the reserve. In the van, they heard a radio station blaring out news about a missing child named Jesse Rinker.

"Until now, news of Jesse's disappearance had gone through different doors in my mind," Rodger said. "But this was a big jolt; a bad dream had become real. All the radio stations played this every hour."

Midnight was close upon them; the wilderness home, normally swallowed up by the silence of the boreal forest all about, was lit up and

---

* The time Rodger Rinker referred to was 1987. It was a transitional time, and in the years since, parents of Native children have become anxious for them to receive a good education.

thrumming with vehicles, with large crowds milling about the house and its extensive grounds. A sinking sensation struck the pit of Rodger's stomach as he saw his family through a prism of publicity. He stepped out of the van to find media personnel waiting to pounce like hungry wolves. All stared at him, but none approached or said a word.

The story of the missing toddler son of Christian missionaries on a Native reserve dominated the news. Rodger, Karen and their eldest four children felt under siege; they read about themselves in newspapers and heard about themselves on hourly radio broadcasts. To a family who lived an isolated existence among Native people on a reserve, devoted to family life, to educating local children and teaching them about the love of God, this was shocking — "a totally unreal feeling, to see ourselves like this," Rodger said. "But we have to put up with it; we have to deal with this," he added, as he gestured with a wave of his hand towards the press with their cameras and the large numbers of people crowding the grounds of the mission compound. "The more publicity the better," he added. "The more pictures, clues, sightings and information given, the more police will work on this case, and the better chance we have that Jesse will be found. We all believe he's been kidnapped."

The police believed otherwise: the Rinkers' big wooden house, the compound, everything within a three-mile radius, became a crime scene, and the family were considered the principal suspects in the disappearance of their own child.

"In eighty percent of all missing children cases, a family member is responsible for abducting the child, or for its murder," a Royal Canadian Mounted Police (RCMP) officer said, quoting current statistics. "We have procedures we must follow in these cases."

While officers from the investigative branch interrogated the family, scrutinized their every move and listened to their conversations all day, every day, officers from the operational detachment set up ground searches, eventually mounting one of the largest search efforts ever recorded in the history of the province. RCMP Constable Richard Smith from the Rocky Mountain House detachment was asked to act as team leader, as search master.

"I was considered qualified to do this because I'd studied search management and had attended the Canadian Forces Survival School course," Richard said. "Assisting me was Ben Shantz of Rocky Mountain House Forestry."

RCMP Constable Jim Thoreson also came to help towards the end of the second week of the search. "But I only had training from the Canadian Forces Survival School on how to take a search team out in the bush — I had no management training," Jim said.

Once appointed, Richard headed out to set up headquarters in a tent near a gravel road on the Sunchild Native reserve. Other officers from across Alberta descended, and then came the volunteers, among them large numbers of local Native people. These First Nations volunteers were among the first to offer to search; they were warm, caring people who never wavered in their support and help for the stricken family. Of all those present, none had search training of any kind. Constables Smith and Thoreson made it their first task to take police officers aside and give them a crash course in how to manage a search team. "At the least, we knew police were disciplined," Richard said.

With the arrival of helicopters, the two officers went out to flag search lines, having already divided the area into twenty-eight segments using probability of detection methods. Each man was dropped down to mark one area, then picked up and dropped off to mark another and another. Boundaries were set and sectioned off with tape. All the while, more volunteers crowded in: Natives with saddle horses, dog handlers, trappers — all were organized and given areas of responsibility.

The search began with an array of sophisticated tools: a hand-held, heat-seeking, thermal-imaging camera, a tool so sensitive it could detect any slight object, even under a foot of mud; side scanners; and sonar devices. Altogether, 1,100 to 1,200 searchers walked in three different directions in a grid pattern over the area where they thought the child might have wandered. The intensive effort involved local police, First Nations people, the RCMP, armies of volunteers, and an organization devoted to locating missing children. For the next fifteen days, more than eight square kilometres of ground were searched. Assistance came also from nearby British soldiers-in-training, from a local trapper, from owners of bloodhound search dogs, crew in additional helicopters, and pilots of boats using side and depth scanners who combed the river depths. A bear was cut open to examine the contents of its stomach. Only roots and berries were found.

A freshly dug grave discovered by the British soldiers brought the RCMP quickly to the site. They immediately contacted reserve chief Tom Bigchild, who hurried to the site, together with a medicine man, to examine it. "A genuine Indian grave," the chief declared.

It was just the beginning of a long struggle for officers of the law: with a landscape that hid a child — assuming he had not been kidnapped; with local Native people who, while supportive of the Rinkers, regarded police, and most white people, with suspicion; and with the family, whom they were required to hold responsible for their missing child. All the while, the untamed natural world beyond the mission was repeatedly trampled: beaver dams were destroyed and lakes drained; sonar devices probed large swaths of muskeg — bog and marshland where Jesse was last sighted — as well as the depths of the Baptiste River; heat-seeking infrared cameras were mounted in helicopters, "equipment sensitive enough to detect a mouse." More bloodhounds were brought in to pick up the boy's scent from the house, track it to the swings, then along a trajectory several hundred yards toward the marshland — "slough — bad place for him to be." Sixty volunteers from a Mennonite group called Christian Disaster Relief came to help comb the woods all around the house yet again. It was a huge search effort that was to span thirteen months, during which time not a single clue to the toddler's whereabouts was found.

"If the small child had been anywhere around that area, something would have been picked up; he would have been found," said a trapper.

Two weeks after the child's disappearance, a spring snowstorm swept through the area. The search was scaled back, to continue only on the weekends.

★

Rhonda Morgan had come home from work late that day and flipped on her television screen.

"Three children abducted," said the CTV news anchor, who proceeded to profile a father's abduction of the couple's child. A devastated mother wept before the cameras as she described how her life had been turned upside down. Rhonda sat, mesmerized and angry, as a spokesperson from Child Find, an organization devoted to locating missing children, discussed the case with the television interviewer.

"I've always loved kids. I can't believe people can take children, hurt them, drag them around the country — it's too shocking," she said. "I ran to the phone to call Child Find. 'I saw your program,' I said. 'How can I help? What can I do? What do you need?'" This was the beginning of her work with this organization, helping to set up its bylaws and establish a mandate. "But I saw that [its mandate] did not include actual searches," she said. "The more I got into this work, the more I saw the gap in the service."

Rhonda left that organization to found another, the Missing Children Society of Canada, dreaming that she could develop a program that would help families more actively. She incorporated in November 1986 and officially opened the society's doors on May 6, 1987.

It was the very same day that she heard about missing toddler Jesse Rinker. Within a few hours she was in her truck, leaving Calgary and speeding north on the three-hour drive to the Sunchild reserve north of Rocky Mountain House. Lonely roads slipped by, long corridors of asphalt crowded to their edges by thick stands of pines, spruce and birch trees. She reached a gravelled road that ran alongside a river, a small creek, large areas of peat bog, marsh and generally swampy land, remote and primeval. Around a corner came the sudden view of a very large house with yards and fields stretching all about — a place carved out of the forest. Several children of various ages stared as she approached. There stood the Rinker family with four of their five children, and Karen pregnant once more, this time with twins.

Rhonda, made welcome and invited indoors, was immediately struck by an atmosphere redolent of a distant time and place; there was no running water or electricity, while a big wood stove in a corner was the heat source.

"Rustic, it was, this whole place," she said. "No modern conveniences, fields and forests in every direction — an old-world missionary compound with a church that was also a school." She looked all around her, then at the open space that stood between the house and the church school. Here the swing stood, the last spot where Jesse had been seen.

Rhonda followed the family down paths they thought he might have wandered, along the lonely logging trail behind the house where Rodger walked in the early mornings seeking the company of his God. In the solitude of this place, the child's father prayed to the Almighty and communed with him. The path he walked eventually led to a swampy area. No sign of the child — but of course, it had been searched before. Rhonda followed the family in another direction, towards the gravel road that led back to the main highway, and towards the road that led to Native homes.

She had earlier contacted the police to tell them her organization was available to help, and they accepted her offer. Within two days of her visit to the Rinker compound, she helped set up a ground search under the direction of constable Richard Smith, created posters, drove back and forth to Rocky Mountain House to distribute them and interviewed the family, the people on the reserve and the police. She realized she would need all the volunteers she could get for ground searches, and initiated a recruitment drive that saw dozens crowding the streets near her doors and saw Greyhound offering its coaches to deliver the volunteers* to the search site. Busloads descended upon the reserve to help scour the ground within a prescribed three-mile radius of the house. Then came boats, a helicopter, a team of tracking dogs — all involved in the search for the toddler in the little red boots.

While the thoughts of many turned to the possibility that the child had been kidnapped, the police, all the while, were forced to regard the family as chief suspects, and each member came under intense around-the-clock scrutiny. Police used the school as an inter-view room where they grilled the parents and their children. After the initial interview had been concluded, police and parents walked down the hall. Karen, her suffering keen, still in shock and disbelief that all of this was happening, let out a nervous laugh as they reached the

---

* Rhonda recorded names and addresses and checked identification, but didn't check their backgrounds for search experience — something she came to regret when she saw volunteers go out to search wearing running shoes and without bug spray or water — volunteers who were to become potential casualties them-selves. This later prompted the establishment of a trained volunteer SAR team.

door. The policeman stopped in the doorway, turned and stepped in front of her. He squatted until his eyes were on a level and inches from hers. His expression twisted cruelly as he enunciated his words slowly and deliberately: "How can you laugh when your baby is missing!" From that moment the officer developed a confrontational attitude to her and Rodger.

"They didn't do this to be nasty or because they suspected us — because after all, they didn't have enough information at the time to know if we were guilty or not," Rodger said. "They did it to get reactions from us, then used it as part of their procedure-oriented methods. I understood this is where they had to place their emphasis so they could try and determine whether or not we were among the eighty percent of parents who did their own kid in. Unfortunately, during this time, they didn't look elsewhere. We were interrogated — and our whole family — and taken to the police station at Rocky Mountain House to undergo lie-detector tests — this they had to do.

"At this time, our minds were saturated with what was happening, and I'm afraid our kids got left in the dust; they were there, but we couldn't sit down and talk to them and counsel them. We were being consumed ourselves — with grief, intense stress and anxiety. We had no one to help us get through it. If Jesse had died and we'd had his body to bury, we would know how to deal with it — we'd figure out how to get through it. This was different: we didn't know what we were dealing with from one day to another. The pressure we were under was tremendous: first, we had to keep the police working on the case, because at times they were inclined to shut it down — this was why we put up with constant and intense scrutiny, had to tolerate the horrible methods they used to try and break us. But I have to say that only a few officers were extremely aggressive, and I understood even then that to have a good investigation, someone had to do this, that the police are forced to follow specific procedures. Many of them were touched by our whole situation and some suffered with us — you could see it in their eyes. We knew they were forced to hold the family responsible — the statistics are there — but at no point in the investigation did any of them say, 'I really think these people are guilty of something.' Karen and I knew they believed us innocent, that they had to do this, but it was horrible, and extremely traumatizing to our children."

Then came the days when Rodger and Karen were taken separately in a police cruiser to the police station for polygraph tests.

"We felt thoroughly intimidated," Rodger said. "We were told that lie-detector tests never fail. We were shown how it worked, and then told to tell a lie. Like, if you don't drink coffee, say that you do. Then they showed us the way the graph responded. They impressed upon us how scientific it was, a perfect tool that would pick up any lie. We felt we were deliberately being scared to death: you worried that if your heart beat at the wrong time, or if you breathed wrong, they would think you guilty. It's mind-bending. It terrorizes you. You think they're going to ask you normal questions, but they start with, 'Did you murder your child?'"

Seth, a gentle, sensitive boy and the eldest Rinker son, was not spared: the police insisted he also be polygraphed. His brothers and sister watched as the twelve-year-old was bundled into a police cruiser and taken to the station — a slim, frightened boy alone in a police cruiser.

"We really didn't want to do this," Rodger said, "but we felt we had no choice; we wanted the investigation speeded up, and needed to get this out of the way. I was driven by a desire to get the police to look at other possibilities, to move the investigation on. If we'd shown any reluctance, it would be interpreted as guilt. We were innocent."

Rodger later felt he had been incredibly naive to allow Seth to go off on his own in the cruiser to Rocky Mountain House, to suffer through all the intimidation and accusations. His children had been raised in isolation from much of the rest of the world; as well, he and Karen had raised them to respect police, to hold them in high regard as special people, trustworthy and caring.

"But here, they frightened our boy, wired him up, walked up to him and said, 'Why did you murder your brother?' When they brought him home, they let him out at the house and just drove off. I looked into the face of my first-born, looked into his eyes, and felt a terrible premonition. I saw the devastation there, and I thought, 'My boy will never live through this. He's not going to survive it — he's very sensitive, a warm-hearted, kind and thoughtful boy.'"*

---

* Seth Rinker, as his father had predicted, did not survive the trauma of this experience, and committed suicide five years later.

Eventually the police did back off their severe aggression towards the Rinker family, and Rodger was to say afterwards, "I don't know how we survived it. It was unutterably, indescribably horrible. From the third day after Jesse went missing, I thought I'd die with it all. It was prayer in the end that pulled me through. Suffering through the agony of a missing child is the worst torture in the world, and then this… But after all the polygraph tests we endured, I can still say, 'God is in control of all things, and this is in his hands.'"

Karen echoed him, adding, "I want my baby back. But I'll accept whatever God chooses."

The tragedy began to affect the other children, who had at first been caught up in the excitement of all the activity: the helicopters, boats, police, soldiers and dogs. Reuben, the youngest, seemed most affected in the early stages by the tragedy of his youngest brother's disappearance. "Jesse is with Jesus. Jesus will look after him," he repeated.

The Rinker family awoke every day to their familiar natural world: the mission church that was also a little school, the great green forest that wrapped itself, unbroken, over the muskeg as far as the naked eye could see. But all the while they lived in a hothouse, walking on egg shells, afraid that their every innocent word, action or expression might be construed as guilt — even to the point that they feared sneezing at the wrong time. All this, while their little boy, smiling at them from his photo on the mantle, might have been wandering in the forest — or in the hands of a stranger. The spotlight on the family never waned, although some of the attention was positive: local Native people cooked for them, sat with them and offered emotional support.

★

The police, meanwhile, were under pressure to follow procedures, to find the person responsible for little Jesse's disappearance, and close the case. Was the Rinker family among the eighty percent of those guilty, or among the twenty percent who were not? This, to them, was the burning question.

"I also understood that they would come to the conclusion they seemed to want," Rodger said. "But we needed them. They were the only ones who could find our baby."

★

While the investigative branch pursued the family in an effort to find guilt close to home, the police and the RCMP's operational branch continued to direct all the details of the physical search from a tent beside the gravel road forty-five miles northwest north of Rocky Mountain House. They had marked out a geographic area comprising five square kilometres for intensive searching. Each search was repeated four separate times. At the same time, close by the tent, Rhonda Morgan interviewed hundreds of potential volunteers and followed up large numbers of tips. None yielded a solid lead.

"I felt tweaked by this case," Richard Smith said. "I'm in this for humanitarian reasons,* but also there's the detective in me — Where did this person go? What happened? It's a puzzle, a mystery to be solved. I *had* to find out what happened — not to know gets under your skin. It had a profound effect on me, and afterwards it changed my focus on police work, made me realize there are more important issues than break-and-entering and theft. There are more important things in life — like serving the community to the fullest and utmost you can, and that means saving a life. This should take priority over all other police activities. We have to remember who are we working for, and why. We have to stay focused on what it's all about."

"We began getting calls about Jesse being sighted off the reserve, about strange vehicles driving the road on the day he disappeared — reports of a red truck in the area that no one had seen before," said one officer. "The truck was sighted before the child's disappearance, and for some days afterward. Once attention turned to the Natives on Sunchild and neighbouring O'chiese reserves, our investigation became much more difficult because many of the local people viewed police as outsiders — they regarded us with suspicion."

Indeed, the Native people had not welcomed the attentions of the investigators, proving helpful only to the Rinker family. Their attitude hardened when one particular RCMP officer, prejudiced against

---

* Many police officers spent their off-duty time assisting in the search.

Native people, announced that he believed them responsible for Jesse's disappearance — that they had kidnapped the boy and killed him.

"He manufactured his own information to try and create a white man–Native conflict," Rodger said. "'The Natives don't want the Rinker family here and want to get rid of them,' he was heard to say. We knew the local people very well. We had lived among them, and lived like them, for a long time — there was no colour difference and we knew the guy was lying. If proof were needed, Chief Bigchild provided it: just before he passed away, he said, 'The church is needed here.'"

★

Rhonda Morgan sat in her office in Calgary, troubled. She had not ceased trying to help this family, but what else could she do? In addition to her previous efforts, she had advertised, plastering hundreds of large posters of the smiling face of the toddler everywhere.

"Missing children are significant because they create publicity," she said. "Someone might see a picture of the child — some private citizen — and let the society know. It's a powerful thing. I suffered for this family. I worried about the children — especially Seth." Indeed, such was her concern that she drove to the mission compound whenever possible, to talk with him — with all the children — to help them deal with the sustained trauma of police intimidation and accusations. Dawn Taylor, a woman from a neighbouring farm, also recognized the boy Seth's difficulties and tried to help the pre-teen.

The family's plight began to ease somewhat when police attention started shifting away from the family. Theories abounded: some insisted the child had simply wandered off and got lost, got injured, or had died; others, that the boy had been kidnapped — but by whom? And why? Stories about the little red pickup truck resurfaced, adding to the parents' belief that their son had been kidnapped. Next came tips from psychics, who thought they knew where the boy was located, but none of these panned out.

"I've been tracking these forest lands for over forty years," said a local trapper. "I've been searching for a week. I've found missing kids before when others have given up, and if this kid was out there, there'd have to be a trace. I'd find it."

Said an RCMP officer, "Without a single clue found in the extensive search of the woods near Jesse's home, kidnapping could be a definite possibility. Unfortunately, we also heard rumours fly about that cults were involved, most likely because some factions on the reserve have been unhappy about the Rinkers' spreading their Christian beliefs there. We doubt there are cults, and the parents themselves doubt anyone on the reserve would do this."

The idea of tragedy striking white Christian missionaries on a Native reserve inevitably fuelled assumptions that there might be a racial dimension to the case. Again, the controversy about a white-Native conflict surfaced, created largely, in Rodger's opinion, by the same RCMP officer who disliked Native people. Rodger, whose restrained demeanour belied his inward frustration, went to the chief administrator at police headquarters.

"This man has to be taken off the case or we are going to file charges," he said. "He's manufacturing false evidence."

The police refused to take action. "If you do this, we're going to close this case and you won't get your baby back," he was told.

Rodger stood firm. "We are part of the reserve; we live among the Natives, and live like them," he said. "We are the only white people there, the only missionaries to do this. Others live close by, but not among the Natives. We've raised our family alongside and among them, worked the same fields, driven the same roads, lived the same life. The local people respect and love us, and we care very deeply for them. Yes, they might hold prejudice towards white people in town and elsewhere — but not to us."

In anger and bitterness, he looked at the officers. "If you don't pull this man off our case, we *will* file a lawsuit."

The search for Jesse Rinker had become increasingly politicized, and the last thing the police wanted was a court action — particularly because of the groundswell of public sympathy for the family. Eventually, the officer was removed from the case, and the RCMP's chief administrator for central Alberta was required to give daily briefings on the search directly to Premier Peter Lougheed.

"The thing about a white-Native conflict was totally wrong," said Rodger. "No one at the local level thought this, other than one or two members of the RCMP. Some politicians and media assumed it because they were removed from the situation and didn't know the local scene. It became a twisted public perception." It also added to the Rinkers' burden of suffering.

In thirteen months, no single clue of the toddler's whereabouts was found. Huge areas of forest wilderness, muskeg and lonely roads were searched intensively several times. More than two hundred people were interviewed, including every single person who had been within an eight-mile radius on or shortly before the day Jesse had gone missing. Paperwork abounded, but no useful information came of it all. Despite all this, the Rinkers remained unwavering in their belief that Jesse was alive somewhere.

Every day, Rodger would walk the old logging path to the trees and the marsh beyond. He carried with him a huge burden.

"I thought, 'God has to step in and solve this, do something about it,'" he said. "'It will take a miracle, I know that. But God is in control of what happens.' It felt like I was lifting a huge load and putting it into his hands, putting it on his table. I spent hours agonizing, trying to get this burden up there and leave it with him. I thought, if I can get to that point, something will happen.

"God was right there," he said. "That was the agony, the terrible pain. The test was not 'Is God real,' because he was right there. But he was not answering our prayer, and I felt it as raw pain. But the side effect of that pain was having my heart completely changed; now I'm doing what I already was doing, but really feeling it."

The police continued to work on the case off and on, retracing all their investigative steps to see if they might have missed something. They might return to the woods to search yet again, or to interview the family, the witnesses or others, one more time. But they got no further ahead. Ultimately, they decided to recruit a new group of RCMP officers to begin the search all over again in the hopes that new eyes would help. From Edmonton and Red Deer they came, all working now on the assumption that someone had taken the child. The parents were questioned once more.

★

Thirteen months had passed. Sporadic searches and some follow-up investigations continued, and all the Rinker family endured a terrible agony. But neither Rhonda Morgan nor Richard Smith had forgotten the family's unresolved and still-burning sorrow. While Rhonda pursued details of her thirty-six other missing-children cases, she also worked on this one. "Regardless of how busy we were, we never forgot that little boy," she said.

As if this tragedy were not enough to crush a family, a forest fire raged over the Sunchild Indian reserve, a fire considered to have been set intentionally. The entire reserve was evacuated for one week while the fire burned over an eight-square mile area all the way to the Saskatchewan River. A local radio station reported that it had received an anonymous phone call before the fire had started, saying that the blaze had been set deliberately to burn out the Rinker family. Rodger himself also suggested that the fire could have been arson, in part because it had originated in a spot about one kilometre from the Rinker's house, directly in the path of the prevailing wind. A member of the RCMP answered that, while it seemed that the fire had indeed been caused by human hands, it could have been an accident.[*]

"What now?" Rhonda sighed when she heard the news. Immediately she called the family, and what she heard shook her: one day after the fire had been subdued, Rodger had gone for one of his solitary walks along the private path beyond his house, praying as he walked. The path, and all about it, had been changed, devastated by the fire. The trees and marshy undergrowth all about the muskeg lay denuded, now a charred and smouldering wasteland. The fire had felled huge areas of trees and all the undergrowth, but had somehow miraculously missed the Rinker house — "truly a miracle," said Karen, "an act of God to spare our house for Jesse's sake. When he comes home, how dreadful it will be for him if everything is gone. It was a miracle from God that our house was saved."

The miracle was assisted by the enormous efforts made by the Rocky Mountain House fire department to protect homes in the area, deploying water bombers to discharge their cargo onto the homes. The denuded area

---

[*] Subsequently, the origin of the fire was believed to have been inadvertently caused by a neighbour preparing to smoke hides, or by someone smoking in the bush.

subsequently became a good place for logging, as the large tree trunks, while scorched, were otherwise untouched, and therefore salvageable for logging, except for those in a few hot spots. Loggers descended. People crowded into the area. Another concern for Rodger: would having all those people there destroy any evidence of the whereabouts of his toddler?

This man continued to walk his lonely path, begging God to bring back his little boy. He reached one of the incendiary hot spots ravaged by the fire, once an isolated place thick with brush and undergrowth, but now wide open and covered in ash. He spotted a moose horn and bent to pick it up, then found another and another. He liked to retrieve them for his flower garden. When he could carry no more, he stood staring at the ground around him.

"I did not hear a voice, but I felt a presence — felt I was looking for something but not yet seeing it," he said. "And then I did: I saw it — a charred object." He reached down and picked it up, to find that in his hand he held a small rubber boot. Slowly he turned it over and saw remnants of red on its sole. His heart catapulted and the blood burned in his brain. He cannot remember how long he stood on the path in the ravaged woodland, but he did search for other evidence of his son in this spot. He found nothing. He cradled the boot in his hands as he carried it home, then called the RCMP. Officers searched the surrounding area, eventually finding the bones and clothes of a small boy.

A forensic examination was unable to determine how Jesse had died, but Rodger said that that wasn't as troubling to him as all the time his child had spent wandering alone, crying for his parents.

Closure at last: the funeral was conducted by Reverend Lazurius Wesley, a Stoney Indian from Morley. During the ceremony the reverend stressed the importance of carrying on the work of the mission: "Jesse will remain a symbol of the Rinkers' efforts," he said. "These will grow a hundredfold because of the spilled blood of baby Jesse."

Karen stood up and said: "God is good; he is loving. He makes no mistakes in the things he allows — I'm speaking as Jesse's mother. Our baby is happy now, and that's all that is important."

Rodger carried the remains of his toddler in a blanket and buried him in a private lot behind the Sunchild mission at the invitation of the Native band.

"It's going to take time to realize it's all over — all the months of uncertainty," he said. "At one point, the police realized they had committed some terrible atrocity towards our family. The officer prejudiced towards Native people eventually lost his job. I think that if the story of how our family was treated were to be known, many others would lose their jobs."

★

A major news conference was later held, and the media were invited to ask questions. The police had no wish to participate in the event, which was not a problem for Rodger. The questions flew: *What had actually happened to your boy? How did he die? Has anyone been found guilty of a crime?*

Rodger quoted Constable Richard Smith, who believed that the little boy must have slipped into the creek; that when the ground was searched, the dogs would not have found him, although it is known that bloodhounds can track underwater. By the time the creek was invaded by the dozen people who had plumbed its murky depths with hands and feet, after divers had raked its bottom, the body had already surfaced and been dragged by a coyote up its banks and into the trees. The searchers had found nothing, but had come within twenty-five feet of the place where Jesse's remains were eventually found. An unbelievable chain of coincidences, and so the media felt.

"It sounds fantastic, I know," Rodger said. "But it is the only scenario possible to explain what happened."

One reporter rolled his eyes and said, "And you expect us to believe this?"

"It was the normal, natural response of a rational person, but where did that leave us?" Rodger said later. The questions continued.

"Are you telling us your toddler simply wandered from the house, got lost, and kept on walking to the place one mile where his remains were found? Are you saying he walked over a mile of muskeg? How could he have gone so far?"

"Why was he not found in any of the searches? The police dog used had never once in thirty searches failed to find what he was looking for, but here, you're telling us he missed finding Jesse by a hundred feet from the place where he was eventually found, and within the first two-week period of searching — what happened?"

"We had few answers," Rodger said afterwards. "It was better for us to say, 'We just don't know what happened.'"

★

To the parents, the finding of Jesse's remains constituted a miracle. God had brought closure to the torment of their uncertainty and thereby afforded them relief. They family no longer had to live a life of not knowing whether they would ever see Jesse again, how he was being brought up, what kind of a person he was becoming, where he lived, what he was like.

"A death is easier to accept," Rodger said. "As parents, the only thing that is important is whether your child is dead or alive."

There was nothing left to say or do: no further investigation was conducted and the family was no longer harassed or intimidated. As Rodger had said, the experience profoundly changed him: he continues to do what he has always done, but feels it more deeply. Karen is comforted in knowing that Jesse is with God, and that all things are under his control.

★

Richard Smith keeps a photo of little Jesse Rinker in his pocket at all times. When he teaches SAR classes, he shows it. "It keeps me, and them, focused on who we are working for, and why," he said. "Since the day Jesse Rinker went missing, I've dedicated myself to helping people, staying focused on what SAR is all about," he said.

As a result of this search effort, Richard, together with Jim Thoreson, Ken Tryon and several others, established a new organization: the Search and Rescue Society of Alberta. A whole new search effort has evolved because of the search for this little boy.

"Little Jesse did not die in vain," he said. "Because of him, much has been learned and incorporated about search and rescue. At the time, the RCMP did well with what they had — but could have done better. I believe there was a failure in the force then, in not putting more time and effort into training volunteers to become proficient and competent in what they had to do — also in not training police officers in what their role, and others' roles, should be."

Richard began writing letters to the officer in command of his division, suggesting that there were better ways to manage the business of search and rescue. "We can be more efficient, more economic, serve the community better with SAR with the interests of public safety in mind," he said. He recalled stepping on toes and jeopardizing his career on the force in the process of trying to effect change. "But the end goal was more important than my career," he said. Others began to agree, and so began the rewriting of the RCMP's nationwide policy on search and rescue. Richard was one of those engaged in the process, which took ten years. In 1995, the RCMP established a SAR policy that is one of the best in Canada.

"The RCMP now has a high standard of care in public safety and SAR," Richard said. "They have dedicated officers who take basic SAR skills courses, and SAR management training. They now do a fine job serving the public safety as a result."

As well as all this, Richard, together with Dave Hanna and Lloyd Gallagher, formed and trained SAR teams in their spare time and taught classes in how to search for missing persons all over the province. Their efforts were a catalyst for training to begin in earnest throughout Alberta. Each of these men is also involved in training forestry, Parks Canada, military and law enforcement personnel. Notably, the policy of not reporting a person missing for twenty-four hours has changed. "We have an urgent-response team that goes out immediately," Richard said. "People can be found alive within this time."

On a personal level, Richard has never ceased his SAR courses. He pursued specialized programs in the field in the United States and brought experts north to teach how to track and how to conduct SAR management efficiently, effectively and economically.

"We were years behind the U.S. in this," Richard said, "in first theory, initial response, containment confinement, use of the most appropriate resources, searching the most likely places, studying lost-person behaviour, development of a criminal profile... If a person is not found in the first twenty-four hours, it means there's something wrong: SAR methods are wrong, or a criminal element has come into it. I still carry Jesse's photo with me. I say to my classes, 'This is why I do this work.' Something good has come out of this family's tragedy. Jesse was not just somebody's child, but everybody's… You have to remember you're not working for the RCMP, or Parks or police; not even for the family, but for the child."

Richard retired from the force in 1997 and now devotes himself full time to SAR. He lives in a log house with his family and his twenty-five husky dogs in Clearwater County.

Constable Jim Thoreson also found himself in trouble because of his outspoken comments, most specifically about how the force had not been qualified to manage a search such as Jesse Rinker's.

"We were hanging out our shingle and saying we could do this, but we were not trained. We could run search teams, but not manage a search," he said. As Jesse's case had dragged on, he requested permission to attend a course at the Emergency Response Institute in Seattle, and went as far as to file an application. But the RCMP refused to send him, assessing the course as unnecessary. Undaunted, Jim went on his own initiative, at his own expense, and returned with a whole new approach to SAR. Back in Edmonton, he approached the force and related what he had learned — the rationale for it, and how it should apply to their operations. "We do not have this training and we need it," he insisted.

The RCMP appeared uninterested, telling him a course he had attended with the military was sufficient.

"They knew nothing about SAR," Jim said. "I was beating my drums; I got into hot water." Still, he insisted that things were not good enough, and he began talking to the people who ran the provincial emergency program in British Columbia (PEP), obtaining blueprints of their operations. Once he had done this, he proposed to members of Alberta's legislative assembly that Alberta establish an umbrella SAR organization along the lines of the one existing in B.C.

The RCMP remained uninterested. "I had rockets coming at me for that," Jim said. "My proposal was considered radical — my boss wanted me transferred out." To his superiors, "I was a troublemaker and a nuisance; the old-school thinking was that we didn't need it." Eventually, he was transferred out — to Beaver Lodge, north of Grand Prairie. But Jim had pensionable service, so he retired.

"It took fourteen years from the time I presented my proposal for a volunteer umbrella organization to its realization," he said, but added, "Since the conclusion of the search for Jesse, effort has been made by the RCMP to fulfill the duties of their ground search-and-rescue mandate. Some, if not much of it, is because of this search and others like it."

At the present time, Jim is a national vice president of the Civil Air Search and Rescue Association and a director for the Alberta branch. He remains a SAR pilot. He lives with his family in Red Deer.

Both Richard Smith and Jim Thoreson believe that SAR has to give everything to the finding of lost and missing persons, and indeed a whole team of people have done this since Jesse's search. Much time, effort and money have been spent to achieve it. As a result of their efforts, today there are highly trained individuals in the field, people who are skilled and dedicated in their practices. The results reflect this.

Also, "To be a good searcher, to be a good survivor, you have to move on," each man said. "This means both searchers and family. Little Jesse's death was not in vain."

Jesse Rinker.

IN THE NAME OF FRIENDSHIP
Estevan, Saskatchewan, and Brandon, Manitoba

Friendship's a noble name, 'tis love refined. — Susannah Centlivre

It began in a small prairie town when he was not much more than a boy, really.

Dana Quewezance, or Iron Eagle, was a young man just one step beyond his teenage years and already planning his career as a sports medicine specialist. For now, he was a sports-loving daredevil who liked to jump from tall buildings into snow banks. He brimmed with life's joys, his ever-present smile symbolizing a huge capacity for friendship, and it was known that Dana would do anything for his friends. Energized by all sports and a superb soccer player, he formed a slim, lithe arrow, his early years slipping away on the sports fields of Estevan, Saskatchewan.

On a cold night in late October, Dana, the only son of Delmer and Rita Quewezance and a son of the Keeseekoose band, plunged into the Assiniboine River in Brandon, Manitoba, then tried to cross it. The Iron Eagle felt invincible that night: young, with the joy of being alive, at a party with good friends. After a few drinks he thought he could do anything: run fast as a hurricane, climb mountains — or swim rivers.

It had begun innocently enough. Dana and a group of friends had made the trip from Estevan to Brandon to celebrate the birthday of their friend, Rob.* In all, there were three young men and three young women.

The group from Estevan decided to rent rooms at the Redwood Inn near Brandon, and there they celebrated with music, food and drink. The witching hour of midnight rolled around, and two of the young men took off to fool around on the river flats close by Eleanor Kidd Park. Headlights were seen on the road through the trees. They thought it might be the police, and Rob — having no desire for an impromptu meeting with a law enforcement officer — froze in the headlights.

Thinking only that he must protect his friend, Dana headed for the river to act as a decoy, calling over his shoulder, "Don't worry, I'll cover for you." He ran out in front of the car, thinking that the police would come after him, then headed for the river to draw them in his direction — after all, he'd done nothing wrong.

Rob fled in the opposite direction through the trees. When Dana reached the river, he slipped down the muddy banks, right into it. Once submerged, he struck out across the murky water that flowed among the recently formed ice chunks.

Rob saw that the headlights did not belong to a police car after all, and he ran to the river after Dana, only to find him thrashing about near the middle of it. He plunged in after Dana and struggled towards him, getting close enough to grab his hoodie. It slipped from his grasp. Rob felt himself begin to freeze up, then suddenly he was standing in the shallows, looking over a now-empty river — which was betraying no sign that someone had disappeared into it. Frantically, Rob climbed up the bank and sprinted the two blocks back to the Redwood Inn, screaming for help. "Call 911!" he yelled to the women, and he and Craig raced back to the river. They reached the spot where Dana plunged in, stood on its banks, and stared out over waters that now lay quiet.

★

---

* The names Rob and Craig are used to protect the identity of two young men involved in this story.

The Assiniboine River snakes its way placidly through Brandon, its banks trimmed and lined with parks, open fields, gravel roads, a livestock yard and grazing cattle. In places it is heavily treed, with scrub and weeds near the water's edge. In summer, local people drop their fishing lines into it; in winter, they play upon its surface. But the dark, murky surface hides a veritable junkyard of people's discarded property beneath. And on this night it entombs the body of a young man. Police cars, fire trucks and ambulance roar to its banks. Powerful lights from a fire truck illuminate dark leafless trees over black water. A distraught young man on the bank chatters about his friend who has fallen into the river. It is a surreal scene.

The fire department — a multipurpose unit primarily responsible for search and rescue — is first to respond to the rescue call. The firemen's faces are taut with urgency as they ask key questions: "Where was he standing? Where exactly did he climb down the banks? Where is the spot you saw him go in?"

"Our most urgent need is to determine exactly where Dana entered the water," says the deputy fire chief, Brent Dane. "It's critical. Only within the first few minutes — longer is miraculous — is it possible to effect a rescue." But the witnesses' replies are shifting and contradictory; not only have the young people been drinking, but they are consumed with the first pangs of grief. The police are no less urgent in their need to know such details as where Dana entered the water, what he'd been wearing, and his height and weight. The party of young people from the inn, little more than teenagers, weep uncontrollably. Rob, who had run into the river after Dana, stands soaking wet and shivering.

The investigative branch of the local police also needs to question them about what has taken place, but the first step is to take them into a police cruiser to warm up after their exposure to the chill night air. Then, into an ambulance to carry them back to the Redwood Inn. There, the police, in the face of their unrestrained grief, radio for the Victim Services Unit to come and assist them.

Meanwhile, the operational branch of the Brandon Police comb the riverbanks, scrambling through and over scrub and weed and fallen logs. Flashlights probe the darkness, pinpoints of light penetrating the moonless night, as the constables rummage the banks and stare, hawk-eyed, over the water, as if willing it to give up the man within it. Hope flickers, dies, then flickers again. Fortunately, the police unit has a special project running this night, and a large number of officers are on duty to help search both sides of river. If Dana has made it to its other side, he will quickly succumb to hypothermia; they have to find him fast. Canine dogs are brought to the scene, while officers from the fire department launch their Zodiac boat. More police officers arrive.

"It's hard — lots of tension," says Brent Dane. "Time is critical. A young man is in the river drowning — or on its banks, dying of hypothermia. His friends, just kids really, are very emotional. First we have to make sure they don't run back to the river in their extreme [state] and slip into it, to become casualties themselves — we have to get them out of the place. We also have ongoing concern about danger to the police who are crawling the riverbanks; we need to make sure they don't fall in, either. A lot of people, a lot of emotions, lots of grief. You have to step outside of this, find out exactly what happened — keep focused." The blackness of a prairie night that had been upon and all about them continues to be banished by floodlights. The police continue their search of the river and trample its banks throughout a night that slowly creeps towards its end. An autumnal morning yawns its awakening, but there is no sign of Dana. The police contact the Royal Canadian Mounted Police (RCMP) to request that its dive team attend the tragedy as neither they nor the fire department, have divers of their own. The police and firemen remain while the morning unfolds, none of them ceasing their efforts to find the young fellow or to sight his body. Hope that he might have crawled out of the river, and be alive somewhere, has died.

★

Delmer Quewezance is at work on this October 16, working as customs inspector on the Canada–U.S. border south of the town of Estevan. He likes people and enjoys his job, likes helping the people and goods move across the border.

"There are fourteen border crossings between Saskatchewan and North Dakota," he says. "I work at North Portal, where sometimes a lot of activity goes on. It's a good job; I came here from Saskatoon looking for a change from my work as a conservation officer for the province, and have been here for fifteen years now. My son, Dana, he's not sure yet what he will do. He's finished high school and he's deciding to take a year off… sometimes he talks about doing the same job as I'm doing, other times maybe getting into sports medicine, seeing that he loves sports so much. He's very good at them all, too, and an especially good soccer player — he's crazy about that game. They say he has enormous talent. He's my only child — mine and my wife, Rita.

"This day, someone comes asking for me — a police officer from Estevan called Kevin Reed. He says he's sorry to have to tell me that my son, Dana, has met with an accident. He fell into the Assiniboine River, and he's still missing."

Delmer experiences instant denial. *This can't be… it's not possible. Dana's a sportsman, he can swim. How could he drown? Of course he's alive; he's climbed out of the river and is right now wandering about its banks, trying to hitch a ride home.* "Why would he drown?" repeats his father in bewilderment. Now comes the onset of inexpressible shock, grief and trauma that will engulf Dana's parents, his extended family — indeed, the entire First Nations bands of Keeseekoose and Cote — over the interminable months to come.

From left: Dana Quewezance and his parents, Delmer and Rita Quewezance.

Rooms are booked at the Midway Motel, and the three-hour drive from Estevan to Brandon begins. Grandmother Frances is included, along with aunts, uncles, nephews, nieces, cousins and friends from the Keeseekoose Native Reserve. Each wakens now to bleak and empty mornings, with nothing to do but wait: in small rooms, in an unfamiliar town, in an impersonal environment. The only structure in their lives comes from daily trips to the riverbanks to search for their tribal son. They receive briefings from the police to learn what has been done, what has been found, and what next is planned. But no word of sighting has come to the desolate family. The autumn days crunch on and became colder.

An entire city rallies: the Brandon Police and the community at large remain committed to the search for this young man. It is the beginning of an all-encompassing effort to coax the river to give up its dead, or for its banks to reveal him. A plan is made for the RCMP to bring its dive team to the river.

★

"The police in Brandon advise us that they have a possibility of a young person who has gone into the river and drowned," says Corporal Andy Pulo, diving supervisor for the RCMP's D Division in Manitoba. "They've asked us to dive, to do a search for the body and recover it if possible. This is part of our mandate — to perform body recoveries."

Because the Mounties' divers are scattered over various detachments throughout the province, and because a team of four members must be assembled before a dive can proceed, Pulo's job is to locate available officers and organize them as quickly as possible. Within a few short hours they have convened in Brandon, where they meet with local police and learn the details of the drowning. But the RCMP divers are at a disadvantage: they need to have at least one witness show them the exact spot where Dana entered the water, but his friends have all returned home to Estevan.

"To have direct witnesses is like [the difference between] night and day," says one officer. "We have to ask local police to show us what they themselves have been shown, and what they have been told — it's secondhand."

The divers make a plan: first they will conduct a pendulum search of the shoreline. A single diver is attached to one end of a rope, while a tender remains stationed on the shore. The diver in the water moves in concentric arcs, each one taking him farther and farther from the shore, towards the middle of the river. The rope to which the diver is tethered is one hundred and twenty-five feet long — making this the maximum extent of the search area.

Crowds line the banks, then drift away; a December sun shines weakly through the leafless trees onto the sombre scene below. One diver enters the water, then another, and another. Disappointment is keen when all they find is debris on the river bottom. With some frustration, the dive team moves to the opposite bank and repeats this manoeuvre — an overlapping pattern that covers the heart of the search area twice. The effort is intense and draining. It is not only discouraging to the divers, but to the family and the spectators. The afternoon wanes; the divers have not yet located the body, and time becomes a constraint: two team members have to return to their detachments to work their regular shifts, while others who work out of a different base of operations are summoned to attend to a break-and-enter. It's time now to sit down and talk to the family, to break some unwelcome news: they cannot help any further today, and perhaps not at all.

The police arrange a meeting. Frank McKay, the chief of the Dakota Objiwa band, has come to the meeting, too, to act as liaison. The mood is apprehensive: the family does not know what they are about to hear, while the officers aren't sure what reaction their message will elicit. Will they be upset? Angry? Frustrated? Gingerly, the police tell Dana's family there is nothing else they can do to recover Dana's body if the RCMP divers cannot return for another search.

"There are dangers to the firefighters out on the ice, so this part of operation will be winding down," an officer explains. "But we will continue to comb the riverbanks. Recovery efforts will have to be put on hold until spring, when ice retreats from the river. However, it might still be possible for the RCMP divers can come back. We'll all do our best."

"A very honourable family," Inspector Grant will say afterwards. "Very proud and noble people. They sit quietly, accepting the news with understanding and appreciation for all we've tried to do. With our news, there is a collective sigh of relief because the family feels it is not being abandoned, that the police will continue to do everything they can. Their thanks are warm and profuse."

Because the RCMP dive team have not been able yet to return, because time is passing and winter approaching, the Brandon Police now make preliminary enquiries to the Winnipeg force about the possibility of having its dive team come to Brandon.

All the while, the family, understanding that they have not been forgotten, still feel bereft. "Dana would have contacted us by now if… if he'd got out. Now we have to figure he won't be coming back," Delmer says, his voice full of sorrow. He has never ceased looking for his son: every day he and his extended family trample the riverbanks, the still and silent world of spruce and pine that are the park and farmland echoing with their calls and the sounds of their searching. All around them the boreal forest stands, imperturbable witness to their grief.

Meanwhile, the chiefs of the two Saskatchewan Native bands — both of whom are related to Rita Quewezance and therefore feel an additional degree of personal involvement — continue to send more and more people to help search the riverbanks. And at any one time, eight to ten people remain at the Midway Motel with the parents.

A young man's remains lie hidden within the depths of the Assiniboine River, but his family must have him home to bury him. It is unspeakable that he lies disintegrating there, in another town, another province. There is pressure to hold a memorial service for him, but the family must stay longer — must continue its sojourn in the Midway Motel and conduct its shoreline searches, to find some other way to have their son's body recovered.

"They say the body eventually rises to the surface," says Delmer, "but because this is October, with the water very cold and ice forming, it may not happen. We're doing these walks every day; we're watching the river freeze over, knowing our boy is down there. We're watching it trap him — such a helpless feeling, and it goes on and on. We hear of a shaman,* and decide to try him, see if he can help. This man lives eighty to ninety miles from here; it's a long river, and he can't travel — there are problems. But he's a medicine man who also acts as a clairvoyant; he can 'see' things.

---

* A medicine man, a spiritual advisor, a clairvoyant.

"We're willing to try because we're desperate. After everything has been tried and done, and after the RCMP tells us we will have to wait until spring to find our son's body, we say, 'No way, we have to do something.' Dana could be anywhere; he might never be found, especially in spring when the river is high with runoff. Also, we don't want to see our boy's body in that state. We say to the RCMP, 'We're not leaving him here, we're taking him home. We'll find a way.'"

The RCMP divers very much want to return for a second dive, and eventually an opportunity is found to gather a team. The shaman advises that he's had a vision of the body lying in another area of the river, about a mile or so from the original area where he was thought to have gone in. He indicates two spots, and both are searched.

"Out of respect for the family, and sensitive to their cultural beliefs, we examine these places," says Corporal Pulo. "The family takes comfort in this. Unfortunately, this search, too, is unsuccessful."

While these efforts take place on the river bottom, firemen are on the surface taking care of other boaters and fishers. They look for any possible chance to help police and divers and make their facilities available. Brent Dane attends every meeting held with the family when progress reports are given, explaining what each person's role entails. "A tough thing to do," he says. "You're feeling for a family that has lost a young son with a bright future; I sense their despair as the river starts to freeze up. Once it gets solid, we'll have to leave the body until spring, and I had to tell them this, knowing how I would feel if I were in their shoes. I have three children of my own. But I feel this to be part of my job as a human being, and I try to give some comfort to this family."

What now? Dana's extended family continues to meet with the police for daily briefings. After one such meeting, Brandon police officer Ed Riglin says: "Great people. A family in its truest sense — very close and deeply caring of each other. This young man, Dana, he was the son of the entire tribe — the community's son. His family comes from all over Saskatchewan, particularly from Yorkton, the Keeseekoose and Cote reserves. Very traumatic, too, for other kids who were with Dana — I believe they were very close to his parents. Here in Brandon, the family knows nothing of the place, have no connections, no roots, no contacts, nothing — there's just themselves. They're in rented rooms for weeks at a time, uprooted, and suffering this tragedy — it's a dreadful time for them."

It is admirable but unfortunate for the RCMP divers that they have followed the shaman's advice; they know they will not find the body where he says it might be, and this search takes up valuable time — time that has become critical: ice has formed on the river and made diving difficult and risky. As well, they have other tasks: once they have completed the search of the sites the shaman has indicated, their time has run out. Still, they very much want to help. When they finish that day, they ask to be allowed to return to search the original site once more. Unfortunately, it cannot be done: a hierarchy exists within their organization, and it must be respected.

"Our agency takes precedence. If we are called to another case, we have to go," Pulo explains. "The original case has to be put on hold until we can get back to it. Each officer has to be released from regular duties and is freed for one day only. Also, each has to do two shifts in the one day: one as part of the dive operation, the other as a regular policeman."

"I cannot forget the plight of this family," he adds. "We all hold profound respect for them, for the quiet and respectful manner in which they conduct themselves. We can see their extra grief and despair at this non-closure to their tragedy. What further can we do to help them? There's a police services officer speaking to me about wanting to go back and dive at the original site, but our board was under negotiations with [the city of] Brandon about a memorandum of understanding: if RCMP divers perform work for another [police] agency, that agency will incur the costs. I was not sure about the need for this [memorandum], and was told to hold off for the moment. I had to say no."

While Delmer does not give up his belief that there must be other options, he's under pressure to hold a memorial service for Dana. More than a month has passed, his extended family and friends on the reserve tell him. He relents: a service is held. Between two and three hundred people attend, and it provides some comfort. The tributes flow: the exuberance and talents of this young man are recalled, as are his famous smile, his personal warmth and his enduring friendships. "How precious he was... just a child... the child of all of us..." These sentiments formed part of Delmer's elegy to his son.

When it is over, the grieving father contacts Winnipeg's Dominion commercial divers for help. They reply that they try not to get involved in recoveries and refer him to a private organization called the Canadian Amphibious Search Team.

"I've never heard of these people," Delmer says, but he immediately contacts Ken Lugg, the founder and leader of the Manitoba Central Region branch of the search-and-recovery organization. The two arrange to meet at the Redwood Inn, where CAST members have already taken up residence. The two men are a study in contrasts: Delmer is small and slim, while Lugg towers above him at six feet six, with equally substantial proportions.

"This man, this group — they're a godsend," the relieved father says after the meeting. "They understand how important it is to us to have our boy back; we can't bury him without the body because there would be no ending."

What follows is a tale that is heartwarming and inspiring. It is about almost-unprecedented co-operation among all the groups and professional organizations in Winnipeg and Brandon — indeed, among all the players in this tragedy. It is about the willingness to share expertise and information across professions and jurisdictions that elsewhere often compete; the wishing of success to others when one has failed. The RCMP shares what it knows and offers assistance to the Brandon and Winnipeg police, to the Winnipeg Dominion Divers and, finally, to CAST. The fire department and police do likewise. Not least, local businesses in Brandon offer equipment, heated rooms, supplies — whatever they think will help.

"It's not about who recovers the body," said Sergeant Wayne Balcaen. "Not about who did what or about who gets the credit — that doesn't exist here. Police units function as one; they all work together. There are no boundaries. The RCMP officers say, 'Whatever you guys need, let us know; we're there for you. We'll do whatever we can.' They expend their resources willingly on behalf of others. Not only this, but police from all the different divisions share resources and help each other — 'If you need a dog, I'll spare a dog unit out of the city. If you need an undercover agent, Winnipeg will lend you one; I'll send it to your jurisdiction to give you a hand.' This is how it is."

★

Officer Ed Riglin has been going about his duties, yet he feels haunted by the tragedy. He sees the family suffering and in need of a connection, and he feels keenly for them. He has some understanding of the roots and culture of Dana's family, as he has worked with the Dakota Ojibwa tribal police in the interlake areas. He is married to a treaty Indian woman, and now has a family that includes his wife's fourteen siblings, as well as a father-in-law who lives with them. The Ojibwa language is spoken in their home.

"Usually as an officer, you do not let yourself get connected to your work — you leave it at the office," he said. "But I did on this occasion. I found it hard to park this to the side. I felt like an officer in the traditional ways of policing, where it's a way of life, not a job. It's the Aboriginal way: you choose it as a mantle; you are a very important part of the community."

After contact with Delmer Quewezance, Ken Lugg gets in touch with Inspector Grant, then phones Sergeant Balcaen in Brandon to tell him that the family has asked his group to help them.

"Our team will not dive until the police have abandoned their search because we don't want to get in the way," Ken says in his usual co-operative way. "We won't dive until the RCMP declares the search of the river concluded." He also speaks with Corporal Pulo. Sergeant Balcaen confirms all the details of the presumed drowning of Dana Quewezance and invites the caller to send details of his operation.

Briefings go back and forth. Ken explains his team's purpose, its expertise, and what it can do. He repeats that his group will not interfere in any way with the police investigation, and that CAST is willing to stand by and help the Brandon police in any way it can.

"If the family cannot pay costs of the dive operation, I and my crew will try and raise the money to cover costs through donations and private sponsors," he concludes. Then he waits.

On December 3, he is contacted by Inspector Grant, who tells him that the RCMP has abandoned its search at the river, clearing the way for CAST to go ahead. CAST team members emphasize that they dive for the family, while police make it clear that CAST does not represent the force — these assertions are made for reasons of liability.

"Both the fire and police departments are willing to offer you logistical support," Inspector Grant says, generously. "But unfortunately, the police are not able to donate any funds to your team."

Both eager and undaunted, Ken gets on the phone to the members of CAST. First, he dials a number for Cameron Jones, who is sitting on a beach in Hawaii, having gone there to get married. His cell phone rings and, surprised, he answers to Kenny Lugg in Brandon.

"Got a possible job for CAST," the disembodied voice says from across the Pacific Ocean — and then some. "The RCMP dive team has spent three days looking for a young Native man drowned in the Assiniboine River and can't find his body. The family has asked commercial divers to help — they suggested us." Cam listens. He's sitting in the sun on a beach, its sparkling white sands stretching to the horizon, palm trees dotting the edge of a blue lagoon. But he doesn't see any of it; instead, the black waters of a twisting river in a small prairie town press into view.

One week has passed and Cam is home again, resuming his position as a diver in the naval reserves, as a chief petty officer and sergeant on general duty. He learns that the Brandon police have not only given permission for CAST members to go ahead and dive for Dana's body, but have offered all the help they can, including details about where they previously made their dives.

Ken, as the man in charge of the whole operation, is now in full swing. He is responsible for overseeing activities on shore, liaising with the media, the family, police, RCMP, onlookers and passers-by. He elects for the dive to take place on December 6, and on the fifth he sends out an advance team including Simon Haxby, Dave Rowat, Brent Shabbits and Cam Jones to begin investigations. This will be a serious and potentially risky operation known as black-water ice diving. Next he's on the phone to the Redwood Inn, asking about room rates; to the fire department, asking for the use of their main fire hall to dry and warm their equipment and for air for the divers' tanks from their compressor; to Corporal Pulo to ask when they can get together to share information and to sketch the area that has already been explored, the place where the victim was last seen in the water; and finally to interview the witnesses themselves.

"Scott Allingham and I make checklists and look over ice-diving equipment, the modular tentage, the heaters," he says. "And all the while I'm hiking about the city begging for donations and sponsorship of the upcoming dive.* I'm the team scrounger.

"We have to make sure we have direct witnesses," Ken says, echoing the concerns of the RCMP divers before him. "Otherwise it makes for a long, difficult and cumbersome search. I mean, if we rely on others' reports, we'd just be diving in the same place as the police, and likely having no further success. We have to be accurate as to where the body might lie. We need to say to a witness, 'Tell me exactly where you were, what you saw.' To do this takes time — and money. The dive has become risky: anytime you go into moving currents and black water under ice, there's danger. The particular risk here is that the river is littered with bikes, bits and pieces of shopping carts, debris, fallen trees and logs. Then there's working in zero visibility — it creates a very real danger of entanglement."

Ken asks Delmer if he can bring the two witnesses to the accident scene to be interviewed, hoping to enlist their help in pinpointing the spot where Dana ran into the river. Delmer says, "Of course, and I'll be bringing other family members to observe the search." Rob arrives and indicates an area a little further upstream from the spot where the first dives had taken place.

"You locate this spot," explained Cam. "You take the body drop formula — the depth and the flow of the currents — and you equate this into a likely spot where the victim might be. [We call this] the last seen point (LSP). We use a system called DAD — designated area diving."

---

* Among those who offered support: Steve Dennis and Tom Atkinson of Cam Clark Ford in Winnipeg donated a truck; Ken's employers, Canad Inns — particularly CEO Leo Ledohowski and vice president Bryon Temoshawsky — contributed cash, meeting space, and fundraising support; and cash donations came from Delmer and Rita Quewezance, Darren Creighton on behalf of the Brandon Police Association, George Pike from Quest Investigations, John Sinopoli from Film Inc., in Toronto, and the law firm Cassidy Ramsay.

A large communal effort is underway, one that crosses jurisdictional boundaries to include the Brandon Fire Department, local police, the RCMP, area residents and, not least, local businesses. The Redwood Inn provides inexpensive accommodation. Hard copy maps and ortho-imagery files are donated by Atlis Geomatics. The co-operation continues: Corporal Pulo describes the search that the dive team performed, provides sketches of the area searched and offers the RCMP's help. Ken is grateful: this is a challenging technical dive in severe environmental conditions. The help he has received makes it a whole lot easier.

The dive and all its technicalities are planned. Everything is in place, even to the erection of a tent with heaters. Members of CAST's dive team have risen early and drove the two hours from Winnipeg to Brandon. The dive begins: ice screws are planted in the ice and lifelines are attached. An extra, or redundant, screw is added — a precaution against polluted water that creates poor-quality ice. Supervisors make sure that all is in place, that all details are checked, then checked again. "Everything must be perfect to ensure the safety of the divers — no second chances here," Ken says.

Divers walk onto the frozen river with a chainsaw and begin cutting through twenty-three centimetres of ice. Lifelines are run out to the hole, and dive supervisors stand hawklike on the riverbank. The time is eleven in the morning. Scott Allingham, as first diver, enters the water through the hole that has been cut. He drops below the surface but remains connected to another diver with a rope that is used for line signals. All sounds on the riverbank remain muted for the thirty minutes he is under the ice. He surfaces, and another takes his place.

The potential hazards of lifeline diving in extreme water temperatures are many: the polluted black water, for one; diving under the ice and going up against it; and, if stored improperly in the bitterly cold air, moisture can build up in the diving regulators and freeze them solid.

"An ice dive can be a simple but technical one, but because of all these variables, this proved hazardous," Ken says. "A diver has to put himself into an objective position to be able to deal with this."

All the while, Dana's family stands on the riverbank, grateful but expressing concern about the danger to the divers.

"Look, we'll show you how we keep ourselves safe," says Howard Rybuck, explaining what they do. "We have one diver at a time go down. One of us is suited up and ready to go as backup in the event of an emergency."

"How can you find him when the police can't?" Delmer asks now.

"Hindsight is a wonderful thing," answers Roger Windatt. "We know where the Mounties did their search and how they did it, and we benefit from this. We break up the area into zones from 'cold' to 'hot' and search them accordingly." Other team members demonstrate the use of their equipment. The fifteen family members, including Dana's grandmother and an aunt, stand by, silent but interested.

Several dives are made, and it is only two hours before Dave Alderson surfaces, thrusts off his mask, and gives a shout: "I got him!" The frozen body of Dana Quewezance has been found. It is one-forty in the afternoon. The body has been in the water for forty-one days, lying twelve feet below the surface.

Cam gets into the river to help Dave and Howard bring the body to the surface. Team members quickly erect a tarp to cover the entire area, thereby sparing the family the sight of their son, who has become a corpse, and to shield it from the public. Cam performs a forensic examination, and, once completed, he and Dave slide the body into a body bag.

The relief and gratitude knows no bounds; there are hugs from the family for every member of CAST.

Dana Quewezance is buried in St. Philip's Catholic Cemetery on the Keeseekoose First Nations Reserve. He has become a local hero, and the tributes to him are ongoing: a soccer field is named for him, and a trophy bearing his name stands in his old high school.

"He was a lad who loved life," states one of the memorials to him. "He went through his life with a smile, no matter what happened; made the best of everything. Well-liked, Dana was a natural leader with an easygoing personality, and he was particularly known for his capacity for friendship." It was this huge capacity that led indirectly to his death.

"This kind of tragedy is hard on you, hard on all the guys," says Wayne Balcaen. "You have to become hardened to it, even while you're always hoping you'll be successful. You want to see the young person live a happy, long life; all life is to be hallowed. You can either dwell on a case, and it doesn't work for you, or you can say, 'Well, we did our best,' and you know what? Maybe tomorrow we'll be luckier than we were today."

"The RCMP can usually spend only two to three days on an operation, then they have to call it quits, return to their regular work… It was unfortunate for them that they were diverted in their search," Ken says. "The body lay where their officers thought it would be, and they would have found it had they not been diverted elsewhere by being called to other tasks."

Afterwards, Corporal Pulo explains why he engages in this difficult work. "Part of it lies in its variety," he says. "In addition to the regular work, an officer can choose to volunteer for special teams such as emergency response, rescue teams, a containment team, a ground search team, a tactical team for crowd control — there's much variety. Each is considered an extra duty because we are policemen first. A diver — or any other — must work their regular shift before or after the dive, and get paid as they would for regular policing work."

"It's like this," Ken Lugg says. "You know you're skilled at doing something. You have the expertise. You want to challenge yourself, to use your skills to do things for other people. There's really nothing like it in the world, the feeling you get when you find someone thought to be lost or drowned. The family's life has been on hold and nothing's the same. If we who have special skills can use them to help, life can go on for these people."

This sentiment is shared by Dave Alderson, Scott Allingham, and indeed, by all CAST team members. "We are trained by the federal and municipal governments," they say. "Many of us have sought training on our own and have spent much time and money. We have these skills and expertise — at the end of the day, what do you do with it, other than put it on a résumé?"

"You give back to the community; you do something positive. We became members of CAST," finishes another.

"For me, the federal and municipal governments have spent a lot of money training me to be a navy and police diver," Cameron Jones says. "I've got two kids of my own, and if they were to go missing I would want someone to step up and help, to give my family closure. I want to use my experience and training to give something back."

Ken mentions the sponsors, who provide free gasoline, or the loan of a truck; some air for the dive; a free motel room, a few free meals…

"When the lost person is found, or the body recovered and closure achieved for family and friends, the sponsors feel they've had a stake in it, like they've become part of a communal good and have an attachment to the lives of others who were also involved. It's very important."

This is also why he and his dive group work to maintain good relationships with the local police and the RCMP. They share expertise for the common good, and they know that there is much pleasure in co-operating because it gives everybody a good feeling. After this recovery operation, Ken wrote a letter to all who had assisted, to offer thanks on behalf of his team.

★

The two communities that joined in response to this tragic event had perhaps not quite known how strong their bonds were. In the small prairie town of Brandon, police, firemen and businesses large and small rallied to help the stricken family. As did the border town of Estevan, a place of strip mining and coal-fired electric power stations, but also of boreal forest, rolling valleys and rich land that supported farming and ranching. It was here, and on the two nearby Native reserves, that Dana had been born and raised. Inspiration is to be found in the pooling of expertise and resources of public and private organizations — it is exemplary and heartwarming.

"This is a story, not just about an expert dive and recovery, but about a great people, and it is a tribute to all the people in Winnipeg and Brandon who helped," says Ed Riglin. "To a community that shared, cared and co-operated across all jurisdictional boundaries, across tribal, ethnic and multiethnic groups."

Grief-stricken parents Delmer and Rita Quewezance wrote letters of thanks to the Brandon police and fire departments, to the RCMP, to Ken Lugg and his organization and to all who had assisted in the search for their son. A letter from them appeared in the *Brandon Sun*, in which they expressed public appreciation to all the citizens of Brandon for their help, "on behalf of the Quewezance and Musqua families."

The family engaged in fundraising and offered what they raised to CAST to cover their costs for this search — and for others yet to come.

Today, their only — and beloved — son Dana rests in St. Philip's Catholic Cemetery on the Keeseekoose reserve. During the year that has passed since Dana died, tributes to him have continued to flow: "It was a rare pleasure to watch Dana play sports." "… a true privilege to name him as a friend." At the beginning of the new soccer season, the Woodlawn field was renamed in his honour, and is now known as the Dana Quewezance Memorial Field. A commemorative plaque has been erected there. And members of Dana's soccer team — the Strikers — now wear his number on their sleeves to remember him.

"This story is not just about an expert dive and recovery, but about a great people, and it is a tribute to all the people in Winnipeg and Brandon who helped," says Ed Riglin. "To a community that shared, cared and co-operated across all jurisdictional boundaries, across tribal, ethnic and multiethnic groups."

CAST crew preparing for a dive.

Police Officer Karen Murray and Staff Sergeant John Badowski in Toronto Harbour.

MY MATES ARE MY ESTATE
Toronto, Ontario

Serious bodies of water don't have to be large; they can inspire respect because of idiosyncratic moods. — Herb Payson

Police Officer Karen Murray watched the mist rise from the waters of Lake Ontario as she crossed the Burlington Skyway towards Toronto. It was Canada Day, July 1, and even though she had to work on the holiday, her shift would end at five — giving her plenty of time to enjoy the fireworks and all the celebrations.

Moving from the Queen Elizabeth Way onto Lakeshore Boulevard, the shores were nearly deserted in the morning's early light, but she could imagine the crowds that would be gathered there later that evening. She loved to celebrate the national holiday; her father had always told her she was lucky to have been born here, and she believed it. It was, as the saying went, "a great city on a Great Lake."

The waves were high as they slapped against the breakwall, while a chaotic, bubbling froth of whitecaps formed between the lakeshore and the nearby islands.

Karen drew up in front of the Toronto Police Service's marine unit, a square building half-hidden behind the Radisson Hotel at the foot of Spadina Avenue. Here, too, furious waves, five or six feet high, reared themselves against breakwater walls and into the police unit's bay, rocking the fleet of boats moored there.

"Going to be busy today," Karen said as she walked into the large reception area. Heads nodded. The time was not yet seven in the morning.

The weather forecast was calling for the sun to shine — fantastic — but winds out of the southwest were expected to reach gale-force strength before midday. Perhaps the resulting tumult on the water might even call off the Canada Day races planned, although officers knew it would take near-catastrophic conditions to put off anyone determined to participate. The National Yacht Club's races were a highlight of the year, the culmination of a sailor's burning ambition; to enter and to win meant everything, and to those who sail, less-than-ideal weather and conditions only enhanced the challenge. Soon, the harbour and the open waters beyond would be speckled with white-sailed vessels being tossed about roughly.

By ten in the morning, when all vessel and vehicle inspections had been completed, the first call for help had come in: "... sailboat has lost its mast near the Humber River; boat and passengers helpless and in danger." It was an urgent call: officers heard that the boat's mast had been snapped right off in high winds and now lay perpendicular in the water. Within minutes, officers Karen Murray and Tom Hutton, paramedic Allister Keene and Staff Inspector Edward Hegney had cast off the moorings of the unit's fastest vessel, the thirty-foot rubber Zodiac, and proceeded as quickly as conditions allowed towards the Humber River basin. It took between thirty and forty minutes to reach a spot that ordinarily only takes ten. The Western Gap was a witch's cauldron of short, choppy waves thrashing about without rhyme or reason. All around them, small sailboats lay almost perpendicular to the water, their occupants having trouble with rudders, engines and lost sails. Yacht club tenders were everywhere, helping those in trouble, and since the marine unit crew was not needed, they sped on towards the mouth of the river, where they found a thirty-one-foot sailboat wallowing, adrift, without mast or sails. The pallid faces of two adults and one child stared out frantically at the looming police vessel. The Zodiac rode a tempest of wind and wave as it struggled to approach, as police officers tried to get the sailboat under control and free it from the mast still attached at its base. It took an axe, a saw and brute force to cut through it. Staff Inspector Hegney and paramedic Keene decided to board the sailboat and remain with the family while the crippled boat was towed; they considered it too dangerous to try and remove the occupants and transfer them into the police boat. It would be tough, too, to get a line attached so they could tow it to safety. Shouts in the air accompanied the intricate manoeuvring of the police boat as its skipper tried to maintain proximity, but not crash into the sailboat, as the crew members struggling to remain on board themselves. All the while, waves slapped and knocked them about.

"We'd sold the boat," the embarrassed father said once he was safely on shore at the Mimico Yacht Club. "This was to be our last run in it before we handed it over to the new owner. We were making for Port Credit. We didn't realize the winds were blowing at forty knots — couldn't tell it was this bad until we were out in it. We just wanted to take the family out one last time…"

"Always the last run," Karen said under her breath. "Two whole hours, it took us. We were back at the station, writing up our notes, about to have lunch, when we got an emergency call on the VHF radio from National Yacht Club — an unconscious man on board a sailboat approximately two miles south of Gibraltar Point near Hanlon's Point Beach. Four of us responded: myself, Allister Keene, Tom Hutton and Carl Braun — lucky for us that we had Carl, because he was the best boat operator at the station at the time. The victim had been struck on the head by the boom as it swung about during a tack — a guy who'd got himself on board as crew at the last minute that day."

The police vessel — the same soft-sided Zodiac and the unit's quickest response boat — swung out of the Police Basin to make the crossing to Gibraltar Point, a slow and treacherous ride given the high winds. In spite of the conditions, a massed army of white sails scattered themselves about the lake: the famous National Yacht Club Canada Day Regatta had commenced.

"When you get winds blowing at forty-seven knots — that's fifty miles per hour — it's dangerous. You know accidents will happen," one of the officers said. "Why do people go out in such conditions? Because they're sailors — sailors who want to win." Now a crew member lay unconscious and seriously injured in the cockpit of a small sailboat, far from shore.

The helmsman of the thirty-five-foot white sailboat that carried the injured sailor had tried to head towards Ontario Place, on the mainland. Its motors chugged valiantly, but it made little headway.

"Conditions were horrific," Karen said. "The sailboat was a mile and a half off the mainland, and that skipper wasn't going to get to land any time soon — he was making just seven knots an hour. We had somehow to get on board their boat and take the injured man off. First we had to come alongside their boat and board it. Over and over we tried. Couldn't do it — it was too dangerous. Finally our skipper decided to ride up on the sailboat, to ram it from behind. He did. Our rubberized bow rose up and onto the stern of their boat until we were six feet in the air and perched right above their cockpit." All the while, waves five to six feet high broke over them. "Once our skipper got the bow of our boat up, he had to keep it there long enough for Allister to get off, and onto the other vessel. Allister aimed for the cockpit, because the rest of the sailboat decks were flat; if he'd landed on them, he'd just have fallen right off. Their skipper shut his motors off and was trying to steer a direct path without power. We pushed Allister off our boat and onto theirs. We pushed, and he jumped. He was on!

"'Okay, you're next,' he said to me. I thought, 'Oh, no, I'm not!'"

"You're the smallest person on board... easiest to get you on," he said.

But I can't do it... I'll fall into the water. Visions of her own mortality played out in her mind's eye. Aloud, she said, "Okay." The performance was repeated: the Zodiac reared up onto the stern of the sailboat. "I put my feet on the rubber transom," Karen said. "I'm ready to jump. Then I saw the pipe pole. I made to grab it, but a howl went up: 'Don't!' I'd been about to grab a free-floating life pole. The skipper had to try again. Finally, he got the boat jammed up on the sailboat and I got tossed onto its side deck." That wasn't all: the Zodiac had to back off the sailboat and repeat the procedure yet again to get the paramedic's pack — which weighed about sixty pounds — to him.

The accident victim lay on the floor in the bottom of the cockpit where he had fallen. Paramedic Allister Keene and Karen Murray hastened below, and there they found a man who appeared to be unconscious, sprawled on the floor in the small space. A shocking sight: his bloodied head was grossly swollen, his eyes bulged from their sockets and one side of his head was smashed in. Allister paused for a moment. He noted the severity of the man's injuries, considered the violence of the wind and waves and made the decision to treat him there on the floor of the sailboat's tiny cockpit rather than try to transfer him to the police boat. Above, the helmsman continued to try to steer towards Ontario Place while Allister radioed to say he needed help, that the victim had suffered serious trauma.

The unfortunate man had come from another country and had lived in Toronto for only a short while. On this Canada Day, an acquaintance was able to get him on board the sailboat to assist as crew in the regatta. Nobody knew whether he'd had much experience as a sailor, but afterwards they surmised that he probably had not, as he had not ducked his head when the boom swung across the bow during a tack. At the least, they figured he had not been familiar with small sailboats.

The first and most urgent order of business was to get the victim on life support. Allister went to work to suction blood from the patient's mouth and airways, and the brain matter protruding from his nose. Next, to get an airway inserted to give him oxygen. There was little room in the cockpit for three people. He placed Karen in charge of handing him the equipment he needed, and when she could, she held the victim's hand. He had a pulse. Karen, who had no medical training, thought he would be okay when she knew this, and she squeezed his hand. He seemed to respond.

"We're going to save you," she said, and she felt the pressure of his hand. "I kept thinking that if I could keep him aware, we could save him — he'd be okay, he's going to live. I kept talking to him."

"You're doing great, Karen," Allister said. "You're doing the right thing." She in turn reassured the patient again that they were going to save him. "He never stopped squeezing my hand," she said. All the while, winds tossed the boat, and water and wind spray blew across the bow to rock it precipitously.

The police boat travelled alongside the sailboat during the forty-five minutes it took to cross the small stretch of water from Hanlon's Point to the Ontario Place marina. The next big hurdle was the question of how to get the victim out of the cockpit and into an ambulance without further injuring him. Allister could not know whether he had neck or spinal damage. He had inserted an airway, and the victim was being bag-valved. Now he must be put into a C-Spine (a tool to immobilize the cervical spine) to support his neck. The logistics of getting enough able-bodied people into the cockpit to lift the victim up proved taxing. Karen followed after them, carrying oxygen tanks and all the other equipment up and out of the cockpit, as there was no room for any others. She understood that the man had suffered brain injury, but was not aware of the severity. Still, she believed he knew what was going on.

"We saved his life," she said to Allister.

"No, Karen. He's going to be a vegetable for the rest of his life."

"But... but we saved his life," she said again, not understanding.

"He'll be on life support; he won't know anything. He sustained severe brain damage," Allister said.

"We saved somebody and now he's going to be life support? So why did we?" She knew why, of course. They had no choice but to go out and save him if they could, even if he would not make it. Still, Karen struggled with this knowledge. She kept thinking that if this man was never going to be normal, never again have consciousness, what had she done?

"Of course, you don't say these things aloud at work," she said. "Others don't want to know, because they don't want to feel these things, either."

For Karen, this event summoned from her far more than she had ever experienced. In her heart, she knew that what they had done that day was phenomenal and extraordinary. But she knew better than to mention this to other officers, for fear they might belittle it.

"It was a call that will remain forever with me," she said. "The biggest call I've had in four years."

The day was not to end for some long time yet, and all the while Karen felt burdened by the man's fate. Meanwhile, conditions on the water did not abate. It was late afternoon when they saw an apparition draw erratically towards them, a boat coming closer and closer, headed straight for the police vessels in the bay. The officers stared as it careered wildly. What's this? they wondered. Why is it coming into the basin — and into our slip?

"We heard a thump," Karen said. "The mast hit the top of our garage door. We ran out, grabbed the man on board and his girlfriend. The guy was acting crazy, sort of delirious. It was because he was severely dehydrated and very stressed by the conditions. He'd been trying to sail from the American side of the lake, and had struggled in the water all this time — hours and hours. All day, in fact. His girlfriend had never been on a boat, but she had tried to steer it because he couldn't do it — couldn't do *anything* anymore because he was so exhausted trying to fight the conditions to get himself into the harbour. He said afterwards that he made for the police basin and garage to get himself help. Allister gave him oxygen to revive him."

Karen did not leave work until ten that night. She would miss out on Canada Day celebrations, "but I saw all these people out celebrating, having a good time, and all I could think was, *Here was a poor man dying.* I felt I could not have celebrated anyway, could not celebrate anything that night."

In her four decades of life, Karen had already dealt with more than her share of personal tragedy: the deaths of a sister and her mother; the loss of her father on her first day on the job as a Toronto police officer; the suicide of a close friend.

"You have to try to be happy with what you have, because you won't always have a chance to hold onto it forever," she said, an appropriate philosophy for someone sustaining such losses within a short range of time.

Why her choice of police work?

"I wanted to do something helpful, but at the same time, to be physical — a police officer's job — or a firefighter's — first came to mind. Yes, an officer's job means sometimes taking people's freedom away and putting them in jail — that's the hard part of the work. But you are helping, too." She went on to recount some of her experiences during the thirteen years she had worked at 14 Division in Parkdale. "I did a variety of jobs there: police cars, undercover, bicycle and foot patrol. Bicycle and foot were great," she said. "You feel close to the community, that you can do something to make changes."

How did she get into the marine unit? Karen described a fight she was embroiled in once, while making an arrest. She suffered a knee injury that required surgery. "It gave me time to think about where I was going in my career," she said. "This was 1999... I was coming up on thirty-nine years of age. A friend said that marine unit was something that might offer me what I was looking for."

It made perfect sense to Karen, who loved the water. And this different kind of work would be both outdoors and physical. She applied, and got the job because of her fitness levels, her considerable experience and her interest in the particular job being offered. Still, for her first two years she felt out of her depth while she scaled a new learning curve. "I'd been doing something for thirteen years; now I had to learn all new things. But I enjoy it. I love the fact that I can operate the police boats — I mean, how great is that? I can spend my time rescuing people, helping them to safety. This job is about rescue, about saving people rather than putting them in jail.

"When you go out on a boat, anything can happen: you can capsize, lose an anchor — you can lose your boat. We get all kinds of calls, like one to the island because someone had a bee sting. You wear lots of different hats. It's also about marine enforcement: you check randomly for compliance with the wearing of life jackets… we might go over to a yacht club and do checks — 'Before you go out, we're going to do a vessel inspection, make sure you're going to be safe.' It's before the fact, not after — proactive rather than reactive. Foot patrol was proactive, too. But this… this gives you a great feeling."

Karen added that she feels happy to be able to feel and show compassion. "I understand people, and they know that I get them. That's fulfilling. Yes, I've had a lot of tragedy in my life, but you can't use that [as a crutch] and say, 'Oh, poor me.' It's part of life, and you have to deal with it, get on with it — especially here in the force."

★

The marine unit patrols four hundred and sixty square miles of open water — the largest patrol area in Canada. Its jurisdiction encompasses the lakefront and the Toronto Islands, and the unit responds to all police and medical calls. It also engages in basic search and rescue.

"Officers in this unit are different," said Staff Sergeant John Badowski, who went on to explain that the unit constitutes a stressful environment, that those who choose to work here might be called adrenaline junkies who actually thrive on the pressure. "Each needs to be very independent, driven by a wish to achieve, and to reach a higher standard than elsewhere," he said. "Officers have to know their own capabilities as well as those of others because they have to rely on each other.

"Many are 'Type A' personalities," he added. "All of them know they will risk themselves to go to the aid of the others on the lake. It's not the average environment that will widely appeal."

The marine unit comprises one of only two tactical units in the city, and its members are the only officers in Canada who are trained in defibrillation and basic trauma life support.

"You need it," Sergeant Badowski says. "If you're thirteen miles out on the lake and someone has a heart attack, no one's going to come and help you. You're not on land where, if your car breaks down, you can get out and stand on the corner of Queen and Jarvis until the tow truck comes. If your boat breaks down and you end up in the water, nobody's coming to help you — not for a long time.

"Our officers are trained at a different level. When the weather's bad and all the other boats are coming in, that's when they go out — a lot of people are not going to like that. If you don't like water or have a phobia about it; if you're not comfortable with some of the technology you have to use — for example, when there's no visibility and you have to rely on radar and have to understand instrumentation — it's not everybody's cup of tea."

As with those in the Emergency Task Force, officers in the marine unit are compelled to work out for one hour in the gym every day. Most remain in the marine unit for a long time, and those who leave usually do so because of family or health-related reasons.

To be accepted for the unit, an officer has to pass a two-day physical test because of the sometimes extreme physical demands of the environment. It differs even from those in the Emergency Task Force because it's a water environment. The necessary technical skills are taught within the unit itself. Officers have to pass a two-week coxswain's course. Each class has eight participants, and only the top two are accepted. They constitute an elite group. Sergeants, too, are required to pass the two-week coxswain's course, and Staff Sergeant Badowski recently found himself practising emergency drills in the water and having to pass courses in radar and boat handling. "Standards here are substantially higher here than elsewhere," he said.

A paramedic is attached to the unit, and he or she has also to pass the coxswain's course and acquire all the other required qualifications, including defibrillation and trauma life support. Cross-training is also necessary: medics train as coxswains, coxswains as medics. For all this, an EMS (emergency medical services) trainer is hired between six to eight times each year to conduct the classes.

In summertime, the unit responds to between ten and fifteen calls a day. Fewer calls come in winter, but those that do involve rescuing people and pets who have fallen through ice, as well as geese that have become frozen to it. The winter season is largely used for training: navigational, radar, ice rescue and river rescue training. Springtime is dominated by the demand for river rescue — sometimes four or five calls in one day. During both seasons, all boating skills are honed. For the winter of 2004–05, intensive training in navigational skills, radar and Global Positioning Systems (GPS) was planned.

★

"The marine unit was once considered to be a bit of a rest hole — a backwater," says Staff Inspector Edward Hegney, the unit's commander. "But within the past six years it has developed into a tactical unit within the Toronto Police Service. It means that the standard has been raised and training is much more extensive. No other police unit requires an entrance exam, a physical exam and interviews. Not only this, but an officer has to be within the top ten per cent of those in the service from which they are coming in order to be considered. After that, there is a competition. The officer then must take a two-week course so they can be evaluated, so we can judge them on teamwork — all before they get to the unit."

The Toronto marine unit is now acknowledged to be one of the premier units of the force. It is considered a tactical unit because everyone is a qualified coxswain, and qualified medically to a level just below a paramedic; skilled and qualified in river and ice rescue, and in defibrillation. It has an underwater bomb disposal unit, and eleven divers who have progressed from scuba to commercial diving where both tanks and surface-supplied air are used. The unit aims for a team of fifteen divers. Each one has a pager and is on permanent call. For each dive, a minimum number of divers is required, but the marine unit insists on five. Dive calls are many and varied and include accidents, homicides, suicides. In 2003, thirty bodies were recovered from the lake.

This is a special unit with special and unique officers.

★

The helmsman of the sailing boat that carried the injured sailor subsequently wrote to Toronto Police Chief Julian Fantino to praise the integrity and professionalism of the officers involved in the rescue. "Together with the ambulance service, had it not been for your police officers, those on board would never have made it to land," he wrote. "The crew member would not have survived" — even if that survival was short-lived. The plaudits were reinforced by the fact that the helmsman was a physician and was therefore able to gauge professionally the skills and expertise of the marine unit staff.

Afterwards, when Staff Inspector Hegney learned about the rescue, he demanded to know: "How come I don't know about this? Tell me what this is all about."

"I want these officers written up," he subsequently said. "I want them documented, their names given to the Toronto Police Services Board for commendation for exceptional performance of duty." The officers were also awarded the St. John Ambulance Lifesaving Award, and were later recommended for an Allied Services Award — the first time such an award had ever been given to a police unit in tandem with the Toronto Ambulance.

"Allister deserves most of the credit," Karen said. "He's so very skilled in his work, and was very supportive of me."

Although the patient succumbed to his injuries a month later, had it not been for the intervention, expertise and bravery of the officers and the paramedic, he would have died much sooner. He had been given a chance of survival.

Jean-Pierre Charbonneau in a Zodiac in the Bay of Sept-Îles.

RELUCTANT HEROES
Sept-Îles and Quebec City, Quebec

It blew day after day; it blew with spite, without interval, without mercy, and without rest. The world was nothing but an immensity of great foaming waves rushing at us. — Joseph Conrad, 1902

Maurice D.* finishes odd jobs around the yard, then stands on his front steps, looking up at the sky. Already the afternoon has begun its slide into early evening, and storm clouds are deepening over the Bay of Sept-Îles. He notices that the wind is rising and feels restless. From his home near the shores of the bay he can see a stretch of its heaving grey waters, catch a glimpse of Grand Basque Island beyond. He realizes that the wind, howling from the north, must be thumping the western beaches, and he imagines the thunderous roar of wind and wave on rocks. It's then that the thought comes: Why not go for a spin on the Sea-Doo for a quick thrill before dark? He's on the phone at once to his buddy, Gilles M., to suggest a couple of hours' fun on the waves of the southwestern reach of the bay.

And so it is: two men from a small city in eastern Quebec go out one late-October afternoon to play about on their Sea-Doos over rough waves being thrown up by an approaching storm in the Gulf of St.

---

* The names of the missing and their wives have been changed to protect their identities

Lawrence — a typical autumn storm. But not only that: they head for a rocky part of the coast where wind and waves are strongest, all for the thrill of fighting the elements. They wear warm, protective clothes, but take little with them: no flares, no phone, no radio or flashlight — only an oar and some rope. "Just a quick bit of fun — be home by six," each calls to his wife as he heads out.

Six o'clock comes, then seven and eight, without the sounds of car and trailer pulling up the driveway, laughing voices or the clattering of boots on asphalt. Thunder splits overhead, and torrents of rain begin to fall on the city and the gulf. As the clock strikes half past eight, Martine D., consumed by slow-burning fear, calls the Sûreté du Québec (provincial police) detachment to report the men missing. The police officer quickly realizes that this is a job for the Canadian Coast Guard in Quebec City, six hundred and fifty kilometres distant.

Because of the decision of two men to have a brief thrill in the bay, all the resources of the Coast Guard and the Department of National Defence across Newfoundland, Nova Scotia and Quebec are about to be called upon, and personnel are to risk their lives in a storm of near-epic proportions.

★

It's been a long day for Hubert Desgagnes — it's time to go home. He picks up his coat and leaves the Canadian Coast Guard building that houses the Quebec Marine Rescue Centre, which looks out over the St. Lawrence River in Quebec City. He drives the near-deserted streets of the Old Capital and, upon arriving home, has dinner and relaxes. Not for long: André Gotty, duty co-ordinator at the rescue centre, is on the phone.

"Search-and-rescue is needed in Sept-Îles for two missing men in the bay," he says. "I've sent out a pan pan call; I have Coast Guard resources in the area — some of the large commercial vessels are coming in for shelter from a big storm, and I've contacted all Coast Guard Auxiliary resources. So far, no one will go; the storm is too severe, or the distance too far to travel. I've called Halifax to request air support, and now I'm calling you. It doesn't look good and I'm going to need your assistance."

Hubert goes out again into the late October night to drive to the Coast Guard base he has left but a few short hours before. Lights twinkle above the shiny rock that slides down into the river, Coast Guard ships tied up at its base. He feels a distinct chill in the air, and he knows it will be colder still in the more northerly city of Sept-Îles.

Inside the rescue centre, André is joined by Alain Martel, who is to relieve him now that his twelve-hour shift is over. But André decides to remain at the centre to help with a search-and-rescue operation that promises to be protracted and far-reaching.

As Hubert arrives at the centre, he learns that vessels large and small, both commercial freighters and lakers, have been called out to search, and he discovers that they refuse to go. It is only then that he, as officer in charge of the Coast Guard's Marine Rescue Centre in faraway Quebec City, begins to understand the enormity of the storm that thunders all about the small city. Sept-Îles is in darkness, and the gulf waters on its doorstep heave violently. Somewhere in the waters of the bay, or around the seven-island archipelago that dots it, two men are hiding from the storm — or they are adrift, perhaps perishing at this very moment in the watery tumult. The rescue co-ordinators must find a way to get the Coast Guard ships there. The nearest is the CCGS *Louisbourg*, but this fishery surveillance patrol boat lies thirteen hours away, tied up in Gaspé because of the storm. Hubert contacts its skipper and asks him to come in and search. He replies that his ship is too far away.

"We're asking you to depart Gaspé and proceed towards Sept-Îles and search anyway," Hubert instructs its master.

A helicopter from Greenwood, Nova Scotia, has been ordered by the Rescue Co-ordination Centre in Halifax to conduct an aerial search. The 'copter is a new Cormorant designed with night-flight capability, a speed of 150 knots (about 170 miles per hour) and a flight distance of 750 nautical miles (860 miles). When Hubert learns it will need at least five hours to arrive in Sept-Îles, and when he considers the very bad weather conditions, he asks for another. He is told that a second helicopter will only be sent if it proves absolutely necessary. "If there are problems with the first one, we'll send another. We don't want all our resources going to one place; we might need them for other rescues," he's told.

What now? The three co-ordinators continue rapidly to page all possible maritime resources. They have begun with the large ships, then smaller, and smaller still, finally reaching out to the owners of seven private boats operated by the Coast Guard Auxiliary — despite the knowledge that few are fit for the conditions.

The answers are nearly all the same.

"No, I don't want to go out there."

"No, I don't want to kill myself."

"No, we're not going out in that storm."

"Are you crazy? It's a storm out there — maybe tomorrow."

All answer no, except for the operator of the only Auxiliary boat that is not privately owned — and that is only because André Charbonneau has not yet answered.

A darkened city is shaken by the storm, its citizens lying awake through avalanches of thunder and lightning that rip through the sky. At the docks, vessels huddle for shelter in port. Their skippers, having refused the call to assist in the search, hold onto hope that the men have found shelter on the island, that this is no distress call — only that two men have been late to return home. They tell themselves this to sustain themselves in their decision not to go and look for them. The collective belief is that it's nonsense to risk a vessel and crew out there; much better to wait until the weather improves, then to go and search the islands.

One vessel does respond to the call to search: the sturdy tug *Pointe aux Basques*. Its master agrees to try and venture out in the storm. Instructions are prepared to direct it towards four of the islands that dot the bay, to conduct surveillance of the coastline as it proceeds.

Hubert and his Coast Guard officers know there are only two possibilities: that the men have found shelter and will be picked up when the storm abates, or they are adrift in the middle of nowhere and are in big trouble. Because of this latter possibility, the Coast Guard must try to find them; this is their mandate and it's what they must do. They bend to their effort, silent and absorbed amid the constant ringing of the phones, continuing to reach out in search of help. All the while they anxiously await news: for the sighting of a flare, for lights on the island to indicate the men are safely there. But no such sign comes — and neither radio nor visual contact. They now pin their hopes on the aircraft from Greenwood, that it will spot some-thing. Then perhaps the *Pointe aux Basques...* and perhaps the Coast Guard ship still can make it. But no: the CCGS *Louisbourg* radios that it is still in Gaspé. Its master says he cannot respond to the call because the conditions are too severe.

The year-round deep-sea port of Sept-Îles, second in size only to Vancouver, has lately been busy with large bulk carriers from England, Japan, Norway and around the world, here to load iron ore and occa-sionally aluminum. Many of the large freighters have only recently headed into port, having been diverted from their courses to seek pro-tection from the sudden storm. Those who have successfully sought refuge — the crews of the *Algonorth, Atlantic Huron* and the ro-ro (roll-on, roll-off) *Aivik* — say they saw nothing on their way in. Their masters are not willing to risk the security of their vessels or their crew; they say they are too large, and the task too risky.

★

André Charbonneau is just twenty-four years of age. He is at home in Sept-Îles, tidying up, on this evening of October 15, 2003. It is eight-thirty, and darkness has long since fallen — how quickly the night steals away the daylight hours. André is vacuuming, so he does not hear the phone. Eventually, he notices the flashing light that indicates a message has been left. It's from the Marine Rescue Centre in Quebec City: "Two missing men in the bay, overdue for two hours, lost in the gulf in high seas and heavy rain."

He returns the call and learns that two men left shore about four-thirty that afternoon to go out into the Gulf of St. Lawrence on their Sea-Doos, intending to return by six. They left from the Quay Maltais in Sept-Îles and headed for Monaghan Beach for a couple of hours' fun.

"Wearing life jackets?"

"Yes," says André Gotty. "The gulf waters were choppy and unsettled when they set out, but they've since blown up to become very rough; little visibility and heavy rain." Indeed, the winds had risen to forty-five knots from the east; the air temperature was a mere eight degrees Celsius, and the water temperature only five. Something that André

Charbonneau is not to know at this moment is that the rescue centre has already contacted many Coast Guard Auxiliary members, and that none are prepared to go out in the conditions — none but the harbour tug.

Sea-Doos — in this weather! As all local sailors and commercial pilots know, the gulf is a dangerous body of water because of its strong currents and opposing winds — "winds blowing against the direction of the currents make for a big, big wave," André's father, Jean Charbonneau, says. The retired professional fisherman describes how, on the north shore, the currents flow from Labrador and the water is very cold; there is an ever-present threat of rapid hypothermia to those exposed to it.

"Are you able to go out and search — to go out in Coast Guard Auxiliary Boat 1275?" André Gotty is asking now.

"I don't know, I can't tell you," Charbonneau says. "I'll have to go down to the boat to look at the conditions. I'll see if I can do something. I'll call you if I can go out."

"Only you can decide if you should go," says the rescue officer. Still, there is the hope that, perhaps at last, this is the beginning of good news: that the Coast Guard has one, even two possible marine resources willing to search. But the promise is short-lived: shortly after this exchange comes a return call from the dispatch office of the Iron Ore Company of Canada. The tug is unable to leave the wharf: it will not go out because the conditions are too violent.

André Charbonneau crab-fishing — a great life!

"This is the only commercial resource we believe can go out, and it will not," Hubert says. As chief controller in charge of the rescue attempt, Hubert is running out of options. How can he fail to send help to two shipwrecked men? "There are people in danger, and you can do nothing; you feel helpless, that you are failing in your job," he says. "You are a SAR person, an organization, and you must send rescue… you are responsible to do so."

★

Back in Sept-Îles, André Charbonneau has picked up the phone to call his brother, who lives at home with his parents. Jean-Pierre is only eighteen and, unlike André, is not a member of the Coast Guard Auxiliary, but André knows he is as experienced and knowledgeable as the best of the sailors there are, and he can't think of anyone he would rather have alongside him in these conditions.

"My brother is the only person I trust with me at sea," he says. "I never go out with other members in bad weather. With Jean-Pierre — we look at each other and we understand one another."

Indeed, Jean Charbonneau's sons are both experienced sailors, rich in knowledge, good judgment and intuition. They know what the seas are like when the winds howl up to thirty knots; they know about strong currents, high winds, rogue waves and the walls of water that can be created. They have lived beside this body of water; have strolled about the splendid natural harbour and its seven-island archipelago.

In a few short minutes, André is at his parents' home to pick up his brother. Carrying heavy coats and spare cans of gasoline, they drive to the yacht club marina, and to the trailer on the dock.

There the brothers stand at the water's edge and look out over a sea that rises to six metres in height, with short, choppy waves at the entrance. Wind from the northwest gusts at forty to fifty knots and visibility is poor. Each brother makes his decision, although there is really none to be made, no time to think. "There are people in danger. We have a job to do," says Charbonneau. "If my brother or friend were in danger, we would have to do something to come to their rescue."

"Not so bad, do you think?" André says to Jean-Pierre. "We can go along the coast and be a little sheltered by it — it's about three miles down from the yacht club."

Jean-Pierre agrees. The two begin an inventory of the equipment they will need to take with them: a hypothermic blanket, a first-aid kit, night-vision goggles and survival clothing. They prepare the Coast Guard Auxiliary's boat — a twenty-one-foot Boston Whaler, a fibreglass vessel with a rigid hull — and leave the quay for the tumult beyond.

And so it is that, on an October night in eastern Quebec, a man and his teenage brother leave home to pilot a boat over the savage sea, hoping to come to the rescue of those who might be perishing upon it. All the while, other vessels — large and small, from commercial freighters to tugs, lakers to fishing vessels of every kind — huddle in port.

The brothers are given instructions about where they should search: "Head north and go towards the sheltered bay at the northwest corner of Grand Basque Island," says the rescue co-ordinator. "Check the chalet, the place where summer camps are held. Boaters often stop there, and Martine D. says the two men have a habit of stopping to rest on its beaches. Check in the shed, have a good look around. Keep in mind their Sea-Doos are Model XPs and can run for one and a half to two hours on a tank of gas."

★

At the rescue centre, Alain Martel eventually succeeds in reaching the excursion boat, the *Petit Pingouin*, and despite the very bad weather, its owner agrees to give it a try and go out and search. His boat, a seven-metre rigid-hulled inflatable craft with one outboard engine, is capable in the large waves. The Coast Guard ship *Louisbourg* has already radioed again from its position in Gaspé that it cannot help search; the large harbour tug, the *Pointe aux Basques*, will remain on standby — will call its crew and head out, but only if conditions permit, and not into the deep area of the bay.

What now? What other resources exist that the Coast Guard might call upon? Ah — the naval reserve. The call is made, but once more the answer is no. Its boat is in Chicoutimi and is not available. Perhaps the

Royal Canadian Mounted Police? Again, no. The conditions are too bad to set out — maybe in the morning. The only ray of hope remains the small 1275 Auxiliary boat and the intrepid Charbonneau brothers — and then, eventually, the Cormorant rescue helicopter from Greenwood.

"This is a very risky operation," says Hubert. "If a tug cannot go out, no one can go. Now I'm afraid for the safety of the Charbonneau brothers." He radios them at once to say, "Look, I want you to know that if you get in trouble, we have no one to help you. No one willing is to go out… you will be entirely alone in the gulf."

There is a pregnant silence, which is broken by Hubert himself. "We have no one but two brothers in a small boat, a ground search team to search the bay on foot, and maybe the *Petit Pingouin* [a tour boat] sometime later on. We've asked Halifax to task a second chopper, and they told us no."

While the Cormorant helicopter, Rescue 914, flies towards the gulf, André and Jean-Pierre struggle up the coast in their small craft in winds that "blow like hell," and in thundering rain and sea spray, trying to reach the western mid-channel buoy. At first, they hug the coast, heading north towards the wharf and the buoys where the tugs are stationed. "We are up the coast from the north shore, opposite the middle of Grande Basque Island, heading for the buoy that lies in the middle of the bay between the shore and the island," says André Charbonneau. "The more we go towards the sea and away from the coast, the greater the wind, and the waves are reaching higher and higher. We can't see more than a few feet in front of us because of the sea spray — the buoy and the dock are the only things we can use to navigate."

Sept-Îles has vanished into the blackness — a main power line has ruptured, cutting power to the entire city. There are, therefore, no lights to help guide the brothers and give them bearings. There is no background, no visibility — just white sea spray against a pitch-black night. The rough waters allow for a speed of only six or seven knots, and the brothers find it impossible to use their craft's instruments because the waves demand too much of their concentration.

"We can't see beyond about a few feet, and it's very dark," André Charbonneau will say afterwards. "We try to head towards the island. Winds blow towards it and hit it, and then we have a mountain! The turbulence makes the winds stronger, and the pull of the tides also is very strong — a very rough place to go."

The two young brothers are engaged in a Herculean struggle with the elements. They fight to stay afloat in waves that curl twelve feet above them, but are short — "they are higher than they are longer — very tough to stay out there and remain upright," André says. He tries to put the wind at his back and go with the sea; he's making for the red buoy, believing that one or both of the shipwrecked men might be clinging to it. They are about five hundred feet from it. Wind and currents push them back. They struggle valiantly, but cannot get closer. They find it nearly impossible to navigate; meanwhile, the buoy for which they are headed appears, then disappears. André realizes its light is not working.

What he doesn't know is that the shipwrecked man who clings to the buoy has removed the wire that connects to the light, in hopes that the lamp's failure will give the Coast Guard a clue that something is wrong, that they will come and check it out — and find him. It has the opposite effect: it keeps the potential rescuers farther away; the Boston Whaler travels wide of it and further west, as Charbonneau is unsure now of where the reefs are. As well, the water between the bay and the island is shallow, creating extremely rough conditions, unruly waves that have no pattern to them.

With sorrow and disappointment, André realizes that he can't make it to the buoy, that he must turn. A man — two men — might be clinging to it, or they might not, but he can't tell, he can't see, and he can't get there! Only the knowledge that, earlier that evening, the tug had passed the buoy twice without seeing anything comforts the Charbonneau brothers. Now they must turn about and try to get back to shore. To make their turn, they need to count the waves, knowing that every seventh one is weaker than the preceding six — both shorter and lower. The brothers wait and count, wait and count, trying to get to the seventh wave, to go though it so that they can make the turn. "But we're not sure, not sure… We begin to turn so we can come back with the wind, get to the east of the reef to avoid the biggest waves," he says. "We're so close to the buoy, yet we must turn away from it; we must find another route, get some protection from Grand Basque Island until we reach an area north of Cyrille. We can't do anything else: the wind is getting stronger all the time, and the sea higher; we are in some danger. We cannot even see the buoy now — only from time to time — and we have trouble maintaining course. It's very dark; we can't see anything and it's impossible to navigate in a sea that is higher than it is longer... our boat is only twenty-one feet."

And then they hit the wall of water: a wave crashes over them, and everything aboard drifts. André and Jean-Pierre look at their swamped vessel, which is filling rapidly with water, and they see that the two engines are being submerged. André almost reflexively stops the bilge pump and gives full throttle to the engines; the boat rears up, allowing some of the water to drain out of it. Winds push them — they've lost their spare gallons of gasoline and one oar, but they are still afloat.

The brothers are one mile from the coast along the north shore, facing the island's midpoint. They have not been able to get to the buoy. The conditions are treacherous, and no other vessel is out in the storm. The sea spray is interfering with their radio — they can receive calls from the Coast Guard, but not transmit; if they should get into trouble... but this is not a good thought. They must return — there is no choice. The two wet and exhausted brothers pull into the marina after midnight, André scarcely believing that nearly four hours have passed. After they dock the boat and prepare it for its next trip out, they return home, but not to sleep. They will take some rest, and go out again if the weather improves.

★

All the while, a man clings to the buoy in the violence of the storm. He sees the brothers in their Coast Guard Auxiliary boat trying to get close, then watches them give up and begin their struggle to return to shore. He sees a tugboat go in and out of the harbour, twice passing closer than five hundred feet, but it does not see him — it can't get close, just as the Charbonneau brothers could not.

The news reaches Quebec City that the Charbonneau brothers are returning because the conditions are too dangerous to remain. Hubert radios the skipper of the *Petit Pingouin* to warn them of this. The skipper says his boat is slightly bigger than the small Auxiliary craft — perhaps he will see if he can go out after all. And he does, leaving shore at 11:00 p.m. The tour boat struggles in the blackness of the night in winds of up to fifty knots and waves that reach up to twenty-one feet. Not much more than an hour passes before he radios to say, "It's getting worse and worse... we have to come back in."

"Some members can go to sea with the wind at twenty-five knots; [anything stronger], they have not the experience, and perhaps not the right kind of craft to do it," says retired sailor Jean Charbonneau, explaining the reluctance or refusal of so many sailors to assist in the search. "My boys — they do what they do because they are fishermen. Yes, they take some risks to help others. They know what the boat can do, and what they themselves can do. Others refuse to go out, most likely because their vessel is not the right type to survive in the conditions."

Just as the Coast Guard radio station is notifying the rescue centre that the Auxiliary boat has had to turn back, another call — this time from the rescue centre in Halifax — is received. The helicopter from Greenwood has mechanical problems and has had to make an emergency landing near Fredericton for repairs. Its pilot doesn't know when it will fly again. The three rescue co-ordinators look at each other, and one exclaims, "It's Murphy's Law tonight!"

The families of the missing men are not forgotten, however: the duty co-ordinator keeps in touch with the wives to give them updates. He is also in contact with Quebec's provincial police.

★

Hubert sits with his head in his hands, deeply troubled — and angry. A tough situation, so many problems, so much time passing — and nothing achieved. What now? He stares out at the night, knowing there is little else they can do. With the loss of the helicopter from Greenwood, the only remaining hope has now vanished.

"I'm mad, really pissed off!" he says. "When we asked Halifax for a second chopper we had a feeling nothing would run the way it should this particular night. We were told no. Now it's all jumping in our face. We call for a second helicopter, this time from Gander in Newfoundland — the squadron had said they will send another Cormorant. But the weather didn't permit it to fly directly. Everything is against us." In anger and frustration, he picks up his coat and leaves for home to get some rest. André Gotty does the same; he also needs at least some rest so he can return in the morning. The chill in the air has deepened and the streets of the Old Capital are deserted.

Inspiration comes the minute Hubert is behind the wheel of his car. Yes! What about the small Coast Guard chopper in transit in Rimouski? He knows it's not used for SAR, that it has no instruments for IFR flight, but perhaps it can cross the river in the first light of morning — if its single pilot is willing. There's no other option — but wait: there's the roll-on, roll-off cargo vessel the *Aivik*. It has good manoeuvrability. Perhaps… perhaps… The instant he arrives home, Hubert asks the duty rescue co-ordinator to call the vessel's master.

"This is the Coast Guard Rescue Centre: we would like you to haul your anchor and go search in the Bay of Sept Îles…"

"Are you crazy? If I heave my anchor, I'll be in big trouble myself. Yes, I'll take a look, but I'm sure I can't go out in this weather."

Meanwhile, the *Petit Pingouin* has just returned to Sept-Îles. No luck. Not a clue about the missing men.

Just as Hubert closes his eyes to get some sleep, the phone rings. "Some good news from Halifax," says Alain Martel's voice. "The chopper's crew in Fredericton fixed their fuel leak and will fly over — ETA six in the morning."

Some good news at last, and this is only the beginning: the captain of the tugboat calls to say he will get underway, as conditions have improved; André and Jean-Pierre Charbonneau will go out again; and the Coast Guard's helicopter pilot will take off at first light of dawn from Rimouski to assist. Even the *Louisbourg* has departed Gaspé, bound for Sept-Îles.

At four-thirty in the morning, the two young brothers get up and go out once more into the night — "How can you sleep when you know two men are lost in a storm?"

Faint streaks in the eastern sky herald the arrival of a hesitant dawn, and with it, other craft join the Charbonneau brothers on the water. The RCMP boat *Grand Roi des Côtes* is out early, together with the tug, *Pointe aux Basques*, and another Auxiliary boat, the *Richard L*. "Now we have some resources," says Hubert, and formulates a plan: the *Pointe aux Basques* will search Pointe-aux-Corbeaux and Pointe-à-la-Chasse; the *Richard L*, the islands of Manowin and Corossol. The RCMP vessel will cover the west coast of the island; the brothers Charbonneau, the south and east of the Basque Islands and the bay itself. They know well the depth of the water and the location of reefs here, given their years of sailing and duck hunting in the area.

All searchers believe that the two men went to Grande Basque Island on their Sea-Doos, and that once the weather began to deteriorate, they surely found shelter in the lodge there.

André and Jean-Pierre begin their travel along the west coast of Grand Basque Island, and on to its south point. At least they can now navigate the waves, because they can see them! But this relief is short-lived: at the south point, angry waves continue to assault each other, creating a sea so choppy they can't get across to the east coast of the island. "High but short waves with no pattern to them," André says. A chopper drones overhead. The brothers look up to see the original helicopter, Rescue 914, flying over the bay, its fuel leak repaired.

A voice comes over the radio. "We've sighted one of the men," says a triumphant police officer. "He's alive — great news! We found him clinging to the D6 buoy anchored in the Reef Basque rocks. About his friend: Monsieur D. says he last saw him adrift in the direction of Wabush. Both their crafts are afloat, but disabled. Would you head there, towards Pointe de la Marmite? The helicopter will cover the Pointe-Noire area…"

"Into the mouth of hell," mutters André under his breath. "None of us dreamed they would go there! This area of the bay is where wind and wave is most ferocious, but they did it."

André and Jean-Pierre reach "the mouth of hell." At first, they see nothing, but then — what's that? They see something: it's not part of a shore, nor the remains of a storm, and it's a sinister sight: two smashed-up Sea-Doos are lying against each other in the shallow waters of the bay, half-hidden among the debris the storm has washed up there. The brothers can't get any closer, so they radio their discovery to the rescue helicopter. As Rescue 914 flies over the wreck of the two crafts, its crew notices something else: a yellow object on the beach, something half-hidden among several feet of storm-blown seaweed, algae and debris. "Did one of the men wear a yellow life jacket?"

Yes, he did! The crew in the helicopter hovers overhead; a SAR technician is lowered onto the beach to check out the yellow speck. It is indeed the second shipwrecked man, no longer alive. He is retrieved by the rescue crew aboard the helicopter, transferred to the airport, and thence to a hospital. It is eight-thirty in the morning.

The rescuers experience a flood of emotions; in the hearts of the Charbonneau brothers, there is much angst. Slowly they make their way back to the marina, cold, wet and completely worn out.

Did they fear for themselves?

"We had no time to be scared," André says afterward. "The time — it raced by. It felt like fifteen minutes, not nearly four hours, and then again another four hours in the morning…

"Some people did not take it well that we went out. They said it was too dangerous, and why did we do it? I said then that it was for a thrill — but I only said that because I didn't know how to answer. People didn't understand that what we did was stronger than ourselves — that we had to go. People in distress were in need of us. It's like having a brother or friend — we had to do something."

★

According to the coroner's report, the deceased person died of drowning. It is learned that the first Sea-Doo became disabled soon after leaving the marina. The second Sea-Doo tried to tow it back to shore, but it, too, became disabled. Both craft drifted rapidly. The men had no means of communication. One man, thrown from his Sea-Doo into the water, made the decision to swim to the nearest buoy — a decision that saved his life.

At the conclusion of this rescue effort, Hubert Desgagnes reviews the entire operation. It confirms that both Charbonneau brothers took great, but calculated, risks in order to search for and rescue the two men. André and Jean-Pierre Charbonneau are to be honoured with a medal of merit from the Canadian Coast Guard Auxiliary Association.

What André and Jean-Pierre Charbonneau have done is an act of great heroism: they have gone out into the night, into a savage storm, in a small boat, when all other vessels remained in port.

Search-and-rescue volunteers on a search.

AFTER THE STORM,
STILLNESS IN THE NIGHT
Wabush, Newfoundland and Labrador

To do search and rescue has become my life's passion. When you endanger yourself to rescue someone, it's almost like you've given life. — Craig Porter

It happened deep in the heart of winter, during a weekend in January 1996. Snow lay in huge white drifts; clouds dropped from the sky and seemed to hang serpent-like on the naked branches of the ubiquitous black spruce trees. The streets of the small town of Wabush, on the western edge of Labrador, seemed silent, devoid of people and vehicles of any kind.

For a group of young people, a temperature of minus-58 degrees Celsius was of no consequence, and neither was the blizzard that was forecast to hit within the next twenty-four hours. Four of them, in their late teens and early twenties, planned a weekend party at a cottage owned by one of their fathers. The shack stood twenty kilometres from town, isolated and half-hidden in a heavily wooded area not far from Mills Lake. A snowmobile trail led through hills and valleys of virginal snow, through drifts that piled high among the trees, right up to their high branches — the perfect spot for a winter weekend party. The young people packed beer — plenty of it — and food, then roared off on their machines into a frigid, hostile world to drink and laugh, to joke, to kid around in rustic isolation, free from adult eyes.

Three other young men set off later to join the party, hiring a taxi to drive them over the ten kilometres of rough gravel road from town.

When the road ended and the terrain became impassable by automobile, they planned to continue on foot for the last ten kilometres. Trekking in these conditions meant little to those used to the Labrador winter. Did they fear they might get disoriented, even lost, in this vast white world? They would tell you "No."

The lonely cottage crouched among the trees, far from other habitation, roads, or any hint that civilization existed. It was roughly furnished inside with a couch, two horsehair armchairs and a worn carpet flung over the floorboards. A portable AM radio and a stereo system sat on a table, and books and magazines lay scattered on rough shelves near the wood-burning stove. Two iron bedsteads and bunks, with rugs, pillows, and thick, downy throws piled on them, filled the two small bedrooms. Winds howled about the small building, blowing snow hard up against the windows, obliterating any view of the lake — or of any part of the outside world at all.

Unabashed by the conditions, whistling and kidding each other, the men unloaded food and beer, board games and playing cards from their snowmobiles. Indoors, the chill of the air was not much different from that of the outside world, but it wouldn't take long to get it heated. In the meantime, there was much stamping of feet and jumping about in attempts to generate warmth.

Time passed. The friends did not arrive, and the storm outdoors raged unabated. The four young men became increasingly restive and bored. They felt confined and a little uneasy inside the rude dwelling where no glimpse of the outside world was to be had. Anxious about their buddies, they ventured outdoors several times, firing up their snowmobiles and slowly traversing the lonely trails in search of them.

The night passed. By the next evening, discouraged by the increasing winds and plummeting temperatures and by the continued absence of their friends, whom they'd assumed had been deterred by the weather, they decided to pack up and go back to town. Dispirited, they again negotiated the twisting trails through the woods back to the road, and to the town. Once home, they telephoned their friends to boast about what a good time they'd missed. They learned, to their astonishment, that the friends had indeed set out, as planned, to join them at the cottage, and that nobody had seen or heard from them since. "Oh, my God … heaven help them." These and other words were muttered as a series of frantic phone calls bounced along the telephone wires, to every person and place where the missing men might conceivably be found. The police were notified, and within a short time the town's volunteer search team was called out.

★

Craig Porter had driven down his quiet residential street in Wabush that evening. An arctic wind whipped around corners of the rows of small bungalows and duplexes that huddled side-by-side. Craig pulled into his driveway and, before entering his home, he plugged his vehicle's block heater into an electrical outlet. His wife, Lori, was in the kitchen. He sniffed in appreciation of the aromas that wafted into the hallway to greet him. Seven-year-old Emily Rose had her homework spread out on the dining table. Craig loved opening the door to his home, especially to a scene such as this. This was the reason he prized his place on the day shift as a mechanic in the local iron ore mines: it left his evenings free for just this — spending time at home with his family. "Not a time to be outdoors," he said to Lori, this veteran of Labrador's harsh winter seasons. "Wouldn't put my dog out in it."

He had scarcely sat down in the cozy warmth of his living room to watch television with his family when the phone rang. Craig looked at his wife and his daughter, shrugged, and picked it up. The message sent chills down his spine.

"Search and rescue — gotta go," he said. "Three young fellows lost in the woods — way out near Mills Lake. They were supposed to be out at a cottage nearby, but never made it. But we'll find them." Craig's outdoor gear and his search-and-rescue bag hung in a closet near the front door. He snatched them up and was out the door, in his truck, and gone in mere moments.

Search-and-rescue volunteers, contacted by the police,* headed for the precinct on the outskirts of Labrador City — for Craig, the trip was a

---

* "The police" refers here to the Royal Newfoundland Constabulary, which polices the province of Newfoundland and Labrador. Since the 1860s it has been the force of choice for the city of St. John's, but it has since broadened its jurisdiction to include most of the Avalon Peninsula and the city of Corner Brook. Since 1984 it has assumed policing duties in Labrador City, Wabush and Churchill.

mere four kilometres. Within twenty-five minutes, a majority of the thirty-nine members had roared into the parking lot and piled into the station. A sense of foreboding hung in the air; it was early evening, and three young men had been missing since early the day before.

Under the direction of Craig Giles, an officer of the Royal Newfoundland Constabulary, the volunteers were grouped into four teams of four searchers each, and a police officer was assigned to each team. All four groups were provided with portable police telephones. Craig's team included his hunting partner Eugene Joy, and a young rookie cop about to encounter his first trip on a snowmobile in Labrador. It was a surreal scene: a massing of machines and their hel- meted, heavily cloaked drivers in the stillness of this bitter evening. Machines were cranked up and, with a roar, two of the teams headed off overland along an old surveyors' trail to check out the cottage the three had intended to visit. The other two teams visited every cottage near the road. This meant stopping at all dwellings, regardless of signs of use or disuse, dismounting, then trudging through heavy snow to knock and shout at each darkened door. Before they imprinted their presence with their own footsteps, they searched the ground for any sign that the three young people might have stopped there. As darkness deepened, the temperature — which had registered minus-58 when they'd first departed town — had dropped to minus-87 when the wind chill was factored in. It was a slow and miserable job, as physical exhaustion added to the anxiety they all felt.

An exhaustive search, spanning two hours, failed to turn up any evi- dence of the men. No prints or smudges disturbed the virginal snow that had piled up about the trees and in black hollows, and no objects such as discarded beer bottles or food wrappers were found. Two teams converged at a fork in the trail to discuss any findings. With cold-stiffened fingers, one of the searchers pulled out his radio to advise the command post of the situation and to ask what to do next. The searchers milled around, constantly moving to try to generate body heat, all the while never ceas- ing to scan the ground for signs of life that might have passed that way, a task made all the more difficult by falling and drifting snow.

Then came a shout shot through the trees; a voice yelling, "Hey, take a look at this!" The forest fell silent for a fraction of a second; then there was a crunching of boots in the snow as a rush of bodies converged on the spot where a searcher had bent over to examine half-buried footprints. Hope flared in the hearts of the rescuers. Re-energized, they immediately took to their snowmobiles to resume the numbing task of following an almost nonexistent trail deeper and deeper into the nearly impenetrable wilds of Labrador.

Many pairs of eyes anxiously scanned the deadened white world as they moved carefully over it, frantically looking for evidence that life that had existed here, even for one brief moment, before passing on. Shouts rang intermittently in the eerie silence among the trees when someone thought they had discovered evidence of a spot where the three had flopped, or had perhaps stopped to summon up reserves of energy to recoup their flagging spirits.

"As we bore deeper and deeper into the night in a wind that bit into us, and a cold that stung, then numbed even the hardiest among us, we wondered in our hearts if the next bend in the trail would bring us face-to-face with a group of bodies slumped together," Craig Porter said afterward. Like so many rescuers, he hoped to find bodies, but only those that were breathing.

Two hours, and seventeen kilometres, from the road, one team came upon another fork in the trail. Four searchers were left at the junction of these two trails to build a fire, while two other searchers and a police officer set off, each in different directions, to continue the search. Severe cold had begun to exact a toll on all.

Craig, Eugene and the rookie officer proceeded cautiously along the surveyors' line trail until they came to Molar Lake, about half a kilometre away. Their hearts grew leaden as they found no sign of footprints or clues that told them others had been there before. Upon reaching the lake, the searchers began a series of zigzag patterns across its frozen surface, trying to cut across any existing trail the lost men might have left behind.

"We were out some several hundred yards on the lake and chanced upon deep holes in the surface snow that covered the ice," said Craig. "We stopped to take a look to try to figure out what it meant. Amazing, really, that we found these marks at all, because they were mostly buried by blowing snow."

They were indeed footprints, and joy would have gladdened the hearts of the men had it not been for a terrible twist: slush was discovered!

"Slush: it's a deep layer of water between the ice and the covering snow," said Craig. "These conditions made walking much harder, with the added danger of searchers suffering frozen feet in the extreme temperatures."

The group pressed on, the slush adding a renewed sense of urgency. They understood that the three lost men would be in serious trouble if they had not been able to find adequate shelter in the twenty-four hours that had passed since they had been dropped off by their taxi driver. The trail they followed now wavered from side to side. Those disoriented in this surreal white world would not realize that the actual trail they had intended to follow was some twelve kilometres behind them.

"As we neared the far end of the lake, our spirits sank again when we knew that the three had obviously not found shelter, that they were about to enter the woods and the endless trails beyond," Craig said. "We were thinking the worst. A small point jutted out into the lake. We came round it, adrenaline pumping and all of us full of foreboding. And there we saw a flicker of light! We couldn't believe it. We all rushed towards it, our hopes soaring high, hoping... praying..."

And then the unbelievable happened: three men — all alive — were found huddled around a small stove, their clothing hung around its pipe to dry. "We shouted and yelled all at the same time — you should have heard. Oh, man, it was great! These men, our neighbours and buddies and friends and family, we'd found them alive."

"We're members of the Labrador West ground search-and-rescue team," one of the searchers said at last, trying to stretch a smile across his frozen face. "We've been looking all over for you."

"Thank God! Are we ever glad to see you! Thank you, thank you, thank you!" Smiles stretched across the visible part of their faces. Craig radioed to tell the remaining team members that their quarry had been found, and not long afterward the other teams roared up to this forsaken spot in the woods on their machines.

The three lost men were checked for injuries, then the rescuers took the opportunity to warm up by the stove and refuel before they began the long trek back to the road.

"We figured we'd missed the trail," said one of the wayward cottagers, "but we kept going in the hopes that our buddies were on their way to get us. We were tired and near total exhaustion, but we pressed on, stopping often to rest — we had to."

"We left our beer buried in the snow when we were too exhausted to carry it any further," said another, with a wry grin on his face. "When we came to the lake, we kept going, believing we were almost there. We kept going, but began to think, *This is it, we're done for.* We didn't have it in us to go any further when we chanced upon a trapper's cabin — that's how we got through the night."

With no provisions, the men were preparing to leave to walk out the next morning. But without the search party, and in the deteriorating conditions, the trek out into an endless, frozen world was a tragedy waiting to happen.

Why, Craig was asked later, does he put himself at additional risk? Isn't life here in this harsh climate tough enough without jeopardizing it further?

"I'll tell you," he said. "When I was a young fellow of just twenty-one, I went fishing with a friend called Joe Snow. We stayed in a cabin near a small lake to see what we could get and, you know, have a good time. I was in the kayak on the lake, going after brook trout. I lifted up a stringer full of fish — I think there were about fourteen of them. The stringer came untied from the kayak and the fish swam away. As I reached out for the stringer, I capsized the kayak.

"Joe had been standing in the doorway of the cabin, watching me. He dropped his coffee, ran for the aluminum boat on the shore, and rowed it the hundred feet or so to get to me — [it took] five minutes or less. Already I was so numbed with cold that I couldn't haul myself into the boat, and he couldn't pull me in without capsizing. So he tied a rope around one of my wrists and towed me to shore. Hypothermia? Oh, yeah. The lakes are always frigid. I knew I would have been a dead man within minutes if he'd not been there. Joe cranked up a good fire, put me in a down-filled sleeping bag, and I was okay. But I never forgot it — about how I was rescued. I knew what my fate would've been had Joe not been there.

"I wanted to do the same for others. When you put yourself out, even endanger yourself to rescue someone, it's almost like you've given life. It makes you feel you're doing some very worthwhile thing." He paused, grinned, then added, "It's easy to get into trouble here."

In 1984, three years after his own accident, Craig saw an advertisement in the local paper inviting people to become involved with the police in an auxiliary capacity. He remembered the time he was rescued from the lake, and thought that how he would really like to be trained to be able to rescue others who got into trouble. Without hesitation, he volunteered to become part of search and rescue, and was accepted into a training program* that would enable him to search for missing people in a wild and rugged terrain, where the climate is also unforgiving for a good part of each year. He undertook additional training so that, after a successful search, he would know how to resuscitate and revive the rescued. His intensive training qualified him to assist the local police on search-and-rescue calls.

For sixteen years, he has made himself available, put himself permanently on call for search and rescue. It has required him to be prepared to abandon whatever he is doing, regardless of whether it was work in the mines, his personal recreation, or his family life. He would drop everything, gear up and go to remote places to search for missing people or to recover those presumed to be dead. He understood he would often have to travel in the most difficult weather winter, to suffer extreme cold, possible frostbite and hypothermia, physical injury and exhaustion.

"To do rescue work has become my life's passion; there's no feeling quite like it in the world," he said. "Nothing makes my day like having a search coming to a successful conclusion, the missing person hugging their family when we get back to the command post."

He explained that young people in Labrador are familiar with the perils of their environment. They do not disregard them, but they refuse to let them deter their pursuit of recreational activities. They unconsciously absorb into their lives the hazards of extreme weather, temperature and isolation. But no matter how careful, no matter what

---

* Training for the volunteer search-and-rescue team includes forty hour of map and compass, winter survival with both in-class and outdoor sessions, St. John Ambulance standard first aid, CPR Level C, search patterns, casualty treatment and evacuation, evidence searches, helicopter and boating safety.

precautions they take, they know that accidents can easily happen and that unforeseen circumstances occur. They know, and still they play. What else can they do? The landscape and the climate will always be there. Young people will not remain indoors on a wintry night when the temperature falls to levels incompatible with the sustaining of life if it means forgoing a party, a hunting trip or a snowmobile venture in the great white outdoors. Many love the challenge, the beating of the odds, the physical thrill.

"For myself, I love this place," Craig says of Wabush in particular, and of Labrador in general. "My parents brought me here when I was six years old — and my three sisters and brother, of course. I've been here for thirty-six years, and I never want to leave.

"Here is everything a person could ever want in life. I have a good, steady job as an industrial mechanic in the nearby iron ore mines. I go fishing for lake and brook trout, sometimes for northern pike and ouaniniche [a landlocked species of salmon]. I hunt for rabbit, grouse, bear and caribou — never for sport, but to feed the family. We all go snowmobiling and get involved in all the sports here. It's a great life in the huge outdoors — lots of physical challenges, and big ones, too. What else could a person want? I don't think there is any place else like it in the world."

Labrador, the place for which Craig expresses such passion, is the northern territory of the province of Newfoundland. Labrador City and Wabush lie on the extreme western border, near Quebec. The bulk of this land, which covers some 293,339 square kilometres, is a vast wilderness. Here, it seems as if one can see forever. To the north, there is tundra, and to the south, vast timber stands. It is one of the last great wilderness areas of the earth, boasting towering mountain ranges, massive rock faces, huge lakes and teeming rivers. Wildlife runs free: moose, caribou, giant Arctic hares, lynx, polar bears, porcupines and wolves. Its remote nature insulates it from most forms of encroachment by modern society. It is an unforgiving place because of its very long and frigid winters and high snowfall, its harsh terrain and its extreme isolation.

When Craig speaks of sports, and the physical challenges that accompany it, he's referring to the excellent alpine and cross-country skiing, and particularly snowmobiling. The season for this activity is a very long one, and the wilderness trails are breathtaking and extensive. Few who have visited would dispute that this one of the earth's greatest and wildest of places.

Craig is at home in this harsh natural world, and he enjoys its challenges. But there is another dimension to his life that is distinct from his home, his work, and all his outdoor recreational pursuits: it is his volunteer search-and-rescue work for the Royal Newfoundland Constabulary. This year, Craig received the Lolly McGregor Volunteer of the Year Award from the town of Wabush as the person best exemplifying the spirit of volunteerism through his dedication and commitment.

A CHILD IS THE WORLD
Moncton, New Brunswick

It's like this: every day you have the people you love around you, is the best. Every time I see a child, I feel, "Gosh, he's okay…he's safe." — Lavell Merritt

The meeting was in full progress when Corporal Terry Higginson's pager beeped. Immediately he retrieved it from his gun belt — part of his Royal Canadian Mounted Police uniform.

"Child in Beaver Dam missing since five this afternoon…" He listened, leaned towards Stephen Moore and whispered, "I might be needing the search team. I'll let you know," and he was gone. The thirty members attending the monthly meeting of the York–Sunbury search-and-rescue team struggled to proceed through their agenda items on this warm summer night, but a certain level of tension had been raised, a half-expectancy that they might be called to a rescue — and that of a child.

Corporal Higginson contacted the Operational Communication Centre for more information as he drove home to pick up his search dog, Dar, and his SAR gear, then continued on towards the Beaver Dam sub-division that lay approximately eighteen kilometres outside Fredericton.

"I'm called first because I'm a Mountie and because I belong to the local search-and-rescue team. As well, I'm a search-dog handler," the corporal said. "I thought I'd probably need the SAR team — it was serendipity that all its members were together at the meeting, but when the

RCMP calls for the dog handler, I like to go on my own to the site first. I need to find out if there is a track for this person, and to get all the important information in detail. Only then will I know if I'll need the SAR team. I also wanted to see how many people were there already — to speak to the mother and to learn about the boy. It was also getting late in the day — I think somewhere between seven and eight in the evening."

★

Susie Stockton* sat in front of the television, engrossed in a soap opera. The room felt warm, so she got up to close the blinds against the afternoon sun that streamed in the windows. From time to time she glanced through the slats to make sure that her four-year-old son was there: yes, on his bike, dawdling in slow circles about the driveway and the unfenced grass beside it, talking to his kitten. *Lost in his own little world, as usual*, thought his mother, smiling. He was a good kid, happy to spend hours out there, on his bike or playing with the cat. Her own mother, Gwen, was just in the next room, sitting at the kitchen table, playing solitaire and smoking. An hour, two hours slipped by — Susie could not remember the exact time when she next looked out the window — perhaps four or five o'clock. The child's bike was there, but not the boy. And there was no sign of the kitten. The silence of the forest that crouched close all around the house suddenly seemed menacing; the only sounds, of a frog croaking and the roar of trucks on the distant highway — emphasized the hush. She ran outside and called, and called again.

"Ritchie... Ritchie... Where are you? Come back inside... *Ritchie, where are you?*" She ran around to the back of the house, to the edge of trees. It seemed to her then that the great hardwood forest stood mocking her, its trees leaning close as if reaching to touch the walls of her house.

No reply came to the increasingly frantic mother and grandmother: Gwen — not old, but stooped — walked up and down the gravelled driveway that led to the street and the subdivision proper, all the while calling to

---

* Susie Stockton, Gwen and Ritchie are pseudonyms.

her grandson. Susie phoned her neighbour, then all her friends and relatives, asking them to help her search for her boy. The late-summer sun was slipping slowly towards its horizon; night would soon be encroaching. Susie picked up the phone and dialled 911.

The Stockton house was one of two homes that at the dead end of a lonely road about a kilometre from a secondary highway. Each house seemed carved out of the forest, as if part of the lush, green world of hardwood trees, water and boggy marshland that overlay rock and shale. A place where reeds and willows dangled over frog ponds, swamp and pools of stagnant water. These rippling surfaces reflected branches of spruce, pine and maple, and of alder so dense as to make the forest almost impenetrable. Bird and insect life flitted about like the boy himself, roaming the creeping stillness, exploring hollow places in tree trunks where lived all the little people — trolls and elves and pixies — before falling asleep beneath an overhanging branch. Perhaps they, too, dreamt uneasy dreams of lurking black bears, coyotes or foxes...

Terry arrived at the Stockton home, astonished at the number of people milling about. He was disappointed; they had contaminated the area for Dar, who would find it harder now to follow the boy's scent. Many of the people had already gone off into the woods, both on foot and astride all-terrain vehicles. He stood looking about him: where was the mother? He needed to talk to her. Susie and Gwen were wandering the driveway, fear etched on their faces, their postures betraying a sense of helplessness. Short, stocky Susie constantly ran her hands through her thick chestnut hair while repeating, "He's only four... so little..." In answer to Terry's questions, she said, "Oh, he's about three feet high; thick, chestnut hair like mine; brown eyes... I saw him out here in the driveway on his bike... he doesn't wander off — not usually..."

She recalled that Ritchie had been chasing his kitten all afternoon, and guessed that this might be the reason he'd gone into the woods. There stood the abandoned bike in the driveway, close to the house... no sign of the kitten. Susie was on verge of tears, with a vacant look in her eyes — that of a person deep in thought, someone desperately trying to recall events. "My boy was fearful of the dark, afraid of the woods," she said. "He's not comfortable there by himself. I know his fears... it hurts me that he might be in there all by himself."

Terry knew now that he needed the SAR team, and he picked up his mobile phone.

Stephen answered. "We'll organize ourselves and get there as soon as we can," he said. While waiting for the team, Terry began an initial search around the house with Dar, then behind it and through patches of nearby woods. He searched abandoned vehicles that had been junked on the uncultivated land behind the house and picked through all the small junk piles. He didn't bother to try for a track, because there were too many people out in the woods. "RCMP dogs track only to the freshest scent," he said.

Terry's call to the SAR team had reached them while their meeting was still in progress. The meeting ended abruptly, a rendezvous point was arranged, and then began a race to get home to collect search gear: a flashlight, warm clothes, compass, GPS, maps, boots, hard hats, rain suits, food, water — all that is needed to make a searcher self-sufficient for twelve hours. Once reconvened, the convoy of cars turned off the highway at Lord Road, then headed towards a subdivision that spread itself out across both sides of the road. A few local businesses appeared among the neat rows of small houses — a residential area surrounded by a dense hard and softwood forest. Then they turned onto the lonely gravelled road that led to the two houses at its end.

"A two-hour period is normally required to prepare for a search," said Stephen, "but we accomplished this in just under one." He picked up the cube van used as a command post, and it was here that the search was planned and the base of communications was established. Attached to the truck was a utility trailer that held equipment: tents, a generator, portable radio, compasses, redi-packs, a string X box (a measuring device), flagging tape and first-aid kits. With the command post organized in this way, the SAR group knew it was self-sufficient while at the search site.

The team parked its vehicles in the driveway and immediately fired up the generator, lit up the area, set up a tent and got the propane heaters going. It was after ten in the evening before everything had been set up, and thirty-five searchers organized.

"We had to understand the family, the little boy, his habits," Stephen said. "But you know, you hear different stories: this kid's mother told us her child didn't mind going through the woods, that he had been there with an uncle the week before. And when he did go, he usually stuck to the trails — he didn't usually wander off. We asked what he looked like, about his health, what he wore (a blue T-shirt with a teddy bear imprint on it; brown shorts) and what he carried with him — perhaps candy wrappers — anything to give us a clue. Did he have experience in the woods? Was the bike missing? When and where exactly did the mother last see him? When did she notice him missing?"

Corporal Higginson searched the house a second time. He went out with a team for an initial quick search, taking with him the boy's uncle, two SAR people and his dog. Together they combed some of the trails, calling to the boy as they skirted bog and marshy ground and trampled through thick forest undergrowth.

Meanwhile, the SAR team members busied themselves by planning the technical details of the operation. The question of where to search first was based on what they thought had happened, taking into account statistical likelihoods as well as knowledge of the child and their gut feelings. They broke up the entire area into manageable segments and assigned each a grade based on the probability of finding the boy there.

SAR members knew the statistics: that it was unlikely a child this young would wander beyond about five hundred metres from his home. They cordoned off sections of the wooded area all about, using datum lines.

"A datum line is used to divide up each segment, making the whole area easier to search," Stephen said. "We use a compass to run the line — to make sure it's straight — and a string X box to lay out a visible line — a piece of string — from point A to B. Each team is given responsibility to search their portion of the forest. We marked off one, then another and another, assigning them to well-rehearsed search teams. Other members were organized to work the trails deeper into the forest, and beyond in all-terrain vehicles."

The Department of Natural Resources arrived with updated maps of the area and brought all-terrain vehicles to help search beyond the immediate area where the child was thought most likely to be. In due course, the Red Cross would also arrive.

The woods posed a number of dangers to a small boy on his own — including black bears and a coyote or two — but the most serious potential threat lay in the very topography of the area.

"The woods are very dense, very thick with undergrowth, the kind you have to fight your way through — very unforgiving," Terry said. "You can get tangled up in it, especially at night, and get snared by dead undergrowth. As well, New Brunswick is very rocky: beneath a thin layer of soil lies shale — sharp and cutting. You might twist your ankle, cut your hands, your feet…"

How far could a small boy walk in eight hours? A kilometre, perhaps a little more; it was possible, but not likely, that he might have crossed over from the confined area — across a railway line or a road. The searchers fanned out over their assigned areas, some to search abandoned cars, small buildings attached to houses, old sheds, rusting cars lying about and abandoned wells that lay behind the houses. The corporal, who had already scouted about, had discovered these wells.

"Need to check them all," he said to Stephen, and immediately a group converged on one and then another and another. All were found to be poorly covered with boards that could easily be removed. Still no child and no kitten.

The summer night was upon them, the temperature hovering about fifteen degrees. Some SAR members walked the forest on foot, covering both the narrow paths as well as the four-wheeler trails that crisscrossed the forest. Each group took with it a string box — containing string like a fishing line — that showed them how far they had travelled, and members marked the way with flagging tape so that they would know where they'd been, and where they would emerge — echoes of Hansel and Gretel and their trail of bread crumbs.

A local woman approached Stephen at the command post to tell him she had seen the boy near the frog pond that lay right off the road leading into the subdivision — "Three o'clock it was when I saw him," she said. As always, this highlighted the perennial difficulty confronting a searcher: the mother's assertion that her son wouldn't leave the trails, while a neighbour reports spotting him near the frog pond.

"I mean, it's easy for the kid to walk to the frog pond. I know I saw him there," this neighbour said. Her insistence that she had sighted the boy there changed the focus of the search. Groups went again to examine the wells, others strode off to the frog pond, while several re-examined the trails around the home.

The boy had left his bike behind. And his kitten was missing... Did he go chasing his cat?

"Well, he's been known to follow it around," said Susie. "Tinker — she was a new kitten... He loved her... I guess it went missing and he chased after it."

The blackness of a near-rural night, illuminated only by the lights powered by the SAR team's generator, enveloped them all. Seventy-five people had been out for hours searching for the child. Included among them were professional volunteer searchers, local people, employees of the Department of Natural Resources, and members of the RCMP and the local volunteer fire department. After the neighbour claimed she had seen the child near the frog pond, firemen worked for the remainder of the night to drain it in case the child had fallen in. The body of water measured forty feet by sixty.

"The local people were potential casualties themselves," said Stephen. "They don't know what they're looking for, and they can unknowingly remove evidence. When they come, we register them, see that they are dressed properly and make sure they know what they are looking for. We do have the Red Cross here to look after them, but not until after twelve hours have passed — that's when they come, those are the rules. Also, we can't get any additional resources without clearance from the RCMP — that's why volunteer SAR has to be self-sufficient for up to twelve hours."

Terry Higginson came back to the house in the middle of the night to find perhaps forty to fifty people still milling about. They had continued to pour down the street and to the house, some bringing their dogs.

"Here's my dog — he can help search for the little boy."

"My dog — he knows how to find people."

"No. I'm sorry, but you can't," Higginson said firmly. "It contaminates the area for me. Thank you for offering, but your dog has no background in searching and I need you to take him off site."

"They are not trained search dogs," Terry later explained. "People think that just because they are dogs they can search."

Terry now had to rest Dar. He also needed to liaise with the official search team and update them as to his progress. He saw that the Red Cross had arrived, that more people kept coming, and that volunteers were returning for water and rest. Then he went out into the night again. First he searched once more near the front lawn of the house, then conducted a more detailed investigation of the area close by, where a creek ran through — a patch of ground that was very wet — like a bog. An hour passed, and another. He found nothing.

For the other SAR team members, the night also passed without clues of any kind. Between five and six in the morning, they began returning to the command post, exhausted. Each shift lasted for twelve hours, after which other searchers were to be brought in to relieve the first group.

In the early hours of the morning, before faint streaks in the sky heralded the dawn of a new day, Stephen called in two other search teams. "There are twelve other teams in all, consisting of five hundred and fifty volunteers," he explained. "All are trained in SAR. I called on the four closest teams and put them on standby because I thought I might need their help. I asked could they get here seven-thirty. They, in turn, called their members and arranged to get them to the site."

By eight in the morning, amid the rustling of the woods and loud birdsong, another benign sunny day dawned, but one belying a sorrowful scene on a small, dead-end street outside Fredericton. Someone had turned on a radio, and news of war, hurricanes and floods spilled from it. No sign of those here. The most important topic in these parts was the little boy had been lost in a vast, lonely forest where paths led every which way. Everyone present could relate to the little boy's fear, to his pain and abandonment, more easily than to the misery of strangers on other continents where catastrophe seemed a continual state of affairs.

No one had slept — not the family, the neighbours, the exhausted search team members, or the extra fifty searchers at the site. Some of the original SAR members — many of them cut by stinging nettles and bruised by low-hanging branches — stayed, while others went home. In view of their lack of success at finding any clues, Terry decided that an aerial search was needed, and he called for a helicopter from the RCMP. None was available. He approached the Department of National Defence and asked for the use of their chopper. Success. By nine, it was droning over the tops of the trees. He then returned to the woods once more with Dar. An hour passed, and another.

Eleven o'clock: the morning was passing by and, as the search proceeded, anxiety and fear for the little boy grew. A frantic mother and grandmother could be found sobbing on the steps of their home. The child's uncle — indefatigable, tight-lipped and silent — tirelessly accompanied the SAR members. But they had been this way before, fighting with the trees and dense undergrowth, calling to Ritchie until their voices were hoarse — so far, to no avail.

But wait... Was that a sound? So very faint. They stopped. They called out. A tiny voice responded. The group thrashed through the trees in the direction of the sound, and finally found a small boy, curled up at the base of a tree, clutching his kitten and a stuffed toy. He was only six hundred metres from his home.

A neighbour, Robert D., saw him first, a tiny figure curled up beneath an overhanging branch. "He was asking us who we were; he said he wouldn't come out until we'd given our names!" Robert said. "I fought my way to him. I was yelling and shaking... That kid — he asked for our names before he would come out.

"I couldn't believe we'd found him. I have an eight-year old boy, so this hit very close to home. It was a huge relief that he hadn't been kid-napped. We're like one big family when it comes to things like this."

Ritchie had suffered nothing more than shock, confusion and a few bug bites. Why had he not responded to the calls to him?

"He could have been asleep, or too afraid to answer, not knowing who was calling him," Stephen said.

"Yes. It's typical of young kids that they don't respond when you call," Terry confirmed. "They're often afraid of being in trouble and not sure of the reaction they'll get. Ritchie was certainly glad to be home, although he looked surprised to see so many strangers at his house. He became subdued. He explained he had gone looking for his kitten, had followed it deeper and deeper into the woods. He told how his grand-father once told him to stay put under a tree if he ever found himself lost in the woods. No, he said, he wasn't scared, not really... He'd used his stuffed animal as a pillow and bedded down for the night under a hang-ing branch, his kitten in his arms. Then his eyes brightened and he said, 'I met a bear and had to punch him in the nose... then a fox came after me and I tripped it up!'"

"The most wonderful feeling in the world," exclaimed Susie, reaching out her arms for her child.

"Now we've got our lives back," said Gwen.

"So often search-and-rescue people are confronted at the end of their search by death and mutilation," said Stephen. "But not this time. This was perfect."

More than a hundred people had helped in this protracted search, one that included the York-Sunbury, Hoyt, Tri-County, Carleton, River Valley and Charlotte County SAR organizations, the RCMP, the Red Cross, the Department of National Defence, the Maryland Volunteer Fire Department, and friends, relatives and neighbours.

"It's always a very good feeling to find someone and get them back to their family," Terry said. "While there is a satisfied sense when you catch a person who has wronged someone else, this has an added dimension — doing something for another person who feels devastated and helpless because they're missing their loved one."

Stephen Moore says of his involvement with volunteer search-and-rescue work: "When you are involved in it, you're always very focused and anxious; your adrenaline pumps and a sense of urgency drives you. Family and neighbours come to you begging for information and help — but you're the one who needs the information! Our York-Sunbury group was formed twenty-one years ago after an incident where the RCMP needed searchers to help locate a missing person. We got a group together, the first group in the province, and here we are all these years later."

Terry explained that police like to maintain close links with the local SAR volunteer group. Working closely together has promoted a good relationship between them.

Terry also particularly prizes the work he does with his search dog, Dar, an eight-year-old male German shepherd purchased and owned by the RCMP. Dar lives with Terry and his family, and the corporal says, "I've trained two previous working dogs for the RCMP, and I can honestly say that Dar had been by far the best of the three, the closest canine partner I've had the honour of working with. Our bonds run very deep — and would be impossible to break.

"Right now I'm training a new police service dog because Dar has developed some medical problems and I know his time as a police dog is coming to an end. Long ago, my wife, two boys and I decided that when this happens, we will keep Dar with us as a pet until the end of his time. He's a great dog in every way: a dedicated working dog, well balanced, very sociable and a really great working partner — the best."

According to Terry, the RCMP obtained Dar in the former Czechoslovakia in 1996. This isn't unusual; the force routinely searches the globe for working dogs. "It costs a lot to raise dogs like this, and there's a worldwide shortage of such good working dogs." Animals are selected carefully for courage and for versatility. "Our dogs can search for missing persons, can track, get involved in criminal apprehension, search crime scenes... Some, like Dar, can detect explosives and do narcotics work — this is different from the many that can do only one thing.

"I've been working with dogs since 1993. It puts me on twenty-four-hour call, but I find it amazing to be able to communicate with an animal. You can't do it verbally, so you use body language, commands, understanding of how they react to certain situations... One of my favourite things is to work with my dog to find missing people, whether Alzheimer patients, suicidal people... there is always someone worried about this person, and it's a great feeling to be able to help them."

Corporal Terry Higginson and Dar.

Left to right: Wayne Dowling, Kenny Fraser, Lorne Calvert.

THE RIME OF THE
ANCIENT LIFEBOAT COXSWAIN
Louisbourg, Nova Scotia

And now there came both mist and snow,
And it grew wondrous cold:
And ice, mast high, came floating by
As green as emerald.
       — Samuel Taylor Coleridge, "The Rime of the Ancient Mariner"

"Afterwards, this fellow comes up and says to me, 'If my son was on your boat and something woulda happened because of the icing situation, there woulda been someone having to answer a few questions.'

"I said to him, I said, 'It's like this: what if your son had been on that fishing boat? What if I never went out — then who would be asking the questions?' The fellow couldn't answer; he had nothing to say to that. For me, I go out when I'm called. I do what I can to the best of my abilities, and I hope and pray to God everything will be all right. Knock on wood, I haven't lost anybody yet — but it's not to say it couldn't happen."

Wayne Dowling is an old man of the sea: for thirty-two years he has served on the Coast Guard lifeboat station on the rocky coast around Louisbourg on Cape Breton Island. As he had done this day, he sets out in his little lifeboat to face the wrath of the Atlantic Ocean, when all other boats make haste for safe harbour.

It is February 21, 2001. Wayne stands at the window of the trailer that functions as a Coast Guard lifeboat station. He's a short, stocky man with a receding hairline; there's the look of the ancient mariner about him. The ocean laps gently close by, a placid North Atlantic that at this moment is largely free of ice. The rocks that guard the entrance to the harbour stand silhouetted in the soft morning light. This tranquil scene belies the extremity of the cold temperature outdoors, a frigidity that blankets Cape Breton Island, immobilizing the landscape into a peculiar stillness. *The infamous calm before the storm,* Wayne thinks afterwards. He muses about other times, about storms that had thrust the sea almost to the trailer door. The station has had few calls this winter — and none today: few vessels, aside from the occasional fishing boat, would venture upon the sea in these temperatures. At four in the afternoon he closes the station. He and his crew retreat home, pagers in their pockets in the event of a call.

It is dinner time — 6:17 p.m. — when the Rescue Co-ordination Centre in Halifax intrudes upon the Dowlings' evening.

"Sixty-five-foot fishing vessel, the *I. V.Y.*, has radioed that they have steering problems… having trouble staying on course. Have only the use of their emergency steering. Will the lifeboat crew go out and assist."

Just another call to rescue, but what a call! And what a night! Wayne learns that the fishing boat is far out on the ocean, close to the banks of St. Pierre, one of the Magdalen Islands eighty or more miles from Louisbourg. The captain is using emergency steering — "Someone's in the back end of the boat with a tiller stick," Wayne says. At this point he has nothing more to go on.

Other crew members drop their activities, bid a quick farewell to their families and hasten to the station: Wayne Dowling, Lorne Calvert, Kenny Fraser and James Bates. They greet each other silently, then simultaneously spring to action to prepare the lifeboat — the forty-four-foot *Spindrift* — for the frigid conditions and a long tow. A mere twenty minutes from the time of their summons, they are on their way to the rescue of the large fishing boat. The coastal waters lie calm as they leave the station, the wind to stern, but the thermometer reads minus-50 degrees Celsius. Yes, there is a heated cabin, and heated window panels with windshield wipers that move briskly back and forth, but a chilled area around them leaves only a four-inch hole in each panel through which the pilot can see.

At the halfway point, conditions change abruptly: the sea has reared itself up in spitting green fury and the lifeboat lunges, rocks, dips and flies on the crests and valleys of the rocking waves. Crew members look at each other in silence; they know they have a further thirty to forty miles yet to travel in this manner to reach the stricken fishing vessel. This is going to be quite a night.

"A storm comes up and it begins to blow like the dickens," Wayne says. And so begins an ordeal of a kind the crew has seldom endured in all their years of rescue work.

"I feel for these fellas," Wayne says. "I was a fisherman once." He stands at the wheel, straining to see through the frost buildup, rubbing his hands for warmth, straining again to see. He notes that ice is beginning to accumulate on deck and the boat is starting to list. Winds howl, waves slap up against the hull, water and sea spray thrash over decks, ice floes crunch and the boat increases its listing. Another hour passes, and another, yet it feels like no time at all.

The darkness of night has long since swallowed up any glimpse of the watery landscape, and six hours elapse before the fishing vessel is sighted. The men cheer. In the gloom, Wayne struggles to manoeuvre the lifeboat alongside the larger vessel. His men are on deck, grabbing at the railings to keep upright — and on board as they prepare to throw a tow line to the

The Canadian Coast Guard's Arun lifeboat, Spindrift, *after its rescue of the fishing boat* I.V.Y.

fishing vessel. The decks are slick with ice, the sea is thrusting, and the men are almost blinded by sea spray as the line is thrown. It arcs up and across the howling space between the boats. Arms are outstretched as it flies across, landing right on the deck of the crippled vessel! It is snatched up by a waiting fisherman and attached. Again the sound of cheering erupts, and then begins the long and crippling trek back to shore in the implacable cold. Like a tiny tugboat pulling a giant tanker to dock, the lifeboat lugs the large fishing vessel towards the safety of the shore.

On the way back, more ice accumulates on deck and around the windshields of the lifeboat. The seas are still high. Then, abruptly, the lifeboat's engines stall.

"Something — maybe a plastic bag — is wound around the pro-pellers, binding them up tight and stalling the engines," Wayne will later explain. "We have no steering, no power." A struggle that is to last two hours has just begun. Wayne pushes the engine into reverse, then drive, back and forth, until, just as suddenly, the foreign object seems to come free, the engines turn over and the lifeboat plows ahead.

Wayne now looks with alarm at his boat's worsening list, which has become so severe that the little lifeboat is almost on its side. He knows that he and his crew are in imminent jeopardy, so he tries to reach Sydney's Coast Guard radio station to ask for help.

Sydney can hear him, but Wayne doesn't know this because his radio is not receiving properly. With increasing frustration he tries to make himself heard, to send out messages for help. His vessel is now almost completely iced up and is listing at an angle of twenty to thirty degrees; he has slowed to a crawl. Nothing to do now but send his three crewmen on deck with wooden mallets to clear the ice — a treacherous business on the steeply sloping decks in the bitter cold. As the men attend to the task, they look like they're from another planet: three orange-clad aliens, banging with mallets on a frozen surface.

Ice has now formed on the water, the chunks resembling thick islands that surround the lifeboat, which is still twenty-six miles from home. The *Spindrift* struggles on in silence, fear in the hearts of her crew. The men are afraid for themselves *and* for the fishing vessel. Suddenly, they let out a cheer as a shape looms up ahead: it is the Coast Guard's icebreaker *Sir William Alexander*, which now comes alongside.

"We're doing all right," Wayne radios laconically, "but we'd like you to go ahead and take some of the heat off us, bear the brunt of the storm. We'll ride behind you…" The icebreaker does just this: it forges a path for the lifeboat through a rough sea of ice and storm.

Louisbourg looms ahead, as noon approaches. The crew of the lifeboat has endured nine hours of towing in the bitter sea. The ice-breaker and the lifeboat approach the harbour shoal buoy. The *Sir William Alexander* is no longer needed, so it stands down and continues on to Sydney to resume its icebreaking work in the harbour there. Wayne begins shortening up the tow lines. "We have two big lines together — one six hundred feet, the other nine hundred," he says. "Fifteen hundred feet altogether. There's a shackle between the two of them, but one of them must have taken the other line down when we were backing up. I'm about to go ahead when one line gets stuck in the propeller. I'm stalled. I try to tow the *I.V.Y.* with one engine, but can't manoeuvre. I find myself having to radio the *Sir William Alexander* to ask it to please turn back and help me — and I'm only half a mile from shore! The thing is, with one propeller and engine working, I'm steering and handling the boat myself, but as soon as I take the fishing boat in tow — and because of his rudder angle, to starboard — he can't steer. I can't manoeuvre, and the fishing boat just keeps going around in circles."

Wayne lets the line go and asks the *Sir William Alexander* to tow it into Louisbourg's harbour. When the icebreaker gets as close as its size allows, another fishing vessel takes over and tows the *Spindrift* to dock. "First time in my life I ever had a rope in my [propeller] blade," Wayne says.

For this rescue, Wayne Dowling receives the Commissioner's Commendation "in recognition of your outstanding efforts… [Y]our professionalism and dedication exemplify the finest tradition of the Canadian Coast Guard."

★

A man and his crew have little fear of heavy ice buildup on the decks of their lifeboat to the point of its capsizing, have little fear of perishing in the extreme cold of icy seas — but they fear a summer storm. The one on July 5, 1979, was no ordinary storm — "Never seen the likes of it before," local people said, their voices full of awe as they spoke of the big seas that thrashed the coast, swamped the government dock and all but obliterated the entire landscape the day the little lifeboat went out from Louisbourg to the rescue of a fishing boat and towed it to safety. The winds blew up to sixty or seventy knots (seventy to eighty miles per hour), and torrents of rain and thunderstorms punished the east coast of Cape Breton Island. A local fishing vessel was out longlining in that storm when its engines failed. The pilot's father, and the crew of the Coast Guard's lifeboat, both set out on the seething seas to bring them in. The question was, would any of them return?

"When I left that day, light winds were called for and the outlook good," George Le Moine, owner of the fishing boat *Lady Marilyn*, said. "Lovely day when we went out. We set our gear — about eight miles of it — longlining for cod. We set our lines at night and planned to haul them in next morning — you have to let it soak awhile. It took us a whole day to haul it, and our three-man crew had begun at daybreak. All was going well until one of the crew heard a radio broadcast from Sydney radio — they'd revised the weather forecast."

George didn't pay much attention. "When they change a forecast, they just step it up a bit," he said. And this was July, he might have added, not a time of the year when you expect high winds and storms.

"Then we heard another forecast — winds to blow up to fifteen to twenty knots, and next thing they're telling us it's up to thirty," he said. "When they call for high winds like this, you don't take any chances — you head back in. The wind was hitting elsewhere — we could see it. We anchored out our lines and marked them with a buoy so we could retrieve them some other time, and then we prepared to head in.

"All of the vessels were starting to get in," George said. "You could almost see the wind coming, at fifty to sixty miles an hour from the southeast. We came closer to shore, where the sea depth is only about thirty to fifty fathoms — not a lot of water — and it makes it much rougher the closer you get in. The wind was behind us and the seas got big — thirty- to forty-foot waves — and our boat was only forty feet. I had to slow her down. What happened was, she tossed around so much she stirred up my fuel tanks, stirred up dirt or rust — anything that was in the tank — and plugged up the line. I tried to clear it, but I ended up twisting the fuel line clean from the tank. No way I could fix this."

In this freak storm, the winds shifted, now coming from the southwest, but this did nothing to improve conditions. George tried to guide his boat away from shore and run parallel to it. But high winds and tide fast blew him towards it. Worried now, he threw over his anchor, then he added the trawl anchors as well, about seven in total. Like a leering devil the fretted coast of Cape Breton loomed: jagged, slick and menacing. George saw other fishing boats hastening to the safety of the shore — among them his own father in his sixty-foot fishing vessel. At the mercy of a violent and shallow sea, and feeling very nervous now, George radioed the Coast Guard.

"We're about dead in the water," he told the Regional Control Centre in Halifax. "Fuel line's off, and we have no power." George's father heard this broadcast, turned around and headed straight back out to sea to help rescue his son. At the same moment, the Coast Guard lifeboat headed into the storm to help the fishing boat.

"I had the throttle wide open, gave it whatever it could do," said Wayne Dowling, the coxswain of the lifeboat. "I had the engines right to the floor of our boat — the Canadian Coast Guard 118. That guy was soon to be up on the rocks."

On the shore, and all over the government dock, people stood to observe the drama of a freak summer storm. They would have noticed that the lighthouse was invisible, obscured by the waves. "Never seen such big seas," they said. They saw that the government wharf, too, lay completely covered in water.

The spectators watched the lifeboat and its crew set out on the water, a blip upon a thrashing sea. Its engines roared and it seemed to jump right out of the water.

"That fishing boat in trouble — it stood four miles out from shore," Wayne said. "But when we got to it, it was just two hundred feet from the rocks — very close. In big trouble, it was. We made it out to them fast as we could."

George, frightened for himself and his crew, and worried about his father, felt an even greater fear as one of the crew of the lifeboat stood, about to throw a heaving line.

"They had to get very close to us because the line had to be hauled in by hand," he said. "With the waves so high, I got scared they were going to crash down and go right through us."

One boat stood on the crest of a wave thirty to forty feet above, the other in its trough. "The wave could hit our boat and push it to one side," George said. "We tried to go head-on through the waves; we looked up at the lifeboat from very far below — looked up and saw one giant green fist of a wave that could knock us sideways, that could come right through us... That lifeboat crew, they had to watch that they didn't hit us, had to watch out to avoid all our anchors, and at the same time, get the towline aboard us."

Crew member William Hunt, drenched and buffeted by wind and waves as he slithered about the bow of the lifeboat, waited for that split second when the lifeboat was roughly on the same level as the fishing vessel, when one was on the upswing and the other on a downswing. It was only then he had a chance to throw — and he had but one chance: if he missed, he wouldn't get another. The fishing boat would be on the rocks. Out of the corner of his eye he saw them: jagged, rocky outcrops that loomed ever closer, their vessels on a forward gallop towards this terrible horizon.

William made a monkey fist (the end knot for a heaving line). He waited, then threw.

"We got him first throw!" exalted the crew. A *Lady Marilyn* crewmember grabbed the small line and pulled it in.

"They were just holding on for dear life," Wayne said. "If we hadn't made good on that first throw, their boat would have been blown on the rocks. They were in the surf, and we couldn't have got into it — not where they were. Very lucky for him, it was. We were out on the sea, where the waves stood at thirty to forty feet, and I was afraid of pulling the fishing boat under while we were towing — I was really afraid this time," he said. "I'm climbing a wave, like scaling a mountaintop, and cutting down the power so I don't drag him under by pulling his bow down. He could have had all his windows smashed out... his boat could've sunk right under. And I had to keep my engines running at half-speed just to keep head to the wind."

The captain of the *Lady Marilyn*, once the tow line was attached, had to abandon all his anchors — anchors that hadn't even hooked the ocean bottom, so fast was the drift. He marked them with a buoy, so that he might return at a later date and retrieve them.

The lifeboat first pulled the fishing boat off the land a little and towed it out from shore. On board the *Lady Marilyn*, George worried that the brute force of wind and wave would pull the cleat right off his boat — or the lifeboat. "With that much wind and that much strain... if you think you're going to be hit hard, you slow your boat right down, but I had no control over that once I was under tow. We had to take everything that was coming back at us: no steering, no engine power... there was one time when one of my crew stood on the north side of the wheelhouse and I stood on the other. The wind just picked him up and threw him right across the deck. He landed in a chair, and he crushed it.

"The wind — never seen anything like it in all the years I've been at the station," Wayne said. "I couldn't see the lighthouse when I was coming in, even when I was close up." The coxswain now had trouble pulling the fishing boat in because of winds that blew straight to shore. Unable to tow directly into the harbour, he had to beat a path up — offshore — and to the left of the harbour, keeping the wind to portside. "We had to go in at an angle, run up off the shore, then turn into the harbour," he said. "We were afraid of capsizing, afraid of towing and having the heavy seas beat the wheelhouse off the boat we had under tow. Very heavy seas, they were."

He mused afterwards that perhaps he and his crew should not have gone out that time, should not have been in that storm. Could he have refused? When a call to a rescue appears as a potentially risky one, he asks his crewmembers are they willing to go out. Invariably they answer yes. If one refuses, another can always be found. But this has never happened: no one has ever refused. Wayne has never refused.

"Some days I think I will just pack my bag and go get a land job," he said. "But here I am, still doing a job I love.

"You get an adrenaline rush — know what I mean?" he says. "You say to yourself, 'Maybe I can go and save this person.' You get worked up, your adrenaline pumps and you just go. Everything worked out fine; I'd go back and do it again."

Wayne Dowling and his crew — William Hunt and Harold Fudge — received personal commendation from the Commissioner of the

Canadian Coast Guard for their efforts in this rescue. "I was most impressed with the report of your valiant effort… when the three of you saved three lives… under particularly difficult conditions," he wrote.

"Your unflinching devotion to duty and excellent seamanship was well demonstrated by that fact that the lifeboat set out in sixty-knot winds and high seas… such exemplary service prompts the whole-hearted admiration of your colleagues within the Canadian Coast Guard, and commands the esteem of the seafaring community at large… My personal commendation for a job well done."

★

Wayne Dowling lives with his wife close to the Mira River, near New Boston. He has a son, a daughter and three grandchildren. Clocking in thirty-two years' service with the Coast Guard, he is one of the oldest search-and-rescue workers in eastern Canada.

A WALK IN THE WOODS
O'Leary, Prince Edward Island

The warm August day dawned like so many others, but Sam Cornish was nowhere to be found. No one saw him on the street, greeting his neighbours as he habitually did, or picking up bottles from the road-sides. No sign of him driving around in his truck. Later, they said that he had hidden himself in the woods behind his house. It was the morning after his grandson's wedding, and he would have known his son Billy had come looking for him to say farewell. The family understood: Billy lived far away in Ontario. Sam, elderly now, would have been unsure when — or *if* — he would see his boy again. Best not to hang around to say goodbye.

His indomitable wife, Aletha, had been busy, what with post-wedding events and the many generations of the family around. She last saw Sam shuffle his way across the garden behind the house and head towards the woods beyond, axe in hand. She guessed it to be somewhere around seven-thirty in the morning. At the time she didn't think anything of it; this is what her husband of fifty-five years did after breakfast — when he wasn't walking in the village or splitting wood, he would take a walk in the woods.

The interior of the white, two-storey wooden house that stood beside the main street still hummed with family members, all here for the wedding — many more were at daughter Mae's home a short distance away. At about eight-thirty, Mae received a phone call from her mom to say that Sam had gone for a walk and had not returned. This seemed rather a long time — longer than usual for him to be gone. Mae immediately called all the family and asked them to begin a hunt for Sam. Soon the news spread throughout the small village of O'Leary that Sam was missing. They came to help; everybody knew and loved old Sam.

Children and grandchildren walked about the half-acre of woods and fields that made up part of the Cornish property, all the while calling to Sam. Some looked in the outbuildings: barn, garage, doghouse and a shed for tools and equipment. Others phoned the neighbours to see if he'd been visiting and been waylaid. They drove to all the places they thought he might conceivably be, and to Carleton, Lot 6 — the place where Sam had grown up. Still others stood shielding their eyes against the blazing sun to scan the vacant lot next door and the woods beyond. No response. And no Sam.

"Granddad didn't come to the dance after the reception — maybe he wasn't feeling well," said one of the many grandchildren irrelevantly.

"He said he was just too old," said another. "His knees were bothering him."

Mae, a public-health nurse, considered the probabilities: her father was in his eighties, arthritic and sometimes quite forgetful — "possibly early Alzheimer's," the doctor had said recently. It was a hot, humid day — "enough to get you soaking wet after the slightest exertion," said someone. Mae guessed that her father would be wearing very warm clothing, as he habitually did — "a bit chilly in the early mornings," he'd said. This gave her something else to consider: Sam could have been suffering from heat stroke or dehydration. All agreed that proper help must be sought immediately, and Aletha picked up the phone to call the RCMP.

Billy and his family, meanwhile, had been driving back home to Ontario. They reached Fredericton and phoned to see if Sam had been found. When the reply was negative, Billy turned the car around to return the way they had just come.

★

The small town of Alberton lies next to the village of O'Leary, and it is here that the local police — L Division of the Royal Canadian Mounted Police, staffed by ten constables and two corporals — are located. On this sultry Sunday, the unit's dispatcher listened to an anxious voice relating that old Sam Cornish had been missing from his home since about seven-thirty or eight this morning. "The family and local people have searched, and can't find him anywhere. Even if he takes his cane with him, he can't walk very far, what with the arthritis in his knees," said the caller.

Constable Scott Stevenson, general investigator and search manager, and volunteer search manager Mike DesRoches were alerted, and they officially called out the volunteer ground search-and-rescue team and drove to the Cornish home. Once there, they found large numbers of neighbours, friends and family members — some crying, all frantically searching and praying. Not long afterwards, the volunteer search-and-rescue team arrived.

Stevenson was ultimately responsible for the conduct of the search, but he relied heavily on his civilian counterpart, DesRoches, who was one of the few trained search managers on the island. Together, the two set up a command post on the vacant lot next door, then went to work out of the back of their truck. They set up a table, spread out maps, and interviewed the family about Sam and his habits. Where did they last see him? Where might he go, and why? How long would he be gone? What was he wearing? How was his health? How far could he walk? How easily could he get lost? Is a recent photo available?

"Sam would go for a walk in the mornings," offered Aletha, describing how his slight figure would be seen in the garden (how he loved it!), then along the street chatting with his neighbours. Daughter Jean said he spent much time splitting wood, then stacking it in a wood-pile or building. He was an active member of the legion and helped it set up for bingo or any other event taking place. A war veteran, he took pride in caring for other veterans' tombstones — built white crosses for them and repainted them every year.

With knowledge of Sam's age, habits and the state of his health, the search leaders set up grid searches of the woods, organizing a string line to include several dozen square metres of ground behind the house and parallel to the street — a square grid. They used probability-of-detection (POD) methods to mark off areas of high, medium and low probability and made use of tracks and footprints behind the house that were thought to be his. Neighbours were sent to search fields across the road and along the hedgerows — "gives them something useful to do and it eliminates those places," said Mike. "Besides, we needed to rule out that he hadn't fallen down among the raspberry bushes. They grow about four feet high, and if he had, we wouldn't see him."

Volunteer firemen began arriving. Stevenson and DesRoches looked at them, aghast. Some wore full bunker (firefighting) gear, hastily put on without undergarments, no socks inside their heavy boots. Many had raced from the beach wearing T-shirts, shorts and sandals. "Can't let them go into the woods like that — boots and no socks," Mike said, shaking his head.

Help arrived: Stanley McDonald at the local Guardian drug store freely offered armfuls of socks, gloves — and the T-shirts needed under the harsh cloth of firemen's jackets.

"For a fireman, speed is the critical thing," Mike said. "But not for a search — it needs careful planning. You don't want people screaming off

Sam and Aletha Cornish with their nine children.

into the woods, yelling for Sam, contaminating the area and getting into trouble themselves. Because firemen are not trained in search methods, we had each of our SAR members take three or four of them, together with some local people, on a grid search in the woods. Each was given an area based on POD. By now we had thirteen members of Prince County's ground SAR team present, each responsible for several volunteers. It worked well."

Not much later, a small plane owned by a neighbour droned overhead. At the same time, young people with access to four-by-four all-terrain vehicles searched farm lanes and old railway tracks, places that bordered those search areas that had already marked out. Up and down the tracks they drove, then they struck out across open fields. If Sam had come out of the far end of the woods, they might find him wandering.

"We'll try Don Smith and his search dog," said Constable Stevenson now. Smith wasn't available, so a call was put in to Corporal Mike Landry in Moncton. Stevenson also asked the Criminal Investigations Division for the use of a helicopter from the RCMP's J Division in New Brunswick.

"I'm free to help," the pilot said, "but have no chopper and no crew. Besides, the forward-seeking infrared equipment won't be of any use on a very hot day like this."

Corporal Landry arrived with his dog and was asked to search the back of the house and the perimeter of the areas that had been marked out. This might help contain the search area, and perhaps find a new point from which to look further. Sections were searched, then eliminated, one by one. Meanwhile, a hasty team worked the boundaries, checking streams, fields and trails. Its members moved quickly, cutting across trails, trying to cover off any clues: cigarette butts, clothing items. All they found was a single paper napkin — "used to clean his glasses and probably fallen out of his pocket," a daughter said.

The early afternoon passed. Waves of heat shimmered over the distant potato fields. Clumps of woodland punctuated the soft green swells and dips of the fields that stretched to the edge of low-lying swamp, to scrubland, tangles of wild raspberries and brambles. The inertia of a hot, sultry Sunday lay upon the small village of O'Leary.

★

Heather Pringle, a local veterinarian and SAR member with team leader training, now arrived. She had Austin Perry put out a string line to set up search boundaries, then, taking Paul Hardy and Carl Doucette — both of whom were also trained team leaders — with her, set out through the woods with map and compass in hand to maintain their bearings. In time, teams of searchers would cover the entire grid.

Meanwhile, Brian DeLong, a minister from the local church, stood alongside the family to offer comfort. The nearby G&E Restaurant geared up to supply water and snacks, while at the local fire hall, Firemanettes — the firefighters' wives — gathered to make sandwiches.

"Things were getting serious," said daughter Jean. "I wouldn't wish this on anyone. Evening was coming and our dad was out there somewhere… " her voice trailed off. Into the minds of these middle-aged and older sons and daughters, images of a beloved father flitted, even as they feared for him: the warm-hearted patriarch who cared so deeply for them all, who had supported them in all their needs — and their wants if he had been able — taking two or more jobs to earn the means. The one thing he loved the most was to have his big family and all its generations about him.

"You should have heard the thrill in his voice when he heard one of us was coming home to visit," said daughter Shirley, remembering. "We all cried for him most of the afternoon and evening…" All, perhaps, except for the blue-eyed, brown-haired Aletha, who — as she always did — kept her emotions tightly reined. Still, her children knew that beneath that exterior lay a big heart, warm and generous.

The searchers began straggling in — hot, discouraged and extremely fatigued. Mike saw this. He worried that he might have serious casualties on his hands — and almost immediately after this thought came news that a searcher had suffered a diabetic attack. An ambulance would be needed.

"Dusk approached, and it wasn't looking good," Mike said. "The family — they were all very upset and anxious. We had a forgetful old man who couldn't walk far, who'd had no food or water all day, who had probably fallen and couldn't get up. We'd been searching for six to eight hours… I decided we should order a body bag — that's how we were thinking."

Heather Pringle and her group returned from their search without finding a single clue.

"Look, we'll go out one more time before darkness falls and do a last search," she said. Her group took with them map and compass, set up a string line, and took off to cover the very furthest area that had been marked out.

They searched, called out Sam's name, and searched some more. Finally, they stopped. "I don't think we'll find him here," Heather said. "It's too far, Sam wouldn't —"

"Hey, I've found a footprint!" Paul's shout cut her off. "Here's another one! Okay, let's follow them. Let's do one more sweep." They ran a string line and tracked through woods that butted up against old railway tracks, following them for a distance. They crossed a field, then circumnavigated back to the woods. They were about a hundred metres away when they heard it — a crashing noise in the trees, the sound of someone chopping.

"Sam! Sam!" They yelled in unison.

"Yeah?" A weak voice arose from within the depths of the trees. Amazing: they had not yet searched this area because they didn't believe Sam capable of walking so far. He was a kilometre and a half from his house, and a hundred and fifty metres from Confederation Trail, the old railway bed had become a hiking and snowmobiling trail. The spot lay in an area that had been assigned a medium to low probability. The three searchers brushed through the dense trees and undergrowth, calling out all the while, and finally there, among the trees and brambles and wild forest growth, they found Sam Cornish, not only standing upright, but using his axe to chop off any branches that got in his way.

"It was close to eight o'clock, and Sam was a bit confused," Heather said. "He looked exhausted, and he was soaking wet with sweat. But no wonder! He wore all these warm clothes: a flannel shirt, heavy pants, a jacket, boots and a hat. Paul and Carl picked him up and began carrying him to where I'd parked my van when he said, 'Stop! I left my axe in there.' He wouldn't leave without it."

Intense joy and jubilation greeted Sam and the searchers when the van drew up to the house. Sam looked surprised — and embarrassed —

by the crowds around his home. He denied having been lost; instead he smiled, said he'd had a great walk through the woods — had been having a great time.

Did he realize how long he'd been away?

"No, I went for walk," he said. "I got twisted about a bit, a bit confused about where I was, so I lay down and took a nap. I woke up hungry and ate some wild raspberries… I was on my way home when they found me."

"He'd probably slept away the long, hot afternoon and was in better shape than his rescuers," someone joked.

The immediate aftermath of the successful search was a very emotional time. The family's tears of sorrow became tears of intense joy and relief.

"Best moment of my life," said a searcher.

"This is what it's all about," said another, "finding people alive. We were high-fiving each other, everybody hugging all the others and some had tears in their eyes."

A huge energy rush added to the relief felt by all the SAR team members and firemen. Scott Stevenson and Mike DesRoches were among those with teary eyes, such was the intensity of their relief. Both had endured much pressure, particularly Scott.

"You feel it as a terrible personal failure if you don't find the missing person — or the body," he said. "You always wonder, years later, should you have done something else? It haunts you: should you have done something else, looked elsewhere else first… The community looks to you to be successful, and you're also held accountable for spending money, whether in five minutes, or over several hours. People, even years afterwards, can second-guess you and the decisions you made that day. When people heard we'd asked for a ground SAR team here, there was some reaction. Yes, it's a small island, there are not a lot of roads and trails and other hazards, but people don't realize the extent of our thick wooded areas and how easy it is to get lost in them. The woods where Sam got lost covered four to five kilometres — thick woods of birch, spruce, maple, alders. What if Sam had been down on the ground? What if we hadn't called out the team?"

Sam Cornish was an O'Leary oldtimer, father to nine children, grandfather to twenty-two, and great grandfather to nine. Well known and well liked, he had lived in Prince County all his long life, working variously in a garage as mechanic, as janitor in the post office, and at the local agricultural building. An avid gardener who toiled long and hard among the vegetables on his half-acre, and a generous man, he gave away much of the produce from his gardens.

Aletha had also worked while raising her many children: cleaning the local church and the Credit Union building, planting and picking potatoes; wallpapering the homes of her neighbours. "You do whatever you can do when you have a big family," she said.

In this gentle place of sweeping potato fields, woodlands and dairy farms, an event of this kind galvanizes the community — indeed, a whole county. All those who were able contributed to the finding of Sam Cornish.

Sam died a few months later, but it was not related to his walk in woods. Two years later, he is still missed sorely by his family.

*

"I do this because I like to be outdoors," said Constable Scott Stevenson, an RCMP investigator and the detachment co-ordinator of the SAR team. "I became involved in SAR in 1996 when I first arrived in Alberton's RCMP detachment. This is a great group of people to work and spend time with: fishermen, farmers, engineers... We all get together for this, we bond."

Since this search, Scott has been transferred to the Forensic Identification Unit in Charlottetown.

Mike DesRoches, one of the few trained search managers on the island, explained that PEI has had trained SAR teams only since 1995 — later than most other provinces. The need for it became acute when the RCMP began a search for a missing woman, an effort that proved difficult and chaotic because of a lack of trained people and the absence of anyone with search-management training. "It became a nightmare for the RCMP," he said. "SAR on PEI can be busy, but we can also go for an entire year without a case. We occasionally get called to look for suicidal people, and we do mock searches with the police as training."

Mike is a child and family services worker in O'Leary. He has long been involved in volunteer work — as a fireman and as an auxiliary police worker. In 1996 he became involved in volunteer SAR work, and has served as treasurer and vice president of the Search and Rescue Volunteer Association of Canada.

Asked why she does search-and-rescue work, Heather Pringle answered, "I enjoy the outdoors. I love back-country hiking, adventure racing with map and compass... Then there's the camaraderie, the really wanting to help out. You figure that you have these skills, so why not go out in the woods and search?"

Prince Edward Island, where Lucy Maud Montgomery's Wind Woman sighs over fields and woods and coasts, is not a place accustomed to violence or tragedy. When they do strike, the community of small communities is galvanized. Which is exactly what it did for old Sam Cornish.